never, a Cloud

never A Cloud

For Joslyn Wolfe!

Jo Brunini

JO BRUNINI

IDLE RIDGE
PRESS

Library of Congress Control Number: 2022917988

979-8-9861205-0-8 (paperback)
979-8-9861205-1-5 (hardcover)
979-8-9861205-2-2 (digital)

Set in Dante MT Pro
Cover design: Hyun Min Lee
Cover photograph: © Pete Bushell

Printed in the United States of America

For my father, and cars that grow wings and fly.
For my sister, and rivers of laughter.

To—

As when with downcast eyes we muse and brood,
And ebb into a former life, or seem
To lapse far back in some confused dream
To states of mystical similitude,
If one but speaks or hems or stirs his chair,
Ever the wonder waxeth more and more,
So that we say, 'All this hath been before,
All this hath been, I know not when or where;'
So, friend, when first I looked upon your face,
Our thought gave answer each to each, so true –
Opposed mirrors each reflecting each –
That, tho' I knew not in what time or place,
Methought that I had often met with you,
And either lived in either's heart and speech.

—Alfred Lord Tennyson

OTYRBURN

CHAPTER ONE

Strange and Wonderful

*"*B*lue Violet," one boyfriend called me. I explained the science behind ultraviolet light. The cowboy from Cheyenne, Wyoming, rode in and christened me "Violent Love." But I kicked him out—his saddle and his horse, Wonky, too. Besides, he insisted on smoking in bed. The barbarian from Barbados who dubbed me "Drooping Violet" did so knowing I was in excellent health. The environmental lawyer from Hoboken who sailed the Sun Odyssey 49 used the cloying nickname "Common Violet" only once. The Beat poet who cleansed his unwanted energy by singing when he asked for a glass of "Violet Water," I encouraged because I liked his voice.*

I tell you this because it is nearly impossible to fully know anyone. Something along the lines of watching cloud formations and attempting to describe them, let alone recount their liveliness or artifice in motion. Even clouds have character. A careful observer can only know the sky if they have taken the time to live beneath it. As your storyteller, I acknowledge my limitations.

My parents should have known that a name like Violet would cause some trouble. My father, Thomas Grey, was a physicist. I do wish he'd left "Violet" suspended at the inner edge of the arc. Instead, I spent a lifetime insisting "indigo" belonged to the color order of the rainbow and, as proof, repeating Sir Isaac Newton's mnemonic device "Richard Of York Gave Battle In Vain." (For my part, I named my daughter Ava.)

Don't tell me about your successes, not just yet, but do guard your story well. This is a novel about a motley crew, who grew into a family, and how I became the matriarch.

We are not different in our private concerns and wishes. I always carry a notepad, jot the date down, and write a sentence or two that accumulate into a number of illegible longhand pages. I am a writer. I had a path that I crisscrossed over Maine's rocky shore with a dog that I named Galaxy.

Archibald Reid was off the road and over the bluff, hiking down to the Atlantic Ocean, before he heard my goodbye. Actually, he missed it altogether because I said nothing. And I was just beginning to like his smell. He fathered my child, and even wilder and stranger than to dream of Shambhala, he never knew it.

In the beginning I collected fragments, but years have flown, and much has happened since I attended my first New Year's celebration at Otyrburn in Wyndham, a sleepy dot of a village on the backside of Perthshire, Scotland. It was then that Archie's daughter, Margot Reid, handed me the letters.

Perhaps I should state clearly why the events that unfolded matter, being of no historical or political import, if one is to judge pinpoints in time by the ushering in of a new pope or the dismissal of a president with tiny hands. I am writing a map for you, complemented by other stories I heard afterward, if my memory serves me. A constellation, if you will, of soul and matter, and truths therein revealed when a bankrupt way of talking to someone is denied. Dear friend, I wasn't headed somewhere to do something, or archive a dream, or achieve a specific goal, per se, but to "be there." Margot is Ava's half sister. One she's never met.

I tried to shield her from this convoluted—at times, admittedly, challenging—family. On sober reflection, my psychoanalyst suggested once that I was riddling my obsessions by recording the transparencies I'd witnessed through others' stories and that this action was a desire to heal, and there could be some truth in this. Let us say it is an act of love. I do not promise you an accomplished design. Sometimes you have to believe things that are in contradiction among themselves.

PERTHSHIRE, SCOTLAND, DECEMBER 27, 2018

Those gathered had witnessed a pink flash at sunset. The party had enjoyed a languorous start. The evening, however, had been far from uneventful. First to rise, Margot lifted a glass half-full and righted a book at rest facedown. How many years had it been? A discarded newspaper and shoes, the worn flipped edge of a cotton runner, scattered petals left by a vase of dried wildflowers, a woodcut print, a sleeping dog, a rumpled throw blanket tossed the night before over the arm of the blue-and-white-striped soft-cushioned sofa in the somewhat-shabby sitting room. The house had always afforded the relaxed charm and invitation of a cozy corner.

Upstairs, Margot washed and dried her face, then glanced out the window at the far field, now heavy with rain. In the familiar front hall below, the furnace clanked in the old stone dwelling, and the dog's unclipped nails tapped eagerly over oak. The path that she and her boyfriend, Owen Fowler, had cleared through these woods in 1989 was long overgrown, but the memory of it was as seductive and captivating as ever.

I met Margot three years, to be precise, after our story begins. She was quiet, quieter than the rest of the extended family or her gathered friends, but when she told me about Owen, I, too, was right back there with her, in the throes of first love.

He had just gotten his license. Owen had worked shirtless in Margot's grandfather's orchard, his jeans frayed, his hair long, and his accent slightly lilting. Earlier that spring, he'd skipped school and read Rumi down by Lewis Creek, and he had given her his copy when they met together at that creek in June—eagerly creating their self-sufficient cosmogony.

For more than ten days, Margot and Owen had not made love, just to see if it was possible. The spring dried up first, sending her grandfather, Alistair, into a tailspin; then the cosmos in the field had drooped day and night, and the birds sang early at an alarming rate, rendering sleep nearly impossible among the three hundred residents in the hidden, happy village of Wyndham. "Who leaves teenagers alone in an orchard of forbidden fruit?" Edwina, Alistair's wife, had asked, and she was right: *precipice, risk, and wisdom go together.*

The morning of the 2018 holiday party, Margot Reid was remembering things she didn't know she'd forgotten, and in her childhood home, her eight international guests were groggy: Ruby

Lowell, her daughter; Will Lowell, her brother-in-law, and his girlfriend, Elisabetta "Lisbet" Giardi; Johnny Franco, the old college roommate and friend of Margot's husband, George Lowell, and Johnny's date, Anna Cavanaugh; and Margot's friend Sybil Ruttenberg and Sybil's husband, Max Mowbray.

Within Otyrburn's kitchen, George was seated at the table, solo, coffee in hand, awaiting the visitors, as two chefs packed hearty lunches and provisions for his hunting party. His eyes fluttered up from the newspaper. He was forty-seven years old and good to look at. The familiarity of his face and his avuncular charm were weighted by the deep wrinkle between his eyes. Bacon fat on the griddle, Margot, with a glance at his countenance, saw his consternation. The beds unmade upstairs, guests' bedroom doors opened and shut, and soon, orders for eggs sunny-side up, over easy, over hard, scrambled, and poached and Friar's omelets with apple would fly out of the pantry. George was clearly preoccupied with something, but she didn't know what.

When Margot gathered a mental picture of her trusted friend Sybil, the beekeeper was singing while working her hive; that way, she was less likely to disturb them. *Honeybees are forgiving. You must force one to sting you. It means the end of their life.* The door banged twice and stuck on the lip of the jamb where early morning snow had collected.

"Such miserable weather." Sybil, a bona fide New Yorker, often complained about the fabric of life, as though it were changeable. "Love the bare stone walls."

"There are worse places to be." The two walked at ten in the morning on a holiday of gathered friends filled with expectation. "And besides, you get to try seaweed lemon butter," Margot added.

"With pickled mussels and kippers."

"Owen hasn't changed all that much."

"How's that?" Sybil asked. "Even our first love grows old and changes."

"If anything, he's more perceptive and honest."

"Your husband reads the *New York Times* book section on Sundays."

"Weekends, Owen paints watercolors of birds," Margot said.

Sybil wiped under her nose with the back of her suede mitten. "Artistic guys seldom maintain the luminous phenomenon."

"I took a detour from 'Do what's sensible.'"

"You paid court to your father, then to your husband," Sybil said.

"Then which is the dream I live, my life before George Lowell or my life after?"

"When you return to a place in your past, it is never the same. We can't trust words." Sybil's hand rested on the sleeve of Margot's boiled-wool jacket. "Egads. What's the matter with you?"

"What's right with me? Emotional debt makes people forget themselves."

"There's a word in Spanish for this—*golpe*—to experience a shock, suddenly, literally, a knock on the head, an awakening." Sybil snugged the double length of wool scarf around her neck. "Take the experience of meeting Owen again and learn what you need to learn without hurting anybody. Don't destroy your marriage. He'll be there in the next lifetime."

Sybil, a deep moral magnet to those seeking guidance—except when she isn't, Margot thought and kicked away an icy rock in their path with the toe of her boot.

"Come on, Sybil, reincarnation answers many things—and what if you're wrong?"

"Without acceptance, there is no commitment. Everything gives in life."

"What will Ruby say?" If Margot lost Ruby, she lost everything.

"She's an independent thinker. Max will say something like, 'What a wicked woman to do that to her husband, after all those years.'"

"My life has been ruined." The white stretch of snow-covered hills seemed to slip away forever. "Owen knows who I am."

"This isn't the right time in life to upset the apple cart." Sybil put her arm around Margot's shoulders and gave her a squeeze.

"You have to pay, even for courage."

"The universe doesn't deliver signs."

"You don't remember, do you, Sybil, when you and Max talked on the phone for hours, and how you eased your hand over the pillow where he would soon lie?"

"I remember."

In the bedroom at the back of the house, over the kitchen, George and Margot's only child, Ruby, kissed the black velvet ear of her terrier mix, Onyx. The morning's view from the north window over the snowy stable yard below now framed her godfather, Max, as he chatted out in the open with her father, their warm breath rising around them.

The start of a new year, and she was eager to leave Paris and return to the States. She'd get a sleeper van, a tiny house with unlimited vistas, and move from town to town, freewheeling across America. Chocolates have a long shelf life, and she could sell them anywhere.

"Morning, Dad." Ruby had borrowed her father's robe, and its hem trailed over the uneven slate floor of the kitchen.

"You look chipper," George said, smiling appreciatively at his daughter while enjoying his eggs. He was seated on the cushioned bench of the paneled breakfast nook, with his back to the window that overlooked the snowy fields beyond, where Margot and Sybil now walked.

"I just had a grapefruit and eucalyptus bath," Ruby said. "Parsley, cedar, rose, yet citrus alone has the power to stimulate women to release pheromones."

"What didn't they teach you in France? Tonight is the trail ride to the Warrior's Head, and I want to say that we pass through the Lost Valley."

"We might disappear altogether." Ruby set the kettle on the stove. Her father wore his flame-orange wool hunting beanie.

"Do you ever take it off?" she asked, nodding at it. "You put it on when you landed."

"I held off on the bulletproof vest." He folded the morning paper. "I promised I'd give Max a lesson on marksmanship before the hunt tomorrow. Agatha has apple scones in the pantry," he said, referring to one of the two cooks hired for the weeklong party. And with that, George kissed Ruby's cheek and was off abruptly to start his day.

Her father was home, and already, there was no laughter in the kitchen, not in New York City or here at her great-grandparents' house in Scotland.

Midmorning, crows wheeling, Margot and Sybil trekked back along a winding tributary to join those gathered. The rain had turned to sleet. Where mud now mixed with snow in the driving wind, the farmers they passed struggled to keep soaked caps down and the thatch in place on the roofs of their barns. The ever-wary, ever-hungry fox on the knoll, his ears tipped skyward, watched wild turkeys forage.

At the farthest reach of the valley, Otyrburn, the largest of the stone houses, seemingly suited to the storm, stood alone against the wooded foothills. A woman in a black coat with a fur collar, her dark hair flowing beneath a knit cap, stood expectantly beneath the vestibule. In the cutting chill of the Scottish winter wind, Sybil and Margot greeted the stranger.

"I'm looking for Alistair and Edwina Reid; they're my grandparents. My name is Ava Kerouac."

CHAPTER TWO

Violets, Maineiacs, Emeralds, and Rubies

*T*he trouble between Ava and I had begun long before she announced herself on the threshold at Otyrburn in December 2018.

It was a star-filled night; we were sailing together on Hopper's
Island. Ava had turned thirty that May, and in July, I had failed to notice the Milky Way creeping up from behind us, before a hatful of wind
hit the sails. Being the traditionalist that she is, though, my millen-
nial daughter insisted on inspecting the rigging, only to discover we
didn't have a fully functional wind vane. When I told her that sailing
separated "the wheat from the chaff," she said that whoever had sold
me this boat must have been an old codger like me because obviously
no young person, in the pursuit of safety, would ever sail without new-
fangled gadgets. "Nothing supplants conservative seamanship," I had
yelled above the sound of rippling sails, the mast and gunnel heeling.

Score one for the geezers. Ava had shook her head, I'd heard it too, a hint of my father's annoying know-it-all manner.

Stay with me. In rotation, every year, poor Vermeer had a new baby to feed. An artist needs three sailing ships, shoved along by the wind. The first carries moons and memories. The second transports the instruments required to avoid a shipwreck, without a star, without a sky. The third carries, in a net, a tangle of hopes and disasters. It is a matter of courage. Not timing or staging—all sheets to the wind. Faculties be damned when time is of the essence. This is why I avoided marriage. Matter has an unruly way of multiplying. Some things are too difficult to talk about, and some things you have to repeat even when no one is listening.

My daughter is going to inherit from me not money, but truth. Lifelong, I have battled against insincerity. When I was a young teen, even with all that had erased me for an undefined period of time, it was my father's whistle, ironically, that time and again called me back home to dinner. One day, I'm going to buy a mountain house on the Great Plains, or maybe a Dutch gable house in Amsterdam, and Ava and I are going to go there and fall in love again beneath the swollen moon.

A story is a little like paddling through backwater. Seaweed tugs at the keel or at the oar equally. I should tell you up front a little about Ava. Our estrangement began when she insisted that fine summer, her thirtieth year of life, on a defined rendition of her father.

What am I looking for in this cast of characters? Integrity. Honest expression. Unabashed originality. The events I am about to relay triggered my falling-out with Ava. But if I am truthful with myself, my choices, made decades earlier, weighed her down. Wind the clock backward with me, shy of two months prior to Ava's arrival in December at Otyrburn, because many people I now love dearly are making overtures to you.

CAMDEN, OCTOBER 2018

In Camden, Maine, the High Street Bookstore shelf had six germane offerings on the Highlands—four on lochs, fishing, and trekking and two on holiday lodging and dining while in "bonny Scotland." At the end of the day, Ava sought something else altogether and stopped her weave down the narrow and dust-laden aisles when she found the Celtic section, specifically the coffee-table, oversize, brag-worthy illustrious editions. The prerequisites of her purchase: enthralling photos, with roughly life-size impressive illustrations of each player, man and beast, that held the promise of definition.

Again I tried to warn her, this daughter of mine: fathers, not just lovers, can be controlling, even in their absence. But she walked home anyway on a fall night, with books tucked under her arm.

NEW YORK CITY, OCTOBER 2018

Margot's daughter, Ruby, had flown home at the close of her studies in Paris. *She looks healthy,* Margot thought. *Dear Ruby, compelled by the chemistry that happens with sweet-smelling liquid natural leaven.* Birthday presents became cookbooks. Visits to "Auntie" Sybil became excursions through the woods skirting her Connecticut property, armed with stout walking sticks and gleaning rose hips, slow cooked and turned into rosehip jam; wild garlic bulbs, crushed in a mortar into wild garlic pesto; and a handful of nettles that, when simmered, became the base for a nettle soup.

She wore a retro sixties minidress over her thin, bare legs ensconced in white Beatle boots. Ninety-five percent of used clothes could be recycled, but 85 percent will end up in landfills. *Buy less—our planet, our future.*

"There's orange barley water in the fridge," Margot said.

Ruby opened cupboards, searching for something to snack on, and settled on the hermetic-roasted pumpkin seeds.

"Dad sent me a link to an article." The late-day sun cut across Ruby's eyes. She closed the wooden shutters. "'Highlights of Oceanic Art.' Seriously?"

The History of Art by George W. Lowell."

Ruby checked the edge on a paring knife and began slicing cheddar cheese. "While Dad and Uncle Will couldn't go barefoot in the house, you and Gramps ran naked through orchards."

"Grandma Lowell's ring broke in two," Margot said, glancing at the naked middle finger on her right hand. "I caught it on the balcony screen door. And I'd just had it restored to 'outlast' future generations."

"She was a battle-ax."

"That's a terrible thing to say." Margot poured herself a glass of water. "She only called you fat once." She flipped through a pile of mail on the kitchen table. "She told me I didn't have the strength to bear or raise a child." Finding nothing of interest, she surveyed the narrow kitchen. The floor needed a wash. "You know that resting bitch face you love so? I wore it that day."

"Way to go, Mom. I was only ten."

"If the Daughters of the American Revolution gave out diplomas, she would've framed it on the wall."

"Rules are rules, especially when membership is exclusive and official documents are few and far between." Ruby removed her jacket, and her ponytail swept her waist, flashing glimpses of the hummingbird tattoo on the nape of her neck. "'*Merica*."

"America's self-love."

The phone rang on a demilune table in the short run of hallway off the kitchen. Margot rose—her small white dog, Wren, at her heels—and answered the landline, was asked to pass along a message, and hung up.

"He's so completely odd," she said.

"Who was it?"

"Heinke Hessel, a Dutch dealer your father does business with occasionally. A Northern Baroque specialist, I think."

"He's probably on Instagram. Everybody's busy posting 'stories.' LB. FB. I have nothing to say and no stories to tell." Ruby slipped cheese to Wren under the table. "I've already wasted far too many Sundays hunting for Fiesta ware at flea markets—and I'm only twenty-three."

"You didn't buy into that?"

"If I don't, I've 'died.'" She ran her fingers through the ends of her hair, checking for split ends. "Have you heard me singing what sounds like a funeral dirge? I'll never sing it quite the same again, and to me, it belongs around a Russian campfire. I swear I know the words to the melody but can't remember." She unbuttoned her boots and sat with her feet tucked beneath her in her stocking feet. "Do you see what's happening here, Mom? I've sabotaged my own future."

Margot slid the pot of black beans that had come to a rolling boil onto the simmer burner—enchiladas for dinner.

"It's okay to live a little in a parallel universe, Ruby, a world of your own. Shepherds and poets do that."

The late western light streamed through the kitchen window. Margot gave Ruby's head a tender kiss. She had laughed so, as a baby, the first time she saw the wipers wag on the car in the rain. Her daughter was special; she counted butter curls in her sleep, not sheep.

"And school?"

"I found an apartment in the sixteenth arrondissement, a better location than last semester. Chocolate making, then graduation." She began mincing onions. "I now can explain the marvel of engineering behind a croissant."

When I first met Margot's husband, George, his blue eyes fascinated me—as if a child had colored the sky on a spring morning. When he was lost in thought, one eye wandered outward a little. He wore brown wool herringbone most days, with brocade lining, from his London tailors, Thomas Warren, and when two fittings of the basted suit, hand-stitched in white thread, were completed, George believed he had found immortality. He could trace his lineage to William Bradford. His too-many-greats-to-list-grandfather was Henry II. Such was the suchness of George. I give George credit for nurturing Margot's art. Yet he had sworn an oath to do so. When he married her, he bought the season pass. I give him grief for corrupting her innermost spirit.

When headed to work, a thought ran through his brain, and it only happened occasionally as George cut through Central Park, specifically (a walk the director of Greek and Roman art had enjoyed for the past quarter century), and entered at the Fifth Avenue entrance of the Metropolitan Museum of Art. He contemplated the day when either he or his wife, Margot, would find the other a heinous individual.

But then a bird would sing, or a taxi would honk, and the pleasant image of classical music and cocktails at six, dinner at seven fifteen, would erase the concern. From his office, he could solve an online crossword puzzle with a friend halfway around the world.

The *"Juno's volute,"* Scaphella junonia, George reminisced at a break in his office, noting the shell's similar spiral in the marzipan swirls that topped his morning's Danish. *The Roman goddess Juno*, he mused further, looking out at a rainy Central Park, punctuated by dots of bright umbrellas. His mother had painted Juno, robed in a goatskin cloak, seated with an iridescent peacock. Hurricanes marked the opportune time to search for the elusive shell. His head bent against the howling wind, the cutting chinstrap on his sou'wester, the hiss of rain, the lobsterman he'd become, miles out at sea, not a boy from High Meadow Day School. By his twelfth summer, his saffron-colored foul-weather gear had fit correctly. He never did land a prized Juno's volute in the town paper. But he'd been sure of it.

George had achieved his goal; now he lived in a hard-won three-bedroom brownstone with his beautiful family. Life was comfortable and unpretentious. He and Margot had even completed bits of the restorative work themselves. He hadn't been happy about that decision, but she had insisted. After eight years, they had a new shower in the master bath, and it leaked.

Entering the foyer, visitors were greeted by a small twelfth-century Dutch welcome plaque carved with griffins, George's twenty-fifth-anniversary gift to Margot. He lived with her obsession with finding the picturesque in decay and dilapidation, in a cemetery or crumbling old house, though for him, stones belonged in temples, not tipped at alarmingly irregular angles. All roads led to Dionysian beauty, which spoke symmetry. He fell in love with her the night she quoted the French philosopher Denis Diderot, "The ideas ruins evoke in me are grand." A line that George, a Pompeii and Herculaneum treasure hunter, would entertain, as if she had known that he had survived an earthquake in Sicily.

The house spoke of busy lives, stacks of letters atop case pieces lined in brightly colored handmade paper. George's favorite: the boldly patterned poppy-red and canary-yellow geometric sheet lining his maple desk, aged warm as clover honey.

George was headed out first to the drafty manor house that Margot had inherited; Otyrburn had been in the family for three generations. Summers, under her grandmother Edwina's liberal watch, Margot had combed the riverbank and stared up at great peaks, and then it was Ruby's turn.

Otyr, *if traced back far enough, to 1300, is Gaelic for "otter," and* burn, *"anything from a large stream to a small river." Where a figure disappeared into the boundary of hedgerows rich with hawthorn, hazel, ash, and oak, the property initiated one into reverie, and so the entire nation of Scotland. Sheltered by ancient species, some dated to the Bronze Age, a soul traveled as he stood still.*

Edwina had dispelled the daydreams Alistair sought, with minor success, and thrown in the towel altogether with Margot. When first married, she had asked her husband to buy himself a winter coat in town, and he'd returned with a pup instead. "A true necessity," Nipper was short on manners, long on drive and longevity. When he reached eighteen, Alistair credited it to the splash of whisky he added to his oats on Sunday mornings.

"*A flower in the forest,*" George thought, *Edwina's snowdrop analogy would've struck Archie down if the stroke hadn't.* The widower had made Margot's home a happy enough one.

Archie's death had hit out of the blue, similar to that of Margot's mother. Both possessed of vigorous health one day, then gone the next. It acted as a double whammy that he doubted Margot would ever fully recover from. Such a needless shame, the way he and Archie had fought just one day prior to his fatal heart attack.

CHAPTER THREE

Blackbird

*T*eenagers are a difficult row to hoe. "This is the story of my life," they say, but it isn't. Life feels like a terrible piece of sculpture, a song with only two notes and one driving, unbroken tempo.

"Turn it down in there!" Ava had screamed from the privacy of her bedroom.

Nobody needs an excuse for a party, but it was so shitty outside. It had rained on Hopper's Island, dependably, well into July.

"What did you say?" I shouted.

Suddenly, above the smoke-filled din in our crowded living room and pounding bass notes of my bigger-than-life subwoofer—I heard her. My little blue-water pollywog, all of sixteen, was wearing her baby-doll jammies, cutting barefoot through the sea of swaying bodies.

"I have homework to do. It'll be your fault if I fail chemistry," Ava said, sounding peeved. "Why can't you be even a little tiny bit like anybody else's mother?"

She reached to brush a long bang, cutting through the center of my left eye, off my glowing cheek. I had been dancing pretty hard. And didn't know where I'd left my bra, or who the guy asleep in the corner chair was.

"Again, I mean no disrespect for the magnitude of a GPA," I said, "or the multitudes of sailing veterans of past Olympics that inhabit this island of ours—and make far more noise than I—but you know, sweetie, how important coming together is to me."

"The house is downright filthy," Ava fumed, sticking out her lower jaw and scratching hard at a bug bite on her arm. "You know what? I fucking hate when you get like this."

She turned and stomped off. I did catch her bedroom door slam.

"Believe in yourself! And leave your doubts at the mooring," I called, blowing a kiss good night to her retreating petite form, just as Janis wound up and wailed into her best-ever rendition of "Piece of My Heart."

In 1969, my small-town college boyfriend at Cornell was drafted. Archie spent his teens in Scotland. He hadn't had to contend directly with the horror of Vietnam. See the white doves fly. I went to Woodstock and dropped out of Cornell, then hopped a bus to the Hog Farm in New Mexico. Stayed long enough to leave, hiked up north, and hauled fishing nets over the sides of trawlers in Halifax. Then hitched back home and sold lobster rolls on Hopper's Island. Part of the "rucksack revolution," I got around.

When Archie was fifteen, he wrote a letter from Otyrburn to President Lyndon B. Johnson and told him in no uncertain terms that if he were waiting to be drafted into the Vietnam War, he'd join the *conscientious objectors. Archie's politics had brought us together over the value of dedicated protest. He dreamed of tall buildings, the tempo of life, and the courage all Americans wore, opening factories and taking on the sky, in a nation where a sense of human frailty and a hatred of injustice is not far-fetched. A daydreamer, like me, where we verged, somewhere, somehow, there lurked the "big deal" that would make Archie rich.*

PERTHSHIRE, OCTOBER 2018

"Dry as dust. That's what Father says Scotland is, dry as dust," Margot had said to her grandfather when she was a teenager.

"There is no time for a lull in his life," Alistair replied.

The two were seated together in the crook of an old apple tree, where bees buzzed.

"Mom and Dad still meditated, once in a while."

"Swami Satchidananda—I should have never let Archie go to Greenwich Village," Alistair said. He plucked an apple and offered her the first bite.

"Then he wouldn't have met Mom at the coffeehouse."

"When he got his first violin, before he went to bed, your father placed it in the case on a pillow on the floor beside him and covered it with a blanket. If he forgot, at night, the mice would creep into the room and wreak havoc, running over the strings."

"That's silly," Margot said.

"When the draft ended in 1973," Alistair continued, "even here in Scotland, things were easier for your father. But that's when he sold out, renounced his recreational fun, and became a materialist."

Alistair and Margot had talked about the cucumber blight, the pack of wolflike wild dogs that no one ever saw stealing the chickens, and life and death. And then again, out of the blue, as though he hadn't done so lifelong, he would tell his granddaughter not to be disappointed when things didn't turn out as she expected. "Find a place to hide away, Margot, and daydream."

Organized gatherings with intellectual aesthetes, Margot thought, *how they challenge and delight George. How they inadvertently raise the bar on his moral postulations.* The London symposium, en route to Scotland, had been a "humdinger."

In the queue for her flight to Scotland, Margot checked her messages. Something from George:

> After a brief layover in Amsterdam to visit Heinke Hessel, had dinner at Olga's in London Saturday night and sat next to an Argentine author who writes treatises about fifteenth-century Spanish poets. Did you see the article in this week's *Heritage Life* on Scotland's castles? Read it. Otyrburn is every bit as I remembered.

Riding the train, Margot answered a call from George; he was driving Alistair's '67 Land Rover down Otyrburn's gravel drive. The heavyset fruit trees in tones of cinnamon russet over gold contained thirteen distinct heritage apple varieties. Margot remembered two. She remembered the night mist that shrouded the orchard when she and Owen had made it their familiar territory and happy hunting ground. She remembered the fireflies.

Beauty of Bath, picked in early August, bore bright-red splashes broken by stripes of brownish crimson. How many times had the sour-sweet juice rolled down her chin and Edwina had insisted, *Straight to the tub, Margot Gaylord Reid; you're covered in dirt and blueberry stains—come back down when you're as rosy and polished as the Beauty of Bath and not before?*

The story was that her father, Archie, had chosen her middle name, Gaylord, after a client who had made a fortune, like falling off a log. She hated the name so much she actually loved it.

Lord Grosvenor was Alistair's pride, as he had told Margot emphatically, stopping their haul on a trek through the pastures. "Lord Grosvenor owns more land than the queen of England but won't hold an apple finer than mine." The best apple was on the highest bough. Lord Grosvenor's apple pie before she returned to school, the sound of the migrant workers' radio sounding through the orchard when they arrived to help Alistair harvest the crop.

Educated in a metropolitan city, George hadn't yet been able to distinguish one apple skin from another. The Aphrodite of Knidos's flesh, the first female nude sculpted in three-dimensional form. Margot visualized the phone call with a coworker, after the "roundtable," George amplifying the magnitude of Aphrodite's abdomen, *the tilt of her hip, her neck, which had driven men to lust since the time of Pliny the Elder.* A high-principled art expert always told friends, and occasional clients alike, what he honestly thought their items were worth.

VENICE, OCTOBER 2018

The Lowell brothers connected through art. William owned a gallery in Venice, Galleria Cacciano di Rondini, "Haunt of Swallows," which represented fine art and sculpture. George had mentioned he'd call, and Will had looked for any excuse to be otherwise detained for the past three hours, including studying the step-by-step directions on how to secure a car roof rack.

The scaffold knot would do, or the wagoner's hitch. When last they spoke by phone, George had, one-handed, replaced an ink cartridge in his favorite pen and blathered on about how well it was made.

George dialed Venice shortly after arriving at Otyrburn.

"How are you?" The connection paused, then crackled like an old landline. "What's next in the life of the Venetian?"

"Harried—there are two weeks till the *Biennale Arte*. I've shut the door on summer. Are you in Scotland?" Will said, answering the call from his gallery's office, already mildly exasperated—that particular Monday left little room for George.

"I just unpacked. What's selling?" George asked.

"Anything and everything that resembles Brâncuşi. He's had a revival."

William scratched at the back of his neck, beneath the collar of his office shirt. Was it just his imagination, or were his pants fitting more snugly?

"Then tickets for the Cycladic Collection will be in demand at the Metropolitan," George said.

"What am I supposed to do with the new crate you had dumped at my gallery?" Will opened the window. Fall in Venice was late summer everywhere else. "What the fuck, George? I'm not a UPS warehouse. And don't run on about how your Italian business associates are all accomplished scholars, admired throughout the European art world. The next time you instruct any one of your art dealers, Italian or not, to ship a package to me, I will refuse it. So what if it saves you the trouble by making their lives easier. I barely have enough space in my storage room for my own rotating collections."

"Agreed—very well, I'll ask Désiree von Goudshan, the beautiful Viennese opera singer, not to stop by the gallery and say hello. She had a small package for me I'd hoped you'd hand-deliver on your next visit."

"Honestly, George. As you carefully inventory your—and the museum's—collection, open that little black notebook of yours and erase my postal code." Will checked his watch again. "I have a luncheon date. Invite me, and I might just come for a single malt."

"The wall calendar here in the kitchen still reads May 2007—the year that Edwina died," George said offhandedly, with an incredulous laugh. "Archie wasn't around the place all that much." He paused. "Obviously, you care not for beauty. But great, come on ahead to Scotland."

Absorbed by the composition of his poetry, Will dreamed of magnificent birds, of kingdoms of solitude ruled by "notes and queries." With a juvenile excitement, just recently, he had turned the pulsing of his blood, visible at rest in his office through his fair-skinned wrist, into a river that spoke any language the swimmer wished. The Lowell hereditary memory, passed generation to generation, was of coffee, biscuits, and silver pitchers of cream; genetically, the brothers shared an abundance of freckles alone. Everything else was seemingly swept clean by the time Will came along.

CHAPTER FOUR

Otyrburn

*A va, my amazing Maineiac—what a little dynamo, little miss
so-and-so, show her the rodeo. Did I forget to tell you that my
daughter is getting her doctorate?*

*When Ava switched out the dead light bulb at home in Camden,
Maine, her computer keyboard flooded with a warm golden glow. Her
fingers flashed over the keys at half past midnight when she called,
hard at work. "Goddess" is "energy in action": no husband or exclusive lover to bother with, at rest with her own "giving" and her "taking" away. She stuck a Post-it to the page and continued. King Arthur
had received his power from the "Lady of the Lake." For a Celt, their
"other world" was neither above nor below, but beside. And could
be entered with instinctive intelligence. In Brittany, France, women*

today have great moral authority and are often head of the family (second Post-it).

Her thesis research would not be complete without a study of the Bretons: the belief that a woman was a priestess of the "goddess," who once had held ultimate power. Brittany was a near neighbor of the Highlands. Perhaps it was time. The cycles of freeze and thaw, millions of years of erupting volcanoes, Jurassic-period floodwaters, dinosaurs that roamed the coast—what had produced the present-day coastline of her fiery being? Ava had lived and breathed on an island, dominated by the force of the weather and the emotional sinkholes within her, at variance with the bright psalm-singing of my New England family. What of her father's? There was a story out there to raise goose bumps on the backs of her arms. Primal and distinctively Celtic, she could almost hear the tribal chanting. How could she begin a career without intimate knowledge of who she was?

Like clockwork, over the decades, her repeat Google search for "Otyrburn" brought up the ninth title in a mystery series by a medio-cre seventies writer from the Dales; one Griffith ap Otyrburn, K. G.; and then a run of derelict houses, "Otyrburn Guest Cottages," for rent in the Hebrides.

The two features of my thin story that struck Ava the most: you were born in a wild, wind-blasted corner of the world, and just like your mother, your high cheeks will certainly get attention. I gave you a name; your father and I both read Hemingway, and at a drive-in movie, we saw Ava Gardner in The Snows of Kilimanjaro. *Charles Darwin's great-grandson, upon meeting her, credited her as the "high-est specimen of the human species." And besides, she did things her way. I made it a point not to keep any Jack Daniel's in the house.*

PERTHSHIRE, OCTOBER 2018

Having arrived at an empty house, George poured a glass of whisky in the pantry at Otyrburn, climbed the stairs, pulled a comforter from his suitcase, and climbed into bed, noting the dampness of the Cairngorms night air. He turned a page in "Unraveling the Etruscan Enigma," hummed the theme song to *Green Acres*, and took his first sip of Blair Athol Single Malt. It hit the back of his throat with a silky swish of fig and vanilla just as he finished the line: "To an Etruscan all was alive."

"*Etruria*," he read softly out loud, an echo of mortality in the empty house, "ancient name of Tuscany, of uncertain origin but containing an element that references 'water,' possibly tied to the rivers in the region, and related to the '*-sk-*' linked to maritime people or sailors, as in the Basque people's name for themselves, *euskara* or *eskuara*."

He poured a refill. *June 13, 1974*, he thought. *The day Will was born and the afternoon I became the "big brother," when the natural rhythm of life was altered irrevocably. Everybody knew Huxley always loved William more. If I came home from New Haven over spring break and drove my brother to soccer practice, the folks would go on holiday, Corfu for two weeks. How Will adored me. What a marvel of invention a big brother was.* Sporadic night calls were the last thing he heard before he drifted off to sleep under the eaves in Otyrburn's bowed master bedroom.

When morning broke, George pulled on his dressing robe, a gift from Margot in gray wool, lined in tobacco medallion silk. He recalled the years of countless New York evenings together with his father-in-law.

"George, do you have time for a game?"

Fridays, Margot cooked dinner for her father, and he and George played chess.

"Castling when you did was brilliant."

"Actually, it was a mistake." Archie nibbled on roasted cashews. "I was just lucky, and lucky to have this family—and a granddaughter who makes cappuccino truffles."

George splashed cold water on his face. *Mr. Archibald Craven and Mr. Archibald Reid,* he thought, *Mary Lennox and her secret garden, Margot and hers. How that man governed my wife's life, and so now, from the grave—the tough son of a bitch.* George searched through his toiletry kit for his Vetiver de Guerlain and headed for the back stair landing. *Archie could never leave well enough alone. He got what was coming to him. His loss. His voice was so sexy "it made women come"—and Wren pee.*

The kitchen's checkerboard stone retained the evening's coolness beneath his feet. Rust marble with white veins abutted squares of slate. The runs of slate, unexpectedly, ran an inch or so off the reds. It struck George as poor execution until he crossed farther and it registered as ingenious, far more interesting than any floor he remembered, and so he spent a moment bent over in study. The black four-oven oil-fired AGA had been lit, and before long, the kitchen would be toasty.

Margot had heard Charles Trenet play over the radio at the train station. Edwina had said that Trenet, specifically the tune "Sur La Mer," was the one thing that got her through World War II. Trenet had serenaded Ruby in her crib.

Was Owen living in a small hotel in Greece? she thought. *He would love little more than to sail every day. When Owen took a trip, he marked his coordinates by the blackbirds spotted.*

Aboard the 7:00 a.m. *Explorer* out of Edinburgh, she noted the midway point of a seventy-five-minute trip to Pitlochry and added what she expected were another sixteen miles to Blair Atholl.

From there a cab would bring her onto the Cairngorms until Otyrburn came into view. A deserted white croft rose on a knoll, crystalline light reflecting off the wheaten landscape. Beneath the morning's pink clouds, petite stone walls weaved along the A9. Mixed apprehension met keen anticipation as the lull of the train mesmerized.

The approach to Otyrburn passed two south-facing paddocks before the drive forked at the clipped hedge, which led into the stable yard. Otyrburn sat in a wind shadow that faced south over the Carse of Tilt, with one corner of the thirty-seven-acre property tipped into a green crag of the Greeley estuary. Alistair had spoken of an artesian spring, but neither George nor Margot remembered where it was hidden. Legend said that a golden apple tree marked the spot. Crowded in the wood, it had grown so tall to catch the sun that the apples hung from the tip of the crown-like clusters of grapes pointing south. Owen might know.

Gooseberries, and a great many dogs, her fingers stained purple, lips bright red, as she'd puckered at the twang of a sour berry she'd plucked too early.

"Margot, you can't pine after every stray dawdling at the door." Edwina's voice had been low and throaty.

Her white hair braided around her head, her arm had made rhythmic turns stirring porridge with a wooden spoon. Lumbering in movement, and slower still in speech, she'd seen the practicalities of living.

"Can I feed him, then, Nana? He has one gray eye and one brown."

"Summer brings a new beast that you name and I inherit. Lay what's left in your bowl under the Kiftsgate rose arbor and crack an egg over it. The moon is none the worse for the dogs' barking at her. Then go and give me a hand carting my pruning basket.

The buttercups are creeping beneath the magnolia and need pulling. Then there are the gooseberries to pick."

"Which one is it, Nana?"

"The rambler rose at the garden shed arbor. The one I'm always hollering about getting in all over. There's no stopping its white blooms as big as your wee face."

How many dogs had she parked at Nana's? Just like Nana to fill her head with Gaelic proverbs about dogs under the yellow moon. She exited the car, tipped the cabbie generously, and closed the door softly. A red cardinal landed on the drive before she entered beneath the columns of an open vestibule, turning the knob on the weathered black door. *Two twists to the right, then a shoulder shove.* Not hearing activity on the ground floor, she climbed the marble stairs, aided underfoot by a threadbare wool runner, her hand sliding along the balustrade railing. Set in a niche stood a three-quarter-size female figure on a plinth, holding fruit and an urn. Margot smiled softly to see her. Edwina called her North and said she could deliver a storm.

Moving through the house, glimpsing through windows the garden gates Edwina had locked and she'd climbed over to reach the broad meadows, she discerned how cut off she'd been. The bedroom's fireplace lay in ashes as morning light bounced off cream-colored golden bee wallpaper.

George folded back the comforter edge in welcome. "Otyrburn is damn nippy."

"Put on a sweater."

"I bought a loaf of bread at the Gristmill. Organic," he added. "They even had spelt. You're going to love that place."

Margot turned the hot tap on the claw-foot tub and opened the window. How many times had her grandfather Alistair tried to convince her he'd hidden a secret message in the orchard's layout, viewable from on high? *Start with the letter* H *in the west, and just keep looking, kiddo.*

George pulled up a chair and set his bread, cheese, and glass on a scarred bureau top. "I saved you the end. Did I tell you already, Margot? The origin of 'upper crust'?"

"I've no doubt you will."

"Bread was baked on a bed of hot ashes," he continued. "The highest-ranking guest got the top crust, and the last piece, sitting on ash, went to the lowest. Picked that up reading *The Origin of Nowhere.*"

Margot put a toe in—too hot—and then added more cold. "*The Origin of Nowhere?*"

"*New York Times* fall 2018 bestseller, a compendium of phrase origins."

"And what's the origin of *nowhere*?" she asked, then sank into the warm water.

"Nowhere is when I give a lecture at the museum and you're not there," George said.

"All your qualifications, the audience that hangs on every word you speak."

"Coming out of left field," George said. He spread orange marmalade over his toast.

"Oh, George. Can't you, just for once, see further than yourself?"

Linnet sang loudly in the thicket.

"When Will changes mistresses, he moves into a new apartment," he continued, "and his taste in art changes."

How many times had he torn his brother, his own friends, to pieces? The unwashed fellow who worked in the museum cafeteria, or the thoroughly dim-witted guy his secretary dated. *Those* people. Even her own father, only to have no recollection he had ever done so.

"Your insistence that his life is to form means you'll always find something wrong with it," Margot said.

"I can't believe we're related."

"Let people be who they need to be."

Caustic and spiteful, when it suits him, she thought, *when his misanthropic side slips through.* The idea of George kicking up a row in college made her laugh. She mulled over the words of her college religion professor: the good and the bad are devilishly braided.

CHAPTER FIVE

The Summer Room

*M*y father—our lives tangled in tenuous, irreconcilable ways. There are many kinds of lies that make sideways leaps in time. But the fuzziness of relations between father and daughter alone can slingshot out the other side of the wind. It is possible for the mark of displacement on the waterline to go unnoticed.

When my father attempted to fondle me at twelve, I recoiled and ran straight to my mother. It only happened once. Or did it happen at all? Was it one of Owen's favorite birds—the proverbial night owl— that swept in the open window one long summer, so long ago, and over my childlike form? Its wings brushing lightly over me? Did he fondle me or not? My vivid imagination, too many adult novels (well before the age of thirteen)—to this day, I'm not sure.

So you see, whatever the origin, repelling anything and every-thing that might adversely affect Ava was paramount. My mother, Anne-Marie, had said, "Don't be ridiculous! Your father would nev-er do such a thing." When we sailed as a family from our home on Hopper's Island, her favorite part was skimming over the water. From that moment forward, I tried not to jury-rig any component of my vessel, or of my life. It takes three days to acclimate to life at sea, and a lifetime to discover a truth.

This is not to say that I was without sympathy for my father. On the contrary, I loved him very much, his shyness, his war with his academic prominence. The countless times our clashes had resulted in an all-out shouting match. "I had a wonderful father" was how I left it, one of many women struggling to understand who they are in the recess of losses they carry but can't quite remember.

My mother was out of place in the New England tract house he bought in the new subdivision. So he bought her an old house on an island in Maine. She always wanted chickens. I live in the farmhouse of my parents. Ava's dream is a goat farm in Vermont. Margot's most insistent discoveries in life were all made at Otyrburn.

PERTHSHIRE, OCTOBER 2018

Earlier in the week, Margot was surprised when Owen stopped by, aiming to say hello. He had swung by the stone house with its black door and pair of iron boot scrapes. *And I couldn't stop smil-ing*, she thought. She had been home alone when she asked him, in the shelter of the overhang, if he would help her with loading logs into the biomass boiler. He'd caught one in midair that she'd dropped, right before it landed squarely on her toe. They couldn't turn away from each other.

"Look at you. You're freezing," he'd said.

She had not seen Owen for twenty-seven years. Time moved in a blur. Margot was afraid her whole life would spill out of her mouth, or his likewise.

"Was it summer 1989 or '90?" she asked, noticing the space between Owen's two front teeth remained. It had foretold he would be a whistler. His face, since childhood, was ruddy, as though he'd just returned from a long walk, beating into November's stiff breeze.

"The summer of the flesh and the spirit? That was '90, followed by '91," he said. "God, how long ago was that? You're gorgeous. Some people age and you can't find them in there anymore. You look just like I remember, only more beautiful." He brushed ash off the lid of the boiler. "Too much sun and drink, and I look like my grandmother."

They both smiled. At sixteen, in 1989, Margot had joked that his dark eyebrows were thick enough to hide a cricket. People who knew him as a child commented that he was oak-like.

"I probably said twelve complete sentences when we dated. I was that serious, quiet, and shy."

"What did you do your nineteenth summer? That's when I lost track of you," Owen asked.

"I was an au pair in Switzerland, hated the place." She straightened the edge of an old sign hung askew on the cellar wall: CHOICE GROCERIES, H. HARRIS. "Are your brothers still hotheads?" She noticed, with awareness, that he moved with an understated virility.

In a nation where the unicorn was the national animal, Owen's family lived on a sea farm. Running from sea level up to eight hundred feet, it caught a glimpse from the highest peak of the steel-gray lochs of Inverness. Where old roses thrived in the short summer months, the farmhouse crawled with Alba Maxima, the Jacobite Rose. The

Fowlers had always considered themselves Scots and proud of it, but there was a share of Welsh that couldn't be dismissed.

"I can't remember their names," she continued.

"Kyle's the eldest, Percy's the youngest, and I'm sandwiched in the middle."

"That's right. Your father, Rhys, raised horses, and your mother made cheese."

"Rhona MacGregor and her white and red dappled Ayrshire herd—the now-infamous hard and white cheese."

"I can still taste it," she said. "Your chore was to pull your head out of a book and make pleasantries with the guy from the Dairy Yard."

"You make it sound so formal." He smiled and busied himself. With half his body facing her, he reached to straighten a log on the woodpile.

"I remember the day Rhona found the Swedish nudist magazine," Margot said, "shipped twice in its—as advertised—plain brown paper wrapper to one sixteen-year-old Owen Fowler."

"She didn't let on."

"Your self-expression was always measured," she said.

"And Percy's naughty streak a mile wide, and he prone to fistfights. Anything Kyle and I could do, Percy could do better. Percy stole the limelight. Rhona's greatest fear, he ran away to Glasgow at fourteen and was hauled back in by his ear. In love one year later, I read maps, studying exotic place names to run away to—together with you."

"Married twenty-four years now," she said. "I kept a photo of the two of us for the first ten, slipped into the back of a cupboard with a stash of random family photos, and I'd take it out and trace my fingers over your face, until one day, I couldn't do it anymore, and I tore it up."

"That's not what I want to hear. My wife was killed on a bicycle, five years into the marriage." He wiped his brow with the back of his gloved hand. "Set it flat on the fire."

"I'm sorry." She looked at him with anxiety. *When and where had their love been marginalized? All the possibilities, those first conversations, how had it come to a screeching halt?* "Remember the last words we said to each other?"

"Don't disappear."

Their hands had brushed as they shuffled logs around. Any action from now on would be viewed seductively. He hadn't stayed long. Their immediacy baffled their intelligence, this simple longing, and their time in life—the years long past, names carved in trees. Their parts still agreed perfectly, even at a distance.

What was it she had said that day? "Scots were as hard grafted and resilient as the stone wall their hands rested upon, and as dogged and intangible as the rough elements of the landscape that their eyes dissected." She'd got that right, but the New Yorker clearly didn't remember what to do with a muddy dog in the house.

Owen had waited out winters before, waited weeks for the wind to change, for one last outing in his wooden dinghy with ox-blood sails. In due course, the southwesterly winds of the British Isles would prevail and gather with tremendous speed and force on descent into winter's violent storms. Heavy and numerous fogs during August had spelled a hard season ahead. He didn't mind the bleak escarpments of land, and the roll of the sea was a lullaby. The frenetic scurry of a field mouse, the ripples in a salmon run, the last day of a musk rose, how a hawk rode a thermal effortlessly, two motifs in life woven together.

A sough, a murmur of Highland wind, rustled the birchwood as Owen lifted the thumb latch and entered his study. The cottage smelled of wood ash. By the time he kicked off his boots, his nose dripped, and his thoughts were of a dram of whisky, and of Margot. It was his last chance with her.

Parted from the crisp fall air, he met the prevailing musty smell of old books in a damp climate. Two rooms of imposed simplicity. The open kitchen in the "winter room" had a hearth where, on either side, linen-upholstered high-back chairs sat on a brick floor. A painted Swedish mirror reflected light between the limewashed plastered walls and gray timber-framed low ceiling. His dog, Rye, claimed the rug of silver-dun Highland cattle hide.

He went to her every day their first summer when they were both sixteen. In this way a month went by, sometimes in silence, just touching, alive with wanting it, and at seventeen, and eighteen, sometimes coupling till sunset. He knew why Margot had moved slowly since childhood. Why her heart beat so slowly, why it took so long to say something, to eat a meal, or to finish a project.

The "summer room" where Owen slept was papered in a faded black floral block print and had seafoam-green trim. Margot's eyes were green. The unfinished wide-board floor, rubbed with beeswax and linseed oil, was more often than not the "beachy floor," when sea-damp Rye brought the loch inside. Sand-washed and sand-scrubbed floors were an obscure art, but Rye got half the work done. The wallpaper should go, but his favorite aunt, Rhona's sister, had placed it there.

Aunt Fiona had raised five girls in the house. Owen had helped out summers after her husband died, splitting his time between there and the near-neighbor Otyrburn. He still heard the ring of his cousins' soup bowls between their laughter. At Fiona's, they were never hungry for long. Two in a bed, head to toe, and three on the floor on a mattress of sheep wool. The steel morals she'd planted in them, as if the earth of their souls was hers alone to till and turn. Rhona had trailed only a few steps behind, hoe in hand.

Owen lit the fire and pulled up his favorite corner chair. He listened as the high-pitched *kleet*, *kleet* of an avocet called as it swung its upturned bill through the shallow water at the loch's edge. The feisty little bird with an elegant profile adopted an uppity attitude, her neck lowered, wings and tail fully extended, as she sauntered toward him and performed her "high-wire" walk to scare him away. But he wasn't fooled. Her bark was worse than her bite.

Margot had spoken to him in secrets and made him swear oaths, their brief reunions unforgettable.

Seated at his wooden desk stained with coffee rings, he wrapped his hand around the small knob and opened the drawer containing his tobacco. He had two adjacent desks. The second, a maple slant-front with a lock, held his art supplies, and this way, if someone popped by unexpectedly, what wasn't fit for show could be hidden. He thought he had little talent but enjoyed the art of watercolors of birds, currently at work on the pinky-gray jewel undertones on a collared dove.

"American women marry for the wrong reason," Margot had said, just days ago. In two short hours, they'd talked about birds and ellipses, and together, they made an ellipse—*sort of like a circle with two centers.* "How perfect," she'd said, and not thought it odd, "a window into the other with a telescope." They'd remembered a past and years and years and years passed as minutes. What were they to make of dreams like this that shake us so phenomenally, awake in our waking as never before?

He tamped down the ribbon tobacco on the pipe bowl and spread the flame of a wooden match in an even circular motion over the surface, drawing with long, purposeful breaths. A habit he knew he had to quit. In a position of prominence above the artist's desk, he displayed his sole work of art, *Young Man in a Broad-Brimmed Hat*. The young Dutchman, poised in his winter "about-town" coat, rested with his chin on the palm of his hand. Gone were Rembrandt's baubles and heaped fortune. The subject was an everyman.

His walnut desk he'd arranged at a right angle to the room so that when seated, he looked through the doorway. In this way, he was captain and pilot of his domain, seated in one room, purveying over two.

Scotland was a hard land with a hard past. A smart person kept things simple in awkward situations. In a nation where everything mattered, where place names for the sea and edifices of stone were writ in anger and bore names like Cape Wrath and Castle Stalker, both man and beast sought the folds and hollows for shelter. The slightest decision could make a wrong.

Margot had returned. Conversation ran easily and quickly, like water through the loch's valley. Where thick torrents coursed between brambles to deliver a baptismal-like whispered echo, after the tumult, the water reflected still as glass. They both liked what they saw. The beauty of the narrative overwhelmed them.

CHAPTER SIX

The Backside of the Moon

*I*n my prime, my dark hair, now silver, rotated through tones of black, then blue, like midnight. My mother's ancestors were the ghosts of French fur trappers past, so she said, and I was the once-in-a-blue-moon, copper-hued, black-eyed baby from the gene pool that included Montagnais.

Ava hasn't shown much interest in my mother's side of the family. Perhaps when she inherits her great-uncle Leo's authentic quarter-scale, birch-bark canoe that he hand-pegged with wooden nails, carved and laced, then things will change. It only takes a small memento of the past to reignite a remembrance.

Inheriting Otyrburn, Margot met an invasion of memories; entering each room, she had crossed a border, as in a long journey. So she

kept her eyes trained on the sky, expecting to avoid triggers by traveling through the movement of clouds.

When I met her, Margot's auburn hair showed early streaks of
silver, just like Owen's. Her eyes were the color of sea glass. When
she had lost her mother, her ninth year, she dreamed often that Adela
would return one day as a mermaid. Archie had told me that he'd always thought Margot and her mother sprang from the sea.

PERTHSHIRE, OCTOBER 2018

When Margot entered the pantry, she found George on the top
rail of a stool, dusting off the feathers of a taxidermy owl he held
gingerly in his hands. She could hear Edwina saying, "A clean
corner is not the worse for being twice searched." One wall, the
entire length of the pantry hall at Otyrburn, bore the original oak
doors of a series of iceboxes, each strap hinged in iron, since con-
verted to cupboards, and it was there he'd unearthed the creature.

"Sweep's sentinel post was my chairback over summers,"
Margot said.

"You never told me."

"You weren't listening." She pulled out a kitchen chair.
"Alistair attached the lead lines to the rail and rigged a makeshift
tripod to the back of the chair that slid over the tiles on felt feet."

George climbed off the stool. "What would your therapist
say?"

Where he now stood, buttering a last corner of toast, dark-
wood open display shelves ran along two walls, filled with
Edwina's copper kettles, jugs, and cake molds.

"Most Scots know the moon phases and the time of day they
are highest in the sky," she said.

It was garden-planning day. Owen rapped on the back door, entered, and parked his muddy, wet boots in the kitchen at Otyrburn as though he had been raised there.

"My grandfather loved working with you." Margot leaned. He looked.

There were no commuters streaming past her on either side, she on her way to buy a newspaper. She wasn't fishing in her purse for a MetroCard; but rather, in the old country, her heart pounding in the one true place she had called home, since the insistent emptiness that had followed her mother's death.

"And I him."

George's phone rang. He nodded a smile in greeting to Owen, excused himself with a wave, and took the call in the Blue Room, the more formal of two living rooms at the front of the house.

"Do you remember Edwina's nesting box in the old dairy," Owen asked, "and how she complained about the ten pounds for taxidermy?" He still stood like a shepherd, used to holding ground while others dodged and darted to and fro. "Too many barn conversions, and then there are the folk without the common sense to leave a share of standing old dead trees."

A midsize gray dog stood between them. Long-coated, with long legs and keen eyes, he wore a three-inch-wide smooth brown leather collar with a brass buckle.

"He's a rare breed. Did you have one of these before?" Margot asked.

"Rye's a lurcher, like my first, Breeze, just a different mix. He sleeps collapsed in the sun all day, though he could take down a deer. Lur, in Romany, means "thief." He's a thief of the kitchen counter."

Owen's voice, with age, sounded raspy and gravelly. There they were, chatting like the upstairs neighbor and the down,

ignoring the smell of wet wool and lanolin emanating from his
bulky sweater as rainwater dripped off his brow. In her mind, they
were crossing a maze of tracks by a river, their hearts pounding.

"Picasso and his dachshund Lump died within days of one another. I'm an unabashed dog person." She watched affectionately
as Wren jumped silently up and down at her feet. "His three re-
plies to commands: 'never,' 'no, ma'am,' and 'no how.'"

They laughed.

"And what of the garden, Margot?"

"I'd like a pond covered in white lilies," she said, "and to have
fish that love to eat food from my hand."

"I'm glad you didn't ask for a door into a mountain." He smiled
with one raised eyebrow. She knew the action instinctively.

George had returned, catching the tail end of the small talk,
his hands clasped together with the morning's ambition. "How
Margot survives in the world."

"Business?" Owen asked.

George paused to wipe a pool of water collecting around the
sink faucet, then refilled his coffee mug. "Yes, I can't find, even
here in remote Scotland, an eleventh-hour escape."

Margot tipped her head at Owen. "His preeminent art dealers."

"One thousand works in one collection," George clarified. "I'll
seek him out at once."

She knew his attention varied according to the prospect, the
scope of the project, the importance of the individual, and the
work to be done. In Scotland, George's interest was broken grad-
ually, as if in a dream. In New York, he would turn on a quarter,
bounding off on a new course. Wherever he was, he stepped no
farther than was necessary, to save time and extra steps, having
thoroughly entered the spirit of the game, and found out what
type of reward someone was after.

The party ventured out. Together Margot, George, and Owen stood by the kitchen garden, having strolled through the old cutting garden in chitchat without even noticing.

"Old thistle, still going strong, far and wide," Owen said, then stooped to pull the weed. "Otyrburn's a haven for wildlife, roe deer, red deer, though, more secretive, pine marten, black cock, badger, and birds of prey, perhaps an otter along the river."

Watching him, Margot had the experience of traveling within parallel dimensions. Like the young people they had once been who drifted to the other side of a room, an implicit complicity existed between them.

The stable yard tucked tight against the rise of the Cairngorms to the north, a long row of two stone and slate-roofed buildings joined together with an addition. A block of mixed woodland included old-specimen oak, lime, beech, conifers, and Scots pine. The long-established cluster of buildings sat directly behind the kitchen, with a dry-stone wall between the two, topped decoratively: every other stone, set on end, jutted upward to resemble a spear tip.

"Alistair dangled me above this wall," she said, "and threatened to leave me on top of the spikes if I misbehaved."

"The mark of clever goat herders, or a mason with sardonic whimsy," Owen said.

"This landscape is in my DNA," Margot said.

The central building had a hip roof with double stone chimneys on either end, palest-blue doors with arched pediments above, and a hay door painted rose at the center. The lintels of accent stone that ran the full length of the building dressed it beyond the ordinary. The western wing held Alistair's cobweb-filled workshop with a hand-hewn stone fireplace, where on wet winter nights he had sat to clean his tack, and to the east, the original bakehouse, long since inoperable, and laundry. A three-bay cow-shed banked the eastern flank. They entered to find a carriage bay with a three-stall stable, tack room, grain room, and hayloft with stairs to the second-floor powerhouse. The threshing floor remained, and a game larder, wood store, and outside water clos-et finished the courtyard.

In three years' time, Alistair had, with his extraordinary strength, single-handedly, without "Babe the Blue Ox," constructed the entire enterprise. And lifted whole trees to rest in new holes. By dinner he had slain Goliath. How it spooked Margot after the accident, all of it, any stone, cold and separate, and angry, restless, rushing rivers. But not anymore; she was more than she used to be.

"One year, Alistair rented a pony, and on Wednesdays, when Edwina made her market run," she continued, "I rode him through the front door and out the back, with Alistair awarding marks for my carriage."

Both Owen and Margot sensed there was no way out. Silence and perception mattered equally.

Margot watched George; he was noticeably heady to learn, notched and comfortable in the present. They were starting a new life. She had no doubt; he'd upload a status update to his "for the love of classical" Instagram page, highlighting the property's registration in the National Heritage List.

They circled west past a line of clipped yew trees that ex-tended from the kitchen east. In the gravel courtyard, before them stretched a half-acre walled garden. The stonework and steps were in good order, with a fountain, now dry, filled with composted plant matter at the center, surrounded by broken for-mations of weather-beaten boxwood. In the back corner of the garden, Margot recalled a bronze of Faunus, the Roman pastoral god with the legs and horns of a goat, twisting his body to peer over his shoulder at his crouched leopard. Even if Margot and George couldn't make out the traditional quadriform layout, Owen could. Six pairs of urns decorated the western wall; the first of them, with elaborately worked scrolled handles, announced the entrance. Below their perch, Owen delineated the Virginia creeper vines where they grew and diminutive espaliered pear trees. Crab apples on a gnarled tree cast dappled late-day shadows.

"*An Gàrradh*, or Scots Gaelic for 'walled garden,'" Owen said. "Give it a fancy name, but it's where the peas and potatoes grew up until 2000, when Edwina had to let it go."

Margot noticed that George and Owen seemed to look everywhere but at each other.

"A five-minute journey," George said, "one they'd made each way four or more times a day for a lifetime. They must have walked it twenty thousand times, and I can't recall them calling it by a name."

Margot received a one-word text on her phone from Ruby: Mum. Cryptic messaging between the mother and daughter— short for "call me." She broke from the two men and said good night, skirted hedgerows, headed home past Edwina's small potting shed. Its tiny courtyard gave the third access to the walled garden; she exited An Gàrradh under an arbor of twining stems. She lingered for a moment, thinking about road trips they'd taken when Ruby was little, nostalgic for the young family they'd been.

Owen and George now stood in the paddock and strategized land management together, briefly, before discussing financial estimates.

"Well, let's take it slow," George said. "We don't want to get in over our heads."

"Set a limit and I'll make a mental note," Owen said.

"This wife of mine is not satisfied with one home," George said in parting.

The garden enclosed the promise of welcome. Margot waited for George on the stair landing. He joined her, *Bacchus on Holiday: An Archaeologist's Exploration of Time*, in tow. Perhaps she'd accompany George at a lone exhibition. The stairs creaked beneath them. In a house that had known a share of upheaval, she was vulnerable inside. It was but the brim of a larger vacancy.

Owen headed for his truck as a tawny owl screeched and Rye ran to relieve himself, before bolting for a hare under elderberry. *George drives some fancy fucking car, and Margot probably collects Old Master drawings now*, he thought, outraged by George's conventionality. The man Margot had married was "cultured and charming." George's pleasant directness had somehow offended Owen. *I live in my scruffy crofter's cottage, and she in a big house.*

He looked afar at the darkening fields, waiting for Rye to finish his business. *Margot had extended her hand at seventeen, as always, like something out of a fairy tale, and I took it and kissed her fingers, here in the orchard. I've always loved her.* And he asked himself, Had she grown older, content to do the ordinary? His focus was momentarily distracted by a pair of small brown birds living in the boxwood; they had taken their exit so quickly, Owen couldn't identify them on the fly. Minutes later, when Rye remembered dinner was easier had at home, they left. It would be rude to refuse George's offer to help with the restoration. Though there was something incongruous about him.

CHAPTER SEVEN

Avalanche

Where there's a will, there's a way. But please don't for an instant suppose that I, Violet Grey, can manage to express the power of desire, even if I bang a two-by-four over your head. You have to have years behind you, and knees that twist in the opposite direction of which you're headed. How kind and persuasive and absolutely delicious life can seem. We have one or two true loves in a lifetime. Our first is seldom forgotten. Is Margot an adulteress, or in the revolving face of male ambitions, wealth and power, and artworks, is the couple speaking truths that she and Owen alone have inherited?

Archie and I were aboard his boat, the Drifter's Escape. That should have told me something. But instead, I focused on how Archie had said that when he thought of anything beautiful, he called it a "Violet visitation." The night that Ava was conceived—a stone's

*throw from my home, yet miles out at sea, on top of the boat's pul-
pit—I believed that in Archie, I had met the personification of poetry.
That he was, if you'll permit me, the male counter of Lucrezia, muse
of satiric poetry, or some such damn thing. But I had given complexity
to his silent character. You don't comprehend what you're getting into
when you fall in love—our blended selves. It trips you up in all the
right places.*

*"There's Venus." I pointed, above deck, where the dark Maine sea
shone emerald and white while his boat bobbed and the sails slept.*

*"Do you know how Venus got in the sky?" Archie asked, lying on
his back, brown mats of seaweed tangled in his hair and his red whis-
kers glistening in the starlight.*

*"Tell me." I wanted to kiss him and say something affectionately
silly in his ear.*

*"Mercury was skipping stones with Neptune. His arm was as fast
as his heel, and his throw looked as though it would go forever until,
finally, it caught the arm of a sleeping starfish, flipping it into the sky,
where it has remained ever since."*

So like Archie, and how I most like to remember him.

PERTHSHIRE, OCTOBER 2018

When Margot asked to borrow his truck, Owen had explained
how the shop was a difficult hole-in-the-wall to find. He waited, at
rest on the opened driver's door. George was in London on Saint
James's Street, expecting to make the winning bid on a landscape
entitled *Between Land and Sea.* Something too good to pass up,
something with a "strong element of the accidental or casual."

She had earth beneath her nails and woke with the sun. Owen
had caught the same robin in the last of the year's raspberries.
She slid in beside Rye and sat with Wren on her lap, a few inches
from Owen.

"One hour if we take the scenic, forty-five minutes on the main."

"I do love the place," she said, then cracked the window.

"As elusive as it is."

"And why's that, Owen Fowler?"

"I was thinking about how we stumbled with pleasure, at seventeen, and how we moved away from each other to get a better view—not believing what had just happened that had made us collapse in joy and awe. About how we waited our sixteenth summer, till we were seventeen. About how all we wanted to do was run away to our secret hidey-holes and experience it all over again."

Silent, she smiled. "You don't wear a watch—and you use a flip phone. I can't believe it. I was sure you'd be working in London. A man of industry and father to five."

"I was sure you'd sell the place," he said.

They passed a crofter's cottage, its tin roof rusted, the windows long gone, and out at the edge of the rock-strewn fold of land was a sliver of a bend, then the turquoise sea. In that calm sea hid dangerous currents. She had never been a careless swimmer.

"I got a little tired of peregrine falcons circling skyscrapers, though Scotland still causes conflicting feelings." Wren squirmed, pressed against the window. His ears needed cleaning.

"The wryness in your voice hasn't changed."

She shifted in her seat, took off her cardigan, and positioned Wren back on her lap. The heater was broken and stuck on eighty-four degrees. It wouldn't shut off till they'd driven an undetermined number of miles, which, he said, varied with each outing.

"Sometimes I envision a two-lane highway," she continued, crossing her legs carefully. "One lane on the Brooklyn Bridge at rush hour, the other, a farm road."

"I like to drive slowly. I don't want to miss a thing." He shifted the gears and stretched out his right leg a bit. "I'll tell you, Margot, that confession just now had me thinking of pulling my truck over to the side of the road and the two of us getting out and finding a soft spot in the field."

She would come to accept what now must occur. They had to make love again, *if only once.* The engine made knocking sounds, sputtered, and regulated itself. The heat kept on the steady. They laughed.

"I'm not an acknowledged artist and only a so-so mother. I should live alone with five large dogs, collecting buttons."

"A good poet walks naked through life," he said. "Me, I scare myself to death taking a bath."

The truck groaned when it took the hills. She asked about a gray, turreted castle ruin. He pulled off the road beneath a run of trees. Just as he surmised, as they rushed to make love, their elbows, shoulders, and legs were not impeded by the jump seat of the truck. It was no longer an invisible awareness, but palpable.

"Beautiful," he said. "More so later in life."

"Why should we be surprised by anything by now?" she asked.

"Don't try to figure it out."

"Until, inevitably, we begin to forget."

"How many years ago was it when you and George last visited Otyrburn?" he asked. "We were going to have tea, and you called to tell me you had a fever and how Edwina had read you the riot act when you asked her for my number. I parked on the side of the road not to miss a word. I remembered the sound of your voice like yesterday."

"What did you mean the other day, in the kitchen, by 'a door into a mountain'?"

"I think we're all looking for one," he said.

Margot gave both dogs a scratch behind the ear. "And then what?"

"A walk down a path," he said, "perhaps a seat in the crook of the tree, where below stretches a river fed by a sulfur spring. The other side of the bank holds a banquet table laid out by the villagers who've awaited our return, and all they want to do is hear your moments of truth telling."

"Life becomes an intricate document of expectations and missteps, while the person that we were in childhood waits on the sidelines to be remembered." She fidgeted in her seat, undid her seat belt, and sat on her folded sweater. "The springs on my side are shot."

"I'll see what I can do about that."

A harrier hawk's spread wings in flight matched the cloud formations beyond, *whoosh, whoosh,* and soar, until its gray-and-chalk-white body disappeared against the undulations in the atmosphere. He gave her his jacket. She slid her hands into the pockets to warm them in October.

They had placed the heavily carved and paint-chipped mirror that she'd purchased beside the room's single small window, amplifying the northern light, and parted. She'd unpacked her books in her studio in the old stable yard. Later that week, everything in disarray on Otyrburn's front step, she opened *Le Nôtre* and a notebook.

She and Owen had an appointment to discuss the gardens. An Gàrradh filled one and a half acres of rugged landscape and would be a place everyone felt comfortable in but no one recognized, a classical garden to feed the body and amuse the senses. Margot penciled, *tree peonies, delphinium, sweet peas, white roses, clematis, and box.*

The finches were back and fluttered in and out of the copse as Wren dashed when Owen's truck drove down the drive. The pair walked as the dogs leaped between them in the reach occupied by two lifetimes.

"You have the 'garden bible' out," he said. "How are you?"

"A wreck."

"I never wanted to break a family. I can wait till it's my turn." They kissed and fondled.

"I have no idea what to do," she said. "I really don't."

"We swerved—we'll be okay, but Wren won't know what to do with himself, meeting a tod or a connie."

"Fox and rabbit," Margot said.

"And—a *puddock*?" he asked, slipping his hands into his pants pockets and throwing back his shoulders as they strode.

"Stumped."

"A frog—don't tread easily, Margot, where unsure. Nothing lands a man flat on his back faster than rubber boots on slippery slopes."

"And we didn't look before we leaped." She turned her gaze skyward and found the sky cloudless. "Why do you charge so little, Owen? If you don't mind my asking."

He broke into an easy smile. "Because that's how I work for whom I choose and not only the muckety-muck."

Off in the distance, the repeated hammer of a hunter at target practice sounded. "Let's go up to the house and have a cup of something," she said, slapping her thigh to catch Wren's attention.

Owen noted that Otyrburn smelled of linseed oil paint and that she still walked lightly. Margot's current canvas rested propped on her easel in the kitchen. The stable-yard studio had no insulation. The charcoal-drafted composition depicted a female figure with a crown of hovering butterflies and dragonflies.

"Is it titled?" Owen asked, standing in the high-ceilinged room in front of the four-foot-square canvas.

"*Just so,*" she replied. "But you're not supposed to ask till it's finished."

"Devil's darning needles." He pointed at a half-finished purple dragonfly.

"And there you had me at sixteen, half believing that while I slept, they'd sew my mouth, eyes, or ears shut for misbehaving."

"You tried to sell me the Brooklyn Bridge."

She set heat to the kettle, and George joined them in a kitchen held over from the fifties. The fridge, just thirty inches wide, had them stacking items in pyramids.

"Do you hunt, George?" Owen asked, acutely aware a piece of him wanted to impress as another part of him wanted to challenge. "Hunting is one arm in the life of a Highlander. He would as much cut it off as not chase the stag and the doe."

"I could be lured. What's the season?"

Owen had taken one long look at him and easily pictured George in a three-piece suit, pompously explaining to visitors at the museum what was right before their eyes. The oiled canvas *Between Land and Sea* had been newly hung on the kitchen wall.

"Red deer stags and roe deer bucks finish the twentieth of October. And game birds we can find well across fall to the New Year."

"I'll pry my brother away," George said.

Margot took a seat on a rickety kitchen chair with a crocheted seat pad, one Edwina had completed. "Everything wild and unspoiled has character here."

The short half of a pillar candle sputtered as Wren surveyed the chair where Sweep perched and Owen slipped cracker halves to dogs stretched out under the table, mulling over whether or not she had already made love that day. He smiled to himself; Margot had a hole in the toe of her canvas sneaker.

"How hard is it, George, in your line of work, to find something new that draws a crowd?"

"The challenge comes in convincing people to step away from their busy lives and engage with art."

George straightened a dried hydrangea bloom, the color of parchment, held in the vase gracing the center of the rectangular kitchen table. "Did you attend university, Owen?"

"I went to St Andrews and read civil engineering, then found myself far away from what I loved. I had but a half side to it."

Their chitchat was brief. When Owen opened the door in parting, a fierce gust of early winter blew in and out again, and he was gone.

Margot heard George call from the living room, riveted by the news. "Paradise, California, burned to the ground."

She listened to the broadcast without hearing anything that was of interest, blanketed in silence. Then began to think about selling Otyrburn, the money pit, a land mine of memories, old and craggy and uniquely hers. Piles of silverware to polish, carpets to beat, she might smash half the dishes and destroy a rosebush or two.

"I have to get back or go mad from disconnect," he added.

"Good God, George, you just arrived. Breathe. People here actually spend time alone. When you see Johnny, ask him to please bring a guest."

"Marvel Comics writer Stan Lee died, sixty-nine years married, did you hear that, M?"

By the following Monday, George was aboard a flight headed to Berlin, and then on from there, he'd make a layover in New York City. He had important work that "simply couldn't wait."

What talents it takes to remain friends. Not even inside the building yet, and we hear the clinking of glasses, "Oh, you damn fool!" Then the lingering last drink, "You'll never give up!"

George had kicked back over whisky with his closest friend, Johnny Franco, at Johnny's place. He was cooking that night. I have a soft spot for Johnny because he can sing the madrigals of his homeland. He had pierced his ear in college, a concession, then, to his young vanity, when even a woman's chance comment about his "ferocious eyes" flattered him, and the hole embarrassingly remained. Playfully, he sometimes fixes a small silver or gold ring to it and calls himself Don Quixote for the day. He values truthfulness, maintaining friendship's duties, and the remembrance of perspective in life. (The photojournalist has an exacting comprehension, and from what I can gather, he hasn't married because he hates to blur identities.)

His aunt Sophia had predicted he would be a prophet. He traveled like one. Many times, he had opened the door of a house he'd never been in before. He'd witnessed an execution; bandaged diseased limbs; been a bystander to biting and hair-pulling, cockfights and dogfights, childbirth, child labor, and child death; attended marriages in hovels and funerals in private, stuccoed chapels—but more to the point, Johnny sympathized with unlikable characters.

Identifying with Margot, he'd lost both parents in a plane crash in Argentina, while they were traveling on business for a natural fibers company they'd founded. Aunt Sophia had raised him as her own with contributions from his paternal grandparents. His mother's family, descendants of the fourteenth-century poet Vélez de Guevara, never left their ranch, not for anybody, and indeed not the child of an engagement they'd opposed. Theirs was a forty-thousand-acre preserve run as an agrotourism retreat, a fabulous place in which Johnny had zero interest.

An only child, he had twin female cousins for sisters, Pilar and Lucia. The three were born the same year. Sophia had divorced and ran a lingerie shop on the Upper East Side. The Franco females did not learn to drive. They had a driver and a cook. There were a handful of dishes that Sophia made on special occasions when the children asked. Johnny's favorite: traditional paella Valencia as his grandmother had made in El Palmar not far from Valencia, Spain.

New York City, October 2018

"George, you're a natural at inviting acquaintances. I'm more hard-edged," Johnny said, busy at work in his Manhattan home, cracking walnuts for a lemon pesto.

When no one is watching, George doesn't have to pick up the stitches, he thought, *have supreme thoughts or inspired musings.*

George sat on a barstool in the well-appointed kitchen. "You're one of Manhattan's most eligible bachelors."

"I'm a mediocre foreign correspondent," Johnny said.

"Margot's in the ascendant." George bit into a black olive soaked in a brine of thyme and rosemary. "Perhaps in Scotland, she's found her nearly perfect world. She's having a moment."

Johnny had moved on to zesting lemon rind. "Your wife's a bit of a flirt."

"Of course she is. The French admire that sort of thing."

"Marriage needs some part isolation and distance, or it loses focus," Johnny said. "Not that I know anything. But I think about it. You and Margot have never had any." He gripped the dark-wood handle of a Japanese chef's knife and sliced through the middle of a giant red onion. George was a bit subdued for so early in the evening.

"A childhood at the beach," George said, "taught me to see the backwash marks in the sand, asymmetric ripples, then symmetric. You could say the sea transcribes emotions along the shore. Sentiments are etched somewhere daily. What percentage of our intuitive intellect do we waste? I wager ninety percent. Worry. Fears, predominately."

"Jesus, deep fucking shit. George, we're back in our journeyman years at the Philosophy Club, and the year's 1989. Yale beat Harvard in tennis. We're studying Heraclites while learning what it's like to lose our reason over a woman. You're dating the brunette from an island in Maine with the lobsterman father. What was her name?"

"Gail Storm." George had made a dent in the black garlic hummus. He helped himself to another rye bread crisp.

"That's right—a doozy, a boarding-school girl. You went to Europe together that summer and survived. Was that the same summer you peddled encyclopedias along the North Shore at Oyster Bay?"

"I took the salary, not the percentage; four of us in jackets and ties, and I was the only one who made any money, carrying a suitcase for a week through the tony town, spieling off, 'Hello, my name is George. I'm doing some combined opinion work in the neighborhood. May I step in?' Anything to get in the door before the curtains have been drawn and the dogs set loose and they find out we've lied to them and have pushed sales in their living room."

"I taught sailing in Truro," Johnny said, "and lived in a beach house on stilts, smoking pot—Springsteen in concert in Boston. Bought button-fly jeans, just like him, and froze my balls all winter."

George, seemingly tense, his drink in hand, now stood in contemplation, admiring a black-and-white photo of a Dust Bowl–era girl on the adjoining hallway wall between the kitchen and living room. Dressed in gingham and white lace, she stared straight ahead at him with one squinty eye, the other closed. Her straight hair was cropped in a pixie cut.

"Magnum, 1936," Johnny said. "Such solemnity for one so young; what has she seen? We both overlap, George, in one critical juncture; we write an academic thesis on an exhibit or event, and then we balance it with the practical experience of the viewer." He had finished topping their glasses and sat with George in overstuffed leather club chairs. "How's Margot? I look forward to Otyrburn."

"To the latter, yes, it's a January party. Block the last week of December and New Year's. I'm glad you're bringing a date: those were Margot's parting orders to me." George lifted a bestseller off the coffee table and peered at the reviews decorating the back cover. "My better self says let it play out."

"Let what play out?" Johnny asked.

"She's infatuated with our Scots gardener. Things aren't as neat and tidy as they used to be."

"Thick socks and bulky sweaters." Johnny smiled.

"The town is raw. Trekkers and pub-sitters. Pawnshops and liquor shops."

"I might build a cabin in Vermont, George. I become a different person when looking west at the Adirondacks."

"Thick socks and bulky sweaters."

"You're lightening up, old friend."

"Did you ever stop to figure out, Johnny, that you repeatedly date whimsical women, only to tire of them?"

"And why I pack my library with the lives of artists—cautionary tales. One day, perhaps, I'll find a surprising overlap with a woman."

Johnny turned on the sound system and selected Dvořák, and they lit up Cuban cigars.

"Margot works harder at a painting when things go poorly." George shot him a glance.

"Like any artist. Being happy and doing good work are two separate things."

Johnny rose from where he sat by the fire, walked to the bookcase, and took down a guidebook, then handed it to George. "I'm headed to southeastern Europe in the spring, where the Danube River meets the Black Sea. The Romanian woods are home to a population of black bears surpassed only by Russia."

He looked at the petite brass clock on the marble mantel. "Dinner in ten minutes."

"No internet or phone?" George asked, then smiled. He glanced at his watch, half past eight. "Isn't that where horse-drawn carriages outnumber cars?"

A retractable ballpoint pen, Johnny thought, *that's what George reminds me of, steady, long-lasting black ink.*

"I'll be at work on reportage for an environmental piece. Join me; I'm renting a small house in the Romanian building complex where Prince Charles takes retreats. He completed the historic restoration himself using local craft and skill."

"Of course he did," George said, drumming his fingers on the padded arm of his chair. "I need no convincing."

CHAPTER EIGHT

Haunt of Swallows

A Luddite, *as far as technology is concerned, I began writing this novel longhand. Then, businesslike, I bought a Hermes 3000 typewriter from a couple of guys in San Francisco who still do that sort of thing, key repairs and switching out ribbons at the "classic typewriter store." Swiss made, 1958. So far, so good—I now have an official excuse for any typos* ~~henceforth~~. *Writer McMurty never turned on a computer, either. Great key sound, handle and carry, created by the Swiss music-box company Paillard with the world's first lightning margins. I have an Etch A Sketch in my cupboard too.*

Ava Blue asked to borrow my Hermes this week, and I said, "Hell no, sorry, I love you, but." She'd just written an entry in her thesis describing how women, and men, stay with people out of fear of change and only leave when they have no other choice. Years after they discover they should have left either job or partner. Until the room they stood in had been made crystal clear. I didn't want to risk that.

It wasn't the woman who was the strongest that survived, or the one with superior smarts, but the one who was the most elastic.

William's life, surrounded by sea, is an unadorned religion, and so for me, there is no stained glass. A puzzle of soft sea glass shines at our feet. Both he and I narrowly escaped highly regulated lives. His typewriter is a Remington. I do like his poetry. The connection between all artists is undeniable.

VENICE, OCTOBER 2018

William crossed walnut parquet and washed up in his master bath. Draped in diminutive marble mosaics, the sepia-brown-and-white pattern portrayed convivial dolphins cresting waves. *She's like a mysterious package*, he thought, *or an envelope hidden away in a desk.* Between the marble basins hung a small oil painting from Naples. It depicted a vermillion Vesuvius erupting beneath a Mars-black sky, one of many canvases from Will's own fiery-hued mountain and volcano period. Her toiletry bag rested beside his on the ledge of the window. *Her frailty, my sexual hunger*, he continued. *No, she's a haiku.*

There was a commotion out on the street, another tourist run-in with a pickpocket. He opened the french doors in the master bedroom and stood on a balcony of 1920s wrought iron, then quick-dialed Lisbet. "I'm running a little late."

"At all cost, when in Venice, remember, *do not eat fish*," Will repeated to himself, crossing cobbles.

A born and bred Venetian, Lisbet managed a Prada shop, a fashion empire run by a woman. A right on Calle de la Vida, and he came into a secluded atrium. In a maze of tourist traps and crowded streets, they met beneath a leafy bower of filtered light provided by a pergola of cream and green trailing ivy, announcing the entrance to La Luce. You could get lost in a relationship. Subsume your identity within the whims of another, or worse, become somebody you no longer recognized.

"Classic in white, swanlike," Will said with a kiss. Tall and bronze-skinned, Lisbet wore tortoiseshell glasses and a fitted skirt.

"What happened to your razor?" She took a step backward in her heels. "The scruffy beard, I'm always unsure about."

"But you like red."

"Are you hungry?" Lisbet asked.

"Dying of hunger and of love, the Italian buttock and the French one." He goosed her playfully. She smiled, Italian in this, as in all things.

They turned heel, giggled like playmates, and strolled in the direction of her apartment.

They listened to the pleasant trills of songbirds.

"My aunt Lena kept a robin in a cage," she said. "But I forgave her because on New Year's Eve, my sister and I were given a steel pot with a big wooden spoon, and she would open the window and, at midnight, ask us to beat the spoon against the pot."

"Mom hosted a book club, once a week, or maybe every other week," he said. "I was still pretty young—young enough to sit in my pajamas on the stairs out of sight and listen, not too worried about getting caught or being in my pj's. And once a month, she would have a professor from the university come over to talk about that meeting's book. *A Night in the Nabokov Hotel*."

"When will we start dreaming about the same things?"

Will plucked a rose hip from a shrub along the path, rolling it over his palm. "The delicate age of memory making."

She was always helping him turn snippets of dialogue into a distilled memory. Two flights up, and lavender oil from Marseilles perfumed the room. Atop the bed linen, she murmured, "Touch me." Will did not have to be invited twice.

Schubert's "Ständchen (Serenade)" played on as he ran his fingers through the end of her long brown hair. She listened more than she spoke. The habit gave Will the impression her thoughts were rarefied, even mystical, and the idea scared him a bit. She was a chilling, but welcome, spray off the canal.

She drew over them the raw-edge coverlet, hand-worked in Puglia, with Leonardo's signature knot embroidered in large running loops laid at the center. The bed, her design, had a headboard shaped from wide, vertical maple boards cut with a swag along the edge to resemble a garden gate.

"How are George and Margot?"

"George, he's shopping for more European finds, 'must-haves.' How much shit can one person need?" He placed one arm behind his head on the pillow. "Margot, she's busy settling Archie's estate."

"And Ruby?"

"As quirky as ever."

Will studied the portfolios of two contemporary Cuban artists. Intently focused, his pencil tapped rhythmically in one hand. He rose, drew another cup of espresso, a double, and did a few quick stretches on the Tibetan wool rug before he returned to work. Galleria Cacciano di Rondini closed for one hour and a half at noon.

William took particular pleasure in surface and texture but hadn't produced a bust that revealed the potent natural force of his model. He'd drawn near to success his thirtieth year when he portrayed a lover, one he'd felt uniquely and temporarily subdued by, but even that had fallen short. Not religious, a part of him wanted to walk into the bowels of the earth alongside van Gogh's coal miners and whisper prayers to the blue Virgin Mary in the niche they'd pass on the way down into an ebony shaft. Workhorses, which accompanied the miners' labors and hauled the loads, got to see daylight once in their lives. The day when, worn out, they were walked out beneath the sun and driven to the slaughterhouse.

Needy, William dialed Lisbet. "Why did Salvador Dalí fill a car to the roof with cauliflower?" he asked, catching her on break, too, on a sparkling Venetian morning.

"How the hell do I know? I have a shop full of Japanese customers," she said, pressing the phone to her ear with her shoulder to work the cash register with two hands. "Well, let's see, it was the age of Freudian and nuclear exploration. That might drive anybody mad."

He got up from his desk, drew a third espresso, single-handedly, with his cell phone held by his shoulder, put it down on speaker, and splashed cold water on his face, still conversing.

"I've tried to shield you, Lisbet, from my worst"—he dried his face—"but you come dangerously close."

"Is that a delivery of encouragement?" she asked pointedly. "I have to go."

He sighed. "I don't know what it is."

In contrast to Lisbet, Isabel Summers was a fellow American without the desire to edit. Life with her was simple, no delving, imposed constraints. They had left the door open. Her boxed belongings weren't parked outside the door. He had to see her again—and book his flight to New York City for TEFAF at the end of October. Will rarely missed the preeminent arts and antique fair.

CHAPTER NINE

Promises to Keep

When Ava asked me to sit for her thesis research interview on how disempowered femininity can skew the self (among other gender-equality issues), I said, "What could I possibly teach you that you don't already know?"

Question number three: "How did the actions of your father serve to strengthen and also diminish you?" My answer: His storytelling gave my imagination a hold. It served as a canopy that I could return to and lie beneath to restore my ownership over the free space in my life. In this way, he strengthened me.

How did my father diminish my life? He read my diary my seventeenth year: Fritz, we will do it. This summer, we will make love. *Then he invited Fritz to a tennis match and forbade him from ever seeing me again. In the version that my father relayed, after he*

had returned home, Fritz had suddenly jumped ship of his own voli-
tion—out of the sweet-joy-of-love blue—when he uttered the words to
me: "I can't see you anymore."

My father, Thomas Grey, had a limited comprehension of the power behind words. He forgot that I was smart and capable. From then
on, no man would control my destiny—cohabitate and nourish, yes;
love and lift, yes; ask the same question every day, yes: What are you
going to do with your life, for meaning, for truth, for self?

Archie had used Margot as his "ambassador" to Otyrburn and his
parents. As she grew, in her absence, he openly took lovers, assuming
she wouldn't notice, feigning ignorance of the fact that her curiosity was more and more aroused. In the end, right when it mattered,
Margot was unable to look where she wished, at Owen.

PERTHSHIRE, OCTOBER 2018

Margot waited for George beneath the worn green-velvet canopy
on Edwina's four-poster bed. In this bed, her grandfather, Alistair,
had spun tales of "Brownies," and Margot, delighted, screamed
while she jabbed him to stop. It was folklore—built of terror, loaded with universal truths—delivered by one who was preternatu-
rally kind and good.

"Why so down in the mouth, Queen of the Orchard?" Alistair
had asked.

"The bowl of oatmeal I left by the stove last night is full."

"There's your mistake. Clothes or porridge left for a Brownie
only serves as an insult."

"But, Grampa."

"You turn a deaf ear. A blue hat and walking staff suffice."

"Where does he live?" she'd asked.

"Brownies live outside in streams and waterfalls, some say
in houses or stable yards, but not in these hills. My mother left

a child's chair at the fire for her Brownie to sit in after he'd helped her with her work. If they work any bit, they only work at night when you're fast asleep, wee darling. They guard their privacy, so you won't be seeing one. The last Brownie lived in Fenwick Forest."

They traveled an invisible bridge; there were spirits of fountainheads and wellheads, lochs and knolls, and spirits of dwellings. Folklore's appeal belonged to folk and not to educated opinion. It retained the power to linger in psyches while facts fell through cracks. Margot always knocked three times.

What did it mean to be a strong person? To lose one's fears? To laugh, to love, to be caressed, not merely admired? And yet somewhere, her father was agonizing over her lack of discretion.

Margot looked at the empty pillow where George would soon lie. *Giggling doesn't get its due*, she thought. *George and I rarely giggle.* She heard an odd cry in the wood, the window open a crack. *The night Archie tore down my bedroom door*—she reeled the years backward—*he'd arrived to visit Edwina and Alistair at the end of August and accompany me home to New York, only to find me ensconced in my bedroom with Owen.* They had locked the door, with Alistair and Edwina in town. *"Get out of here, Owen. Don't come back."* Archie didn't know what he wanted for my life, but he knew what he didn't want. I was his "beautiful creation." Ten days alone together on Hopper's Island couldn't offset his absence.

Adela had called Margot *my bijou*, or "gem." Till the year of Archie's death, *The New Yorker* still arrived with the label addressed to "Mrs. A. J. Reid."

"What were you thinking about?" George asked, climbing into bed, abruptly breaking her train of thought.

"Adela. Archie. Who invented death? Since childhood, my feelings have been too big for my body."

"You lost your mother over thirty years ago."

Shivering, her red hair plaited beneath a black headscarf, she had wanted to go home. After the ceremony, home was a stone circle of dark moods, and those she left behind, somewhere beyond.

"How far does one have to go to forget one's past?"

"As I say in the opening to my lectures," George said, "that which we love in life and watch perish, utterly, in art can survive forever by creating a complex distillation of sensation and memory."

"That's a prescription label without a warning." She sat up in bed. "What did you and Archie fight about the day before he died?"

"I fetched him and we drove. I knew a small café, and we went straight there. He was enjoying himself—a crabmeat sandwich with fries. The bad weather kept visitors away; we had the place to ourselves."

"He wasn't always as indefatigable as you supposed."

She recalled her thirtieth year, when they'd argued and she'd asked Archie, "Why is all of our communication transactional and not empathetic?" *I don't need a cash infusion or help balancing my checkbook,* she'd thought. Such a pale had come over her father's face.

"Archie's been dead for more than eighteen months." George shut off his reading lamp. "It is useless to revisit that miserable afternoon."

"Now tell me what you talked about." Margot, leaning propped on her elbow, looked at him in the darkened room.

"Nothing in particular."

"Do you remember if he said he was just going to loaf away the afternoon?" she asked. "Because that's what he had suggested to me."

"We talked about a Dutch landscape painter we both admired. Why?"

She turned the light back on. "Because when I asked him about the lunch later in the day, he gave me a flippant answer."

"It was a rather mundane meal, not at all awe-inspiring," he said.

"You had a falling-out," Margot insisted, then threw her head back on her pillow.

"Archie always had a definite idea about what he wanted. He didn't have to get so hot over our lunch or paint such a black picture of life."

"I knew it—you laid into him."

"Give it up, Margot."

"After all he did for us," she said.

"Good night, dear."

She woke first as dawn broke. Shared sleep, Margot had only slept in the arms of one person, and that wasn't her husband.

Beyond the forces of marriage, motherhood, history, and expectations conspiring against women, in their relationship, she risked being erased, like summer doors closed in winter, though no matter how she analyzed and reexamined the linear phases of their life together, there were no apparent signs of crisis. George was different. The house, the home, and their family traditions met his oxygen requirements. He was a historian who depended on continuity.

And down the road in a crofter's cottage, not three thousand miles distant, let alone on the flip side of Neptune, Owen slept. Margot could start walking in one direction, reading a map, turn in the opposite direction the next day, and still end up here.

Owen was wide awake, around the bend, staring at the ceiling, thinking of the "magic mushroom summer" that they nearly laughed themselves stupid at eighteen. They'd cooked and eaten a psilocybin mushroom omelet, divided into equal halves with a ruler.

Margot had flown over the Canyon de Chelly, marveling at how a place viewed only in waking—in *National Geographic*—became electrically vivid. He'd been lost in the marsh grass around that loch outside his door for an unknown span of time, watching as water striders skimmed the surface in a wealth of patterns.

He got up with a jolt from the bed and, naked, stepped first in a puddle, then in heavy mud, headed to the loch. He listened as a "bird plow" sounded—creatures had warning systems. He braced and plunged. Disturbed, the snowy egret lifted in takeoff from where she'd been sleeping in the cat-o'-nine-tails. Had he read too many novels, like an old bookseller? He felt slightly ridiculous, but no less in love.

CHAPTER TEN

The Last Palace

A poem is someone's everything. We read one as a sympathet-
ic excursion. Whether you believe in my words or stare off into
space, you have entered my mind, hoping to find out what was happening somewhere else. And yet, I have arranged words with purpose
that are too far ahead of me to understand. Both Ava and Margot are
modeled on the bookshops of Ruby's Paris. Even Ava's observations on
weather carry a dry—prehistoric for this day and age—witty prose.
Boats at rock in the harbor, who begged for the ocean, took corners
without a pause. I choose to think of Ava and Margot concocting adventures from those fastened objects in their line of vision. There is
never only one side of anyone.

PERTHSHIRE, OCTOBER 2018

Owen was close, and she was glad. He laid a grass-stained finger on his landscape blueprint.

"Wind can be a problem, funneling up a valley, but not if we plant for habitat. It'll predominantly be a garden of straight lines."

A dark wall of forest stretched between them.

"I've shaped a sway in the bow that mirrors the arch of hill rise behind," he continued. "We'll plant six hundred yards of box and two hundred of yew."

The one-half-acre walled garden was almost devoid of the understory. Only Edwina's early bulbs remained.

"We both became artists," she said, standing in her studio.

"I wouldn't call myself that. I paint birds, nothing more, and prefer traditional hand-drawn renderings of gardens."

He gave her a distant smile. All things considered, anticipation was both seismic and delicate. Margot's fingers rested on the paper beside his hand. The elaborately detailed drawings revealed a draftsman's sensitive eye.

"Where are you locating Ruby's sweet-pea bamboo teepees?" she asked.

"In the vegetable parterre. I suggest we go with cordon-grown varieties: Gwendoline, Raspberry Flake, April in Paris, Madison, and my favorite, Percy Thrower. She won't want for sweet pea."

"And this purple area here?"

"An iris garden around your koi pool."

"What's the immense foliage indicated along the border?" she asked.

"Walk with me."

Bees were visiting the huge lime tree overhanging the potting shed.

"Despite having five eyes," Owen said, "a bee prefers large patches of an individual plant, and not just any color, but the blues, purples, violet, and white that can be had in nature; that way, the darker centers contrast where the nectar can be found."

"Visiting five thousand flowers in a single day, in fifteen or more travels. In the city, I keep company with a beekeeper."

"When bees stay close to the hive, rain is close by," he said.

Margot smiled and sat down on a rock warmed by the sun. "Alistair began and ended each day with the forecast."

He extended his hand, smelling of earth, saying, "Climb up," and she stood atop the wall. "Along the edge of Edwina's lath house is volunteer *Acanthus mollis*, or Rue Ledan—the plant you asked about. Lustrous, spineless things. I'm partial because slugs and deer detest it, and the foliage persists into winter."

She heard only bits, distracted by his form. She couldn't stand herself. She'd accumulated things, then evolved into a person of substance with things of suchness. One day, she'd start signing off her emails with "Cheers."

A forest of lupines swam in a circle, sealike, around them.

"I repotted geraniums here for Edwina in her 'Glass House.' How will we keep the connies out, Owen?"

"Netting attached to the farthest perimeter keeps the hares at bay."

They moved from the lath house to the west on a beeline, on a fox run, on a ship pointing.

"'Willful waste makes willful want,' Edwina would say. I grew up with that." Margot bent to tie the laces on her boot. "Alistair and I had the thankless job of wheeling the lemon and orange planters in if the weather turned before I left for school in early September—two trees of each, in and back out again. He used to say we were the workhorses that drove Edwina's Moveable Feast, and then he'd whinny, stomp, prance out on heavy steps, snort, and shake his head low, as though his mane swept the pavers. Gramps was a riot."

"Eccentric," Owen said. "He'd say to me 'tell my bride' this or that, with a cut flower in his lapel 'just because.' When Edwina ceased calling on me, Alistair kept on." Owen stole a kiss. "It won't be an exorbitant fee to replace the glass."

"You said you could train a rose to obey you."

He was forty-five years old, and the oily plant resins of the earth still clung on his skin and dripped off his brow, just as she remembered in their youth. He had the same languor and the same farseeing look.

"I did. You want me to train your roses to do anything," Owen said, feigning exasperation, "*that one* to twist this way, and the other to climb higher. You still don't like snakes much, but do like bumblebees. A rose is not a dog—sit, stay, c-o-m-e."

CHAPTER ELEVEN

Tightrope

*T*he Puebloan people would never, ever leave Taos. They knew all the passes through the mountains and talked to their gods on the open plateau that circled the Blue Lake. A band of angels had come down and circled over the Taos Pueblo—I think, but could be wrong, that the drumming of their staying power is why Ava moves around from place to place.

When we left New Mexico, as a youngster on Hopper's Island, Ava developed a reputation for being perpetually lost. Her rambles often led her along the curvature of the two-mile beach until I lit a fire on the rocks to guide her home. Once, a neighbor had stumbled upon seven-year-old Ava asleep on the dune's edge, with a book in the sand, and carried her back to the white porch with a parrot-green Aztec hammock. Being on an island meant she could circumnavigate *the globe and be home for dinner. At the crossroads, where temptation and integrity converged, Ava tiptoed and peeked, but she always took a step. It's hard not to.*

William is much like Ava in one respect: they both would prefer to live in isolation, not alone, but far from the wickedness of the world.

VENICE, LATE OCTOBER 2018

Booked—William would take his old friend, Isabel Summers, to New York City for TEFAF, and say nothing to Lisbet. There wouldn't be an explanation. Will called off affairs; he didn't keep them. *Relationships are manufactured,* he thought. *They exist in the realm without answers. Maybe when I'm an old man with a shock of white hair that falls over my eye.*

The soft earthen olive green, ever present in the Giudecca Canal, was rendered more or less prevalent to the eye by the quality of light. Lisbet was wrong. Revelations about his inner peace or affliction would only disappoint. Yet she persisted, cleverly injecting subtle, wry humor into his life when she sensed he'd taken refuge in his inner sanctum. A flawed poet can't produce art or fixed relationships.

He threw the evening edition of *Corriere della Sera* into his suitcase, closed the shutters in the living room against Venice's persistent glare, and arranged the pair of bergère opposite the fireplace. The back of one had faded from carmine to rose. He opened his desk drawer and slipped a copy of a poem he'd penned into his pocket. He'd leave the piece at Elisabetta's and mark the date of his return. He turned the key in the lock, then ran.

NEW YORK CITY, OCTOBER 28, 2018

Will browsed a collection of French twentieth-century architects' furniture as Isabel stood across the hall in Stand 74: Modern and

Contemporary British Art. There were ninety-three exhibitors at the European Fine Art Fair, TEFAF. They'd only begun their exploration. *Lively recaps,* he thought, *that's what we do best—novellas on life. Whether I nod enthusiastically or not, Isabel will have a fascinating explanation on why I pursued x, y, or z.* Paintings hung in rooms. *Gallerie Baptiste* here, *Issac Jacobsen Fine Art* there. Furniture paraded in others.

"I liked the lines of the Jasper Morrison desk; where did we see that?" Will asked.

"Not sure if it was before or after *Homage to the Square* in frog-pond green." Isabel's dark eyes lifted briefly, then darted back to texting.

"Oh, jeepers. Can you put it aside?"

She made little effort to hide her irritation at being asked to cease multitasking. "Hold your horses, Will. Back it down, whoa, there, mister. Just like your brother, George." She opened her purse and popped a mint into her mouth, handing one off to Will. "I have a callback for a small role on Broadway, *The Inner World of George Sand,* 'plunging the depths of one woman's subconscious,' though I'm not sure that the director's up to the task."

"What are your reservations?" he asked, weaving between exhibit goers.

"Sand had many lives. Toward the end of her life, she said, 'It seems to me that we change from day to day and that after some years, we are a new being.' In *The Journal of Eugène Delacroix,* he wrote of his friendship with her and that Mademoiselle Sand's fame imposed restrictions on her commentary while alive. Then he went on to say the only quality worth publishing is frankness."

"I'm repeatedly at the edge of a two-hundred-acre field, squinting to locate the demarcation where a monochromatic palette changes to luminous color."

"Then you need glasses," she said. "I'll take it on if the director fails."

Isabel adjusted a black-and-white polka-dot silk scarf, knotted at her neck, looking, with her brunette hair piled on top of her head in a beehive chignon, much like a 1958 Coca-Cola model.

"Why did you mention George earlier?" Will asked.

"When did I do that?"

"Just now."

"It's nothing; you're a modern man," Isabel said, then inched her petite frame forward to examine a '40s Art Deco mirror.

"What's nothing?"

"We slept together once." She lifted her eyes to meet Will's. "I can barely remember when or where. You aren't a *things-should-be* person lost in a spent life."

Will's and Isabel's lives lived in each other's memory. And that memory-foam now, apparently, included George.

"I get it. You slept with me and my brother, thinking we were the same man."

Isabel leafed through the exhibit's program. "George gave me a tiny Renaissance master drawing. I had it framed."

"There's a Brâncuşi here and Chagall's *Les Fiancés Au Cirque*," Will said mechanically. He ran his hand along the smooth, curved back rail of a Kaare Klint chair with a black leather seat from Copenhagen. "I always aspire to hear the music inside the poem. But that thought trumpets too loudly. A hill could have grown up to swallow it, but didn't." He took off his sport coat and slung it over his shoulder. "Anyhoo, I'm more interested in the metrical effects of Latin poets."

Will stopped before a booth with the head of an Egyptian block statue in granodiorite.

"Are you by chance related to George Lowell?" the dealer asked, having read Will's name on the exhibit pass clipped to his shirt pocket.

"His brother."

"Imhotep Ahmed." He extended his hand in greeting. "A pleasure to make your acquaintance. Is George here?"

"No."

"Please give him my card and remind him to call me."

"Sure thing."

William pocketed the card. *Another prestigious collection,* he thought. *The sunny world of big money and art swindlers.*

"One of George's oddball friends." He opened his wallet and stashed the card. "How did I end up here?"

"Good question, a little staid for the avant-garde Will."

"It's a dilemma."

"Your most memorable all-time line was, 'Follow the one in the white toga that doesn't quite make it over her ass.'"

"When the hell did I say that?" he asked.

"When the theater department performed *Spartacus.*"

They stood together and watched the few idlers, hesitant to leave the exhibition. Will had known Isabel for twenty years. They'd shared a house in New Haven while at Yale, with two classmates, Isabel in the theater department and William in fine art.

She looked faint. "Food, the other thing people indulge in during moods like this. Let's get out of here and order room service," he said.

Isabel paused before a set of six 1960s silver egg cups from Finland on their way out of the exhibit.

"This is a recovery holiday for me. William—don't snicker at me with a straightlaced face—I see you telling me 'I told you so.'"

She turned a monogrammed egg cup upside down and examined the hallmarks. "No man could've been more perfect than Jim."

"Hmm. That sounds like a problem. You don't believe that?" Will asked.

"So what are your plans for the weekend?" She smiled, stepping off the elevator. "Or are you going to keep that stank face on all day?"

Will slid the room key card in the door lock. He and Isabel talked about going to Barcelona, but it hadn't happened. Standing in awe, jaws dropped on the sidewalk beneath Gaudí's architectural sandcastles had been just that, a castle in the air. The side trip to the beach where Dalí spent his childhood summers hadn't happened either.

"Whom are you seeing these days?" Isabel called, then threw a packet of rose geranium bath salts under the tub's waterfall as he uncorked a bottle of Piedmont red wine. Her voice rose over the splash and resounded off the marble.

"A Venetian woman I like very much," he said.

"I told whomever it was you dated sophomore year that we had had sex in the studio," she said, sliding down beneath the bubbles, submerged, only to playfully pop back up. "Bodies atop a rumpled sheet, entangled in Rodin poses. We might as well have been covered in clay dust, toe to head. I remember the day clearly because you, William Lowell, called me Lady Dorian Gray."

He smiled tenderly, with nostalgia, seated on the closed lid of the toilet while she bathed. A wealth of recollections streamed between the two, and occasionally, a reminiscence recalled by one would express an explicit awareness of the other. He sipped his wine, and she hers from the tub.

"You're not apologizing—far from it—Isabel the Shakespearean cognoscenti. The world's a stage, Ophelia. Did you think I didn't know?"

"I loved you and your car," Isabel said. "What was the model? Try to find a red one again. You get rid of things *too* fast."

Will rose and unpacked his backpack on top of the bed's quilt. "A 1975 Saab 99."

The Belgian comic series *The Adventures of Tintin* had brought the pair together. It featured an androgynous boy-wonder detective. The childhood aficionados, in their youth, had sported *King Ottakar's Sceptre* watches and *The Black Island* backpacks. Isabel had worn a T-shirt with Milou, Tintin's sidekick dog, trotting across her chest to Art History 101 freshman year. She dried off and put on Tintin powder-blue silk pajamas.

"I had to make your day. It's a pajama party. Google search page seventeen, Tintin pj's, vendor Israel."

"Quirky, sexy, kinda weird."

VENICE, OCTOBER 28, 2018

Lisbet lay in her apartment, on her belly, atop a subtly hued bamboo silk and wool rug. She read Will's verse and repeated the opening line to herself, "We are too literal, too graphic; choking jealousies, disappearing truths." She knew his preferences in food, in art, and how to engage his interest. He had become her treasury of joy against life's ills.

Two matched white Turkish towels hung on the nickel towel bar. The walls of the master bath, set with massive slabs of slate, served as a backdrop for a gallery of sculptural artifacts. A piece of marble cornice bought in Rome served as the mantel for a pair of broken verdigris pots balanced on tripod legs they'd bought together in Greece the summer past. And below, three architectural salvage remnants: one gray slab with stone-cut Latin letters (which neither of them had bothered to decipher, though that was the plan); a portion of an ivory frieze depicting carved sheep asleep, attended by a daydreaming shepherd; and one heavily distressed chunk broken off a Doric capital.

Lisbet outlined her blue eyes with a brown liner, dabbed beige opal lipstick, and caught her reflection in the dinner-plate-size concave mirror wreathed with a gilded laurel.

New York City, October 28, 2018

"Come, keep me company," Isabel said, patting the Hungarian goose-down duvet on their king-size bed.

Will sat calmly in a chair by the window while on the sidewalk below, people moved without expression, compelled by urgency. He thought of fig trees in the wind and the cold silver of the sea. "Do you know Rodin's *Gates of Hell*?"

"No, do you know that Mark Rylance is the preeminent living Shakespearean actor, or that he's an expat from Wisconsin who lives in Britain? He attended private school with a friend of mine."

"Rodin made this imposing pair of massive doors." He stared out the window at the dark, reflective gray of the buildings, held against the slip of skyline. He thought of the purest of grays and the depth of a cloud. "One version in plaster, one in bronze, returning to work on them his whole life, and was never satisfied with either interpretation. Like da Vinci and the *Mona Lisa*, which became a part of his personal belongings that traveled with him till the end of his life."

"I bet Rodin's door was a bitch to cart around."

"The more Rodin saw," he said, "the greater his endeavor. Rodin stood before ingots of lead, bronze, and silver; took a molded block of solid material; and made it breathe. And still wasn't content."

"Who uses the word *ingots*?"

Will had stripped down to his boxers and stretched out beside her atop the bedding. "The door doesn't open. Rodin placed nude figures that crawled and clung to the doorframe, rendering it inoperable. They can't get in."

"Sounds Freudian, closed doors, gates that won't open—ascension, massive upright forged members." Isabel flirted, then laid her hand on Will and kissed him; her volcanic impetuosity was predictable and without warning.

A call to love, he thought, and responded to her erotic touch, only to shut it down and grasp what he had to do, apologizing.

In the early-morning cacophony of garbage trucks, produce vendors shouted, and the shop grates clanked. While Isabel slept, William went for a stroll in his slippers, out the door of the hotel, without a shave, and around the corner for a cup of coffee. It hadn't once occurred to him as odd. He had a perception of rare clarity when wandering at home in the grimy city of his birth—thinking fast and thinking slow, as a child speaks openly—this building is taller than another, this patch of sky bluer than another; he thought of all the people who had entered his life in the space of time and the absence of silence.

In Venice, Elisabetta reread the poem she'd taken to work.

SILVERLIGHT

We are too literal, too graphic;
choking jealousy, disappearing truths,

too little oxygen, too late.
But press on, argonauts in space—
if our grasp of another fails,
or has no beginning—
somewhere, our hard-won efforts succeed,
and leave some trace of how we loved.

—W. W. Lowell

CHAPTER TWELVE

Day Trippin'

I cannot write a poem in praise of my husband. If I had one, he would want to play with my hair as if he owned it, and my Leo mane is much too difficult to brush. If you're the kind of person who seeks out a quiet corner before the weekend guests leave and sprawls across the bed with confidence when the western light sinks low and you for once have the house to yourself, and yet you are not lonely, then you have discovered, like me, that you are already wed to the art of the imagination. There's too much risk otherwise. Someone might say something to break your train of thought and make it all vanish as the moon goes over the water.

At seventeen, I began the makings of a novel titled The Profanity Trail. I had intended to tell the story of a Mexican pearl diver, Rosalita, who came face to face with death, encountering a monster of

the deep, and escaped by swimming through the ink of a giant squid.
The experience imbued my protagonist with the power of prophecy.
Friends gathered around the sand she sat upon, and she dispelled their
scattershot theories, there on the beach by the turquoise sea. (Permit
me the pleasure of description.)

The days when no one materialized asking her for advice, "dear
Rosalita" wrote op-eds on lust and penance, sins and forgiveness, for
La Transportar Tribuna. *In English:* The Haul-Away Tribune.
To celebrate her literary accomplishment, she took a small piece of
paper and scratched upon it four words: just over the hump. *Then*
Rosalita stuffed the missive in a bottle, and corked, it bobbed over
the sea. Wherever it rested in the four corners of the world, the four
words gave the recipient the power to marshal *their inner intuition*
like a finely tuned ear. (So, dear reader, later in the story that I'm
telling you, before you say, "Hold on just a minute, Violet," thinking I
digress—don't forget Rosalita.)

PERTHSHIRE, NOVEMBER 2018

"Owen asked me to visit a garden before winter," Margot said,
closing the chimney damper. *Owen and I have been shuffled and*
sifted, like sand, like time in a bottle, since childhood, she thought.

"Glean what genius you can." George folded the newspaper,
seated in the Blue Room. "I make money for your pleasure garden
when I work."

Margot noticed he wasn't disturbed. He never forgot to put
sugar in his lemonade.

"Let's go to the pub," she said, when every other thought was
of Owen, of something, anything, beyond their habitual default
position of banal forays. "I hardly see you anymore; we leave
notes for each other on the coffee machine."

"I'm here before you now."

The river Greeley curled through the heart of Wyndham village, with one general store, church, post, pub, priest, and baker. It threatened to flood its banks with a roar in spring and made peace-striking ambient noise dependably during the other seasons. One could chart the worst years. The watermarks on mossy facades that sat low were dated. Village folk made a competition of it, who stayed through the flood of 1945, 1960, and who left in 1992, the turbulent years writ in blue paint, the lesser storms tallied in black. The pub sat high, as did MacFarlane's Hardware Store. In desperate times, what was needed could still be had. The same wasn't valid for the post, but the village folk appreciated the holiday when the utility bill was missed for a spell.

The west side of buildings was slate-hung or furnished with lime harling to fortify against a southwester heading across the Atlantic. It kept them dry and was an ornamental dressing-up of the crude material beneath, and in this way, houses made of rubble stone and brick survived the elements. *Harling* came from *hurling* the wet mortar on the wall. George's childlike curiosity had compelled him to ask in town. Where pigment was added to the limestone, rosy houses dotted the village of Wyndham.

A traveler marked the approach of the village when the clumps of sycamore began to appear, creating hollows of sheltered houses. The Dance of the Black Cock Pub stood in the lee of an old English oak. George had surprised his family and slowly became able to recognize the common beech, with their smooth-as-stone, silver-gray rolls of bark, and the sticky resin that dripped from the salmon-colored papery scales of the Scots pine. Margot chose a table by the fire, and Wren set off to waggle with the pub owner's fox terrier.

The night they first visited, the proprietor, Robbie MacTavish, had drawn up a chair and tucked his full-bellied stoutness to the table. He laid impressive hands before them that had won the caber toss too many years to count at the Highland Games and then took one look at Margot. "Alistair Reid's grandbairn is a friend of mine!"

And with that introduction, he had stretched his spine backward on his chair spindles and clasped his hands behind his head, his elbows splayed, hawklike.

"A man can do without a brother but not without a neighbor," he continued, "and Alistair was the best neighbor a man could have. I'll never forget the night—a right foul one—Alistair strode in with Nipper. Hung his dripping oilskin on the hook, called out for a house round, and climbed atop a chair with a 'Bottom's up!' Then delivered his tribute to a bad night with the missus hurling hot irons. 'Honey may be sweet,' he said, 'but no one licks it off a briar.' I'da shadowed him to the top of the devil's hot-coal mountain in my slippers and back down the other side if he'd asked."

Alistair had a way with folk.

All pubs attempted to be a place that offered joy and consolation. The keeper made the difference. Robbie, like his father before him, repeated the same stupid jokes. Fortunately, he didn't have a son. With his bald round head and enormous drowsy blue eyes and long lashes, he belonged on the cover of a nursery book entitled Sleep Well, Wee Laddie, and Your Duggie Too.

"My favorite. A lady with kisses!" Robbie grinned at Margot. "How are my American fledglings?"

George occupied the conversational space before Margot had a chance. "Living the Highlands."

"It's an achievement," Robbie said. "Let's see how you do when the wind picks up."

Margot observed the two men and concluded that George would succeed in Scotland but for all the wrong reasons. He was incapable of intuiting her thoughts—or the subtle nuances of anyone, for that matter, or thing or place, remotely quiet. He relied on a different set of tools.

The Highland Games, she thought, and tried to calculate the year she and George had toured the fields. Ruby was about four, so it had been early on. When at both the food vendor and the vendors with Scottish gear, and especially at the sheepdog trials, she had searched for Owen in the crowd. Then, seeing some friendly faces and some new ones, still with no luck, she'd traipsed through the athletic feats of strength and endurance, the Highland dancers, and more than one whisky tasting.

Again when Alistair had died, she'd counted on seeing Owen. He might as well have lived in Hawaii. Such a long stretch of assumed indifference had unraveled between them. Another decade could easily pass, and then what?

His truck had broken down that afternoon, and he'd arrived at the memorial service forty minutes after she departed. Edwina had left her guest book open on the kitchen table the next morning, in between writing responses to her letters of condolence. There he was—Owen Aidan Fowler.

George rested his hand on the pub keeper's shoulder. "Robbie, I have to ask, what sound does a man make when he throws a twenty-six-pound 'Braemar stone'?"

The walls were covered with photos from past Highland Games, the shelves stuffed with silver cups, bronzes, and a plethora of plaques, all of which told the story of the ritual path a Scots boy took to become a man. The path Owen had completed.

"The Braemar stone is thrown practically standing still, one-handed. With a clean palm and a dirty neck. It's held under my ear just so." Robbie lifted the pillar candle off the table to demonstrate. "It's a quiet throw. Mind you, it won't be polite, letting you in on what I think about in mixed company." He winked. "The stone put is the noisy one. *Braaagh!* After thousands of years, the stone culture is our history and myth. Why do you ask, George? Up for a stone throw at the Highland Games this summer?"

"I'll spare you the ineptitude."

"Don't be ridiculous, man. You married a Scots," Robbie said.

"I love this place." George glanced around the boisterous room. "Nowadays, to talk to someone in the street is seen as an act of aggression."

"Aye. You were a sweetheart," Robbie said, taking in the adult Margot. "I remember the girl with auburn hair in red tartan and black velvet. The bee's knees who stepped blithely through the sword dance." His eyes glinted as he flirted.

Owen fashioned beautiful gardens but didn't have much of one of his own. The plants that failed in their intended location, he adopted, carrying home whatever his clients outright sought to lose: *The berries will kill my dog. It attracts too many beetles. The petals get in everywhere. I don't like the color.* In this way, his secret garden prevailed in rocky soil.

Of the many trees in the wood, he loved beech the best. In the fall he found profound isolation below low-arching vaults of boughs. The Norse and the English had called it *bók* or *bóc*. The pewter bark used for writing birthed *book*.

He packed a bag and headed to the bothy. Remote yet open to all, the going was mountainous. There'd be a fireplace, a loft for sleeping above the floor's draft, and a spring or creek. He'd respect the "bothy code" and replace what wood or candles he used, and he'd carry his spade for meeting the elements on the edge of a peat bog or the top of a crag.

The sun set early his first night. He slept fitfully, listening to the north wind knife through a chink in the wall. Got up, wrapped himself in blankets with his boots still on, and paced back and forth in front of the fire, his gaze inward, looking back. Rye hounded his footsteps with the white of one eye cracked his way.

Her name was Uma Alomerovich. She had been raped in Glasgow at fourteen, and in an exodus, her family had jumped from one town in Scotland to the next, always fearful, till they'd settled on the remote post of Inverness, part of the hundreds of Bosnians evacuated to Scotland under the Bosnian Programme in the early 1990s. Owen had been twenty when they married, and she, just nineteen. That young woman with the merry laugh, from a medieval village at the base of the craggy Dinaric Alps, who recited prayers in "Orientalism," uttering a phrase in Turkish, followed by one in Persian and another in Arabic lowlands, went fast. A bike was no match for a car. Alone so long, he'd ceased relying on a world that was crazy, erratic, xenophobic, and selfishly living on a razor's edge. Too many people's charm had held no lasting musical language—if he could hear it at all.

Under the veil of black, he counted stars, searching for markers—the diagonal Orion's belt, the S-shaped plow. If he kept an eye out for Cassiopeia and Pegasus, he might feel right again. He had no luck, though Venus still shone brightly. His strength had been his ability to endure and have patience.

CHAPTER THIRTEEN

Old Friends

*A*va had telephoned. Once we spoke nearly daily. I'll take anything I can get. From one window in either of our houses, she on
land and I on my island, stretched over the sea, in the best of times, we
act as a lighthouse for each other. She expressed a desire to get barefoot
and insane, to decompress. Then return to her thesis and "adulting."
On the open road, she had actualized impressions that no one had
described to her. To collect her most recent interviews, she'd taken a
ferry across the Atlantic and made it all the way down to DC, some
inspiration for the thesis, but not without emotional cost.

Question number ten: "What place makes you feel distilled to your
purest essence?"

Conservationist, Nantucket, Massachusetts: "When I sit with my
husband in our L.L.Bean chairs in the sand, he thinks I'm reading a

novel, but I'm not. I'm writing one. I don't have to exercise caution when the waves of depression wash over me, or be economical with my emotion. My face is in a mirror, and my eyes are in a book."

Question number seven: "Did you ever believe a decision had been forced upon you?"

Counselor, Roanoke, Virginia: "In 1978, a pregnancy out of wedlock my nineteenth year meant my Puerto Rican father insisted I choose between satisfying the immediate family with an abortion or a shotgun marriage to a man I loathed and feared. Shamed and afraid, I knowingly married into an abusive relationship to please my father, and in a year's time, I fled for my life, at the hands of a man in either direction. That's completely the opposite of truth."

Question number five: "What did your father teach you?" Lawyer, Washington, DC: "He was like the Dalai Lama to me. That kind and loving. And he didn't drink booze, just like the Dali Lama. When I picked a feather from a stone in the path, he halted and stuck it in my hair. No fantasy of small talk, though I sought it. Everything was transcendental. I married a DJ."

What would Ava's father be like? Not anything like my side of the family. It didn't work like that. Fishing boats had to figure. How could she have such an overwhelming compulsion toward the sea?

He couldn't have smashed clamshells in a sheltered niche of rock, or she would have found him already. Maybe he was a cowboy. Ava at the rodeo. A cowboy with the best of intentions, and I was the girl who sang the song. Ava was a smudge on my dress, or was it something in my eye? Something super special. Vanishing ink and lemon juice, her father was a spy. We spent the weekend at home. He was an artist, and I made bread. We goofed away an afternoon.

The wind convinces Ava it is her father; the old man in the moon patronizes her. A tale of a wizard, a tale of a god—she's born of the *pulse of LSD, when I asked for a prayer for the future and, instead, got her.*

Early November, and George's hunting party with William was on for the weekend. Venice–London–Edinburgh, Will's flight had arrived after the close of TEFAF. George turned the key; Will buckled in.

"If Le Corbusier said, 'A house is a machine for living in,' he hadn't been to Otyrburn," George said, with forty-five minutes of their drive remaining. He set the heat a notch higher. "It lacks any utilitarian style. Plain and simple it is not." He slipped in a disc of opera arias. "I had to call in Scotland Yard to figure out the breaker panel."

How many hours make a weekend? Will thought. "So the butler is on vacation?"

"And the duchess long dead."

"You're a bolt of the Mediterranean," Margot greeted. "William, you should do some fishing while you're here."

"When I visit Otyrburn, it conjures images of exiled political dissidents."

"I haven't changed my appearance," George said, "but I have learned a new language. If we stand out here long enough, we'll get caught in a *thunder plump* and be battered by a *tousle*; talk about paradigm shifting. That's a thunderstorm and blustery wind." He ushered Margot and Will through the front door. "Must be the origin of a tousled head of hair. What had Owen called the word for *dismal*, Margot?"

"The weather would regrettably make us feel *dowie*."

"Ain't happening," Will said.

He dropped his bag in the foyer. Surprisingly altogether predictable—the bust of Homer, the one on the second hall table embellished with carved lion's paws—tasteful but expected. Where was anything evocative, even something downright ugly?

William encouraged a level of seismic disequilibrium in others' lives—the impetus to get the lazy shit out of a story. (I like that.) In Venice, when the hot, dry sirocco moved in from the Sahara, whipped in whirling dervishes around him, and deposited an inch of red sand on his loggia, it imparted something revelatory to the day. Elemental art rode the wind and forced itself upon us. If Will surrounded himself with the right pieces, he grew exponentially without taking overt pains to do so.

"To the Blue Room," George called. He toted two glasses while *Il Barbieri di Siviglia* played Act II—his favorite—the fanfare finale to Almaviva and Rosina.

Margot had entered; she bent by the windows draped with faded tartan silk curtains in soft rosy red and adjusted the generous hem on the floor, seemingly perturbed, William noticed, by the tangled fringe along the folded edge.

"Not Rossini with a kind of halo again, George." At the end of the day, not the beginning, she lifted the needle and let it waver over a skip, till it rode the groove smoothly on a concerto for cello in D minor.

"Margot's forty-fifth birthday memento." He proudly held the full-figure statuary, turning the bronze to the light. *"Statue of Cupid—when a man, breaking his bow.* You know how she is about jewelry."

"While at art school, I bought an interpretation of Bouguereau's *Cupid and Psyche*," Margot explained.

The Blue Room would benefit from a coat of paint, William thought, and ran through the myriad of possibilities, from deep indigo to pale periwinkle. George had a unique ability to be present but remain on the margins.

"A toast to Pleasure, the couple's daughter." Seated in a brown leather club chair, George's arm had hidden the split in the armrest that exposed horsehair padding below, until he raised his toast.

He seldom missed an opportunity to share his knowledge. *Ritual and propriety consume him,* Will thought. *Even ravens laugh.* He'd heard them. George waged a daily war with himself. Worse than death was humiliation. The desire for something that repelled him yet obsessed him.

"Actually, it's not the sex—it's the mystery of love I'd hate to lose," Will said. "I depend on it."

He watched George, afraid that his interior silence was like sitting through season one of the Mexican soap opera *Reina de Corazones,* without the tequila. *He's silently correcting my grammar,* he thought. William became acutely aware, once again in his life, of a tension at rest within George between truth and representation.

"Did you run across anyone you know at TEFAF?" George asked. "Pick over anything outstanding?"

"Imhotep Ahmed gave me his card and said for you to call him."

The cogs in the art-world machine, the network of buyers and artists—the realized luxury of long-term dealer–buyer relations. Will found it all so tiring.

"Isn't that the Egyptian who wears black suits only and the same dark-purple neck scarf that hangs below his belt?" Margot asked.

"Add to that a mustache," Will said.

"A pharmacist turned gallerist, he represents young hotshots and is known for his acute eye."

"I bumped into Isabel Summers." Will scanned the titles on a stack of Ruby's puzzle boxes: Speak Chicken, Nancy Drew Diaries, and Very Good Boy Vintage Dogs. "She hasn't changed."

"I crashed at the apartment you and Isabel had rented in New Haven while visiting a friend there once, all these many years ago." George swirled his glass. "The humidity was dreadful."

Since childhood, George had slept naked, Will thought, whenever the night air crawled. *Had he climbed in bed with her, or vice versa?* "Bedtime buddies."

"She's a malevolent creature," George added. "I don't trust her as far as I could throw her."

"Why on earth, George?" Will asked, on the ready grab for dirt.

"She ran your Saab to the ground while you were in Paris. And in your absence, rolled that apartment of yours into an opium den."

"That's all you've got?" Will asked. "She must have been all of nineteen or twenty."

The evening carried on with indefinite swipes at definitions of love, and then George went to bed. A Highland hunting morning began early. Will and Margot packed the dishwasher in silence, the kitchen obliquely lit by the range hood lights. Chipped teacups made a bed with crystal; don't forget the serving spoon—it all fit in there. A Lalique bull on the Blue Room mantel, a fire below, fertility, one who speculates, the impetuous male held in crystal, careful not to break.

William leaned with his back pressed against the kitchen counter. He wore a printed flannel bathrobe with hurtling rocket ships, asteroids, and planets. "Ruby slept in a Moses basket. It was you, right, with a wicker baby basket with an accordion hood?"

"Yeah."

He forked another slice of cake on the outside edge with frosting. "Ruby is Cat Stevens's 'boy with the moon and star on his head.'"

"Who?" Margot teased.

"How much we lose when we leave behind the magic of childhood." He studied the dishtowel printed with orange blossom, foxglove, marigold, clover, a beehive, and the three different types of bees (queen, worker, and drone)—a gift from Sybil.

She placed the glass dome carefully over the cake stand. "George has had you pegged since childhood as the author of *Zealot*."

"*The Atlas of Untamed Places* is more apt."

"Some things are not easy to tell. One has to start over and over again," Margot said.

There was an atmosphere of pent-up prohibitions. As each made a visual inventory, the rinsing of a glass and clattering silver, a pot's copper cover spun to rest at the bottom of the sink, forming a backdrop to a familial lullaby moving underfoot. The meditation had erased their mental noise.

CHAPTER FOURTEEN

Rewilded

"*Tomboy.*" *The sound of a name, its immediacy. Luckily, I lived my youth prior to the tomboy-versus-tomgirl conundrum; there's even a quiz. It must be something similar to explaining the difference between liquid honey and crystallized honey to someone who's never tasted honey before.*

In the Jewish tradition, Lilith, the first woman, was created on the sixth day from the same soil as Adam at the same time as Adam (Genesis 1:27). In Adam's version of events, he and his first wife, Lilith, separated because he insisted she play a subservient role when they made love. Lilith, who preferred variety and many spices in her pantry, grew wings, sometimes a tail, and flew away. He then married Eve, created from his rib (Genesis 2:22), with the hope that she would obey.

Lilith flew to a land of demons, birthing countless wronged souls and troubled children who plagued Adam the remainder of his days. When I listen at night, and the screech owl soars and the vampire prowls—I've entered the realm of Adam's shape-shifting females. God had a consort, too, his daughter from that union—Sophia.

Playfulness is an allusion and, so, not fully visible in translation, though, if remarkably resourceful in conveyance, at least some of the lively inventiveness of lovers, and a life well lived together, leaves an imprint.

The willful Lilith and the original tomboy. Ava is a symbol of hope for me, and Margot, of realization.

PERTHSHIRE, NOVEMBER 2018

The clouds, she'd hardly stood beneath better. There had to be one hundred ways to celebrate them, every cloud, breeze, animal, and dewdrop. *Our now-vanished childhood forms,* she thought, *are like clouds. I'm looking for the remnants of what can be found today.*

"I fear an open winter," Owen said as a skirl, the high-pitched sound of strong wind, rustled dry grass and William, George, and Margot began their ascent, "when the horses will get around easily and the cows graze on corn stubs. But when the fields remain open, they dry out. Perhaps I'm wrong." He looked at the earth below him. "If you don't like the weather in Scotland, wait half an hour, and it will change. We aren't *drookit* and stepping through *dubs.*"

"Come again, Owen?" George, at rest on his walking stick, used the tip to scrape mud off the sole of his boot.

"Drenched and skirting puddles."

"I'm waiting on a *pish-out,*" Will said. "A downpour."

Owen pointed to William's attire. "You bought your choice wooly weekender 'out-in the-field' pants before flying." He nodded approvingly, then turned to follow the horizon. "That wind picking up right now. It's a *flaff* hitting us, a right gusty wind. There are more names here for wind and rain than there are salmon in the river Tummel."

A herd stood on the far ridge. By the early shimmers of light from the eastern arch, they treaded through the oaks. When the acorns were falling, the horns of the deer were fully hardened. Owen's presence gave Margot a sense of vertigo. The group crossed river stones in a burn and climbed out of the small stream to swaths of knee-high aubergine heather and began to crawl on all fours, imitating children, or *bairns*, doing what Owen called "glassing of the hillside." Reaching the ridge, they used optics to scan the rise. It went on just so for the better part of the morning, with Owen's reminder to keep the wind in their faces.

Margot dug her hands deep in her pockets. "I've never liked this."

"There are half a dozen photos in Otyrburn of you and Alistair and Archie in hunting attire," Will said.

"I was a tomboy," Margot said, "but never brought anything down. It was my duty to hunt. To have an 'immersive' experience with wildlife."

George's phone rang, and he strode off. "Put it on silent," Will called. "Tell the world you're unreachable."

Owen's hands are, more often than not, a bit dirty, Margot thought. *George's never so. Owen and I had "trampled the heather." His "morning woody." And I, his "volunteer garden." We had talked about farming and the kids we would have without mentioning their names. That rainy afternoon, Owen had baked sweet potatoes with honey when Fiona went to town. The first time I took a pee in the bathroom in a boy's presence. How grown up it seemed.*

"Heinke Hessel," Margot said. "Whenever he calls, George is out the door."

"And whenever the FedEx man knocks, George is at the door," Will said. "Lean on him for me, Margot; take away his checkbook. The next box goes in the canal."

A stag and hind reached the top of the ridge. The six-pointer rutted and bellowed in the mist, stopped, wheeled half around, and turned his mulish ears and dark-blue eyes upon them. Then moved through the gray sage but couldn't see them. The stag hugged the high ridge, affording no safe shot, and they broke for lunch on the fourteen-thousand-acre preserve.

"A green, nurturing United Kingdom is the making of James Herriot and Wordsworth," Owen said. "Half of Scotland's countryside is owned by four hundred and fifty people."

"Billionaires call it 'rewilding' in the Swedish Lapland and the Côa Valley of Portugal, and I presume so here," Will said.

"Aye, with contention," Owen agreed. "So whether they like or not, farmers stand by watching. The farming way of life is on the way out. Sheep farming is an ecological disaster. And if you lose your neighbor—everything starts to fall away."

"From an airplane," Margot said, "in the wind, the crown of a forest resembles coral in the sea."

Fog rolled in. Owen called it a *haar*, an east-coast mist from the sea. There were times, he said, when on the street below, Edinburgh Castle disappeared in the haar before your eyes. Blankets of mist folded in swirls around them. Two could see each other one minute, and the next, the party vanished in a waking wonder. The blackened ridgeline flashed below the haar with an occasional ruffled grouse in flight. Weather moved on its own accord, and the Highlands were the proving. The ground continued slippery on the rise of the slope, and they worked to steady themselves. Both Owen and George reached out their hand for Margot to hold. She took George's.

"No different than kids *skiting* on the ice," he said.

"I got that one," Margot said.

"If you're going down in a *hunker-slide*, just crouch and take it spread-eagle on your arse."

She walked into a grouping of grasshoppers, and she and Owen smiled together as they watched one land on her upper thigh, then one on her hand and one on the top of her head.

They settled sights on a stag and watched it from the knoll, Rye held by the lead. The stag collapsed from Owen's shot. He said a dedication, but mostly they were reverent and still.

"The learning in youth is the pretty learning," Owen said. "Heard that one all my life."

"*Is e 'n t-ionnsachadh òg an t-ionnsachadh biòdheach*," he repeated in Gaelic. A white pony, strong and steady on the ground, was called in to carry the stag down. It appeared medieval to the three visitors, both poetic and ageless; the pony did his job, the stag his, the man and dog all in concert. "Bagpipes escort the spirit of the dead to the other side."

As the steading was free for the night, Owen had suggested they sky-gaze under the stars of the Great Bear, Saturn by evening, and if they rose early enough, Venus by morning. *Foolhardy*, he thought, *the three of them together. Whose idea was that?* He tended the fire.

"Have you ever married, Owen?" George asked.

The party of four sat hugging their knees, and the flame danced higher.

"We had five years together; married at twenty. I'm a widower. I figure love is something akin to a constellation; some stars hold and others fly apart."

"The Venetians sail at sunset, chasing a 'green flash' to open portals, and only a faint blue appears," Will said.

Rye stretched out beside him, belly up, vying for a rub.

"It's arguably a deeply private life we live." Margot threw back her sheepskin collar and leaned into the fire. "In the end, it's ourselves we get to know most intimately."

She didn't need to tell him. Margot and George had welded their incongruities into a marriage of platonic friendship, at the risk of breakage. You could posit the personal, or you could stand concretely in it.

An owl screeched, *tu-whit-tu-whoo.*

"Tawny owls," Owen said, "pair for life, establishing residence, and never leave their territory. Pairing is natural to survival. It is what we expect to see. Anything else is an aberration."

"Margot believes we pull ourselves out of a hole—in her case a pile of rock, not earth—no, correct that, a ring of standing menhir," George said. "We can peer in the hole and walk on by, or pull someone out and go it together."

"Without apology, George, my life's been an open-ended kinda story." Owen lifted his eyes from the fire to rest on Margot, serene as he remembered. He had forgotten the pain in his hip that day from digging too many plants. Age crept up on all of us.

He piled the logs in the center of the ring.

At five in the afternoon, he thought, *when the moon rises, and when the sun sets, a seaman forgets, and a banker remembers, but she and I, we have a hard time figuring out whose leg is whose.*

"A round of rummy," Will said, "and open that bottle, George, I saw you tuck in your saddlebag."

George rose and wiped dry grass and mud from his dewy pant bottom. "This one? From one of the most storied distilleries in Scotland? The one tasting of peat, lemon zest, and just a hint of pecan and hazelnut?"

"All that's missing is the chocolate crème brûlée."

CHAPTER FIFTEEN

Tied to the Mast

*I*n *the sixth extinction, when things change, insects will scream louder, and it will get hotter and hotter, but we will not sleep in the wilderness beside a ghost or a myth, or a white buffalo, nay a white horse. No, we will sit in our squeezed comfort and watch the dog lick himself, my beloved Whimsy, your Rye, and all the dogs at the ASPCA, and in those dizzying heights, the end of our journey upended, we will sing, "Look at those eyes! The spitting image of her grandmother!" The seventh generation rescues the first, before they realize they need a divorce from all that the union failed to recognize. We all have to get on with our lives.*

One day, one of the many will see us coming down the street and do something right. Your house, your children, your broken destiny,

*my vision, my wrinkles, our endless love. Blind windows still see in
the dark. Lies have a beginning and an end.*

VENICE, NOVEMBER 2018

In the soft light of afternoon, Will sculpted as Lisbet posed naked
in his studio, hands on her hips, and looked directly at him.

"When we made love this morning," she said, "splayed in an
x position, with my foot and calf by your face, did you invent that
pose or learn it somewhere? Geometry was my weakest subject."

"I played jacks as a kid with George." He caressed her ankle
and kissed her. "When we're bed-surfing, I just move you around
without thinking about it—onesies, twosies."

*His composition was on its way to a half-size bronze. He'd initially
decided on a blocked bust of Elisabetta, a head-and-shoulders cast,
though the process became his pentimenti, and swanlike, her shoulders seductively rolled to her breasts. In the sexual union, the difference between the perceived and the actual experience rests with a
partner's expectations. Articulate and confident in bed, Will elicited
a positive response from his partners. What bird eats half the worm?*

They headed to Lisbet's apartment. It had been her grandmother's,
and like "Nonna," she fed *gli orfani*, "orphans," out on the small
balcony. A pair of foundling kittens landed into her sphere daily and navigated a stretch of boughs and limbs woven from the
courtyard below onto the lower roof. And then there were the
songbirds, not to mention her collection of "flying carpets." Will
couldn't pass a vendor of Persian carpets, or Anatolian kilim,
without thinking of her and giving the stack a perusal. Five feet
by thirty-two inches of carpet was ideal for a solo flight. *Acts of
kindness,* he thought, *which I neglect.*

The next morning they took the Eurostar to Rome, where Will had first lived in Italy. Having booked a room in the neighborhood of the Pantheon, they would be served café made with *Aqua Virgo*, or Virgin Water, carried eternally, via aqueduct, from a fabled hidden spring beyond the hills of Rome. They rented a robin's-egg-blue Vespa, which they left parked; walking, district by district, passing oranges, myrtle, and rose, was the best way to see Rome. A lovers' weekend getaway. He stopped in a doorway with the sun on his face, impromptu.

> "The sirocco rides the wind,
> the umber earth paints the bark,
> the blush of ages births desire,
> and I'm beneath the cork tree,
> listening for you."

"If I leave the window open, my life gets messy," Lisbet said.

A trumpet of Roman drivers laid into their horns.

"We won't buy a house; we'll buy a boat with an anchor," he said.

Outward momentum had defined his teenage years. They wove between tourists, with the sun overhead. He took her hand and grazed it with a kiss.

"Maybe I'll write a novel with deckled edges," she said.

"Hashtag messy-but-brilliant."

"Theoretically, one can be overwhelmed by loveliness," she said.

"And walk too fast." He picked a pebble out of his shoe. "I wanted to live in a geodesic dome like Buckminster Fuller."

"I got as far as camping a few hundred yards from a river mouth."

"Where?" William asked.

"Marchese, the birthplace of malaria." She hummed when she walked if it was a perfect day. "I wore a sand dollar on a leather cord around my neck."

They would go off-grid, he thought, *The Call of the Wild*, *White Fang*, a compass, a flashlight, and a pup tent. Lisbet did walk fast. A pair of Carabinieri strolled past. Do not apply unless tall, handsome, and immaculate—must live at home with mama.

"Milksops all, like George," he said, "too delicate to go out in the world without excess finery. And like George, in love with hard-and-fast rules."

"That I can see." Every now and then, the Venetian moistened a finger and held it in the wind. "Hard to picture you as a rangy guy, though." The wind in Rome was most often from the south.

They entered at the northern reach of the Forum. So much history in Rome; later, when the heat of the day cooled, they would join the tour guided by Lorenzo, with a PhD in archaeology.

"It's an old, dusty watering hole, Will, where men buried alive the Vestal Virgins who laughed at something funny a boy had said, then bought and traded slaves, counted gold, and encouraged and enabled its power." She adjusted the brim on her straw sun hat. "Let me see." Then tightened the blue ribbon that held a hawk feather. "Men think wrong."

"The disconnect caused by the severing of the corpus callosum?" Will teased. She had a way with words.

She paused, removed her sunglasses, and wiped the lenses with a soft cloth. "It's hard to find a gauge of everything one conceived. I'm a poorly paid sales manager of frivolity," she continued, brushing her hair off her face, the wind showcasing her widow's peak.

"Remember shortly after we met," she asked, "and I had found you writing, and you opened the oven door to warm the room? Your ears ached from the cold in that miserly apartment, but you were burning inside with creativity." She gestured eastward, over the Capitoline Hill and over the ruins of Ostia, toward the Mediterranean Sea. "Ever since childhood, I've saved pieces of a story, like a scavenger hunt on the beach." He crossed his legs; his face tipped to the sun.

"I think I'll write a play instead," she said. "Once invented, a character is persistent."

"I'm still trying to catch a trout with my fingers."

"Eventually, the wall surfaces will be covered with writers' notes to myself, scribbled so quickly, I struggle to read them."

Will took her in his arms and kissed her cheeks many times, stopping passersby in the street—Rome, another couple kissing. They had found their way to Piazza Navona, not realizing how far they'd traveled. *Our classic love story*, he thought, *now fully restored*.

"I was working scooping gelato," Lisbet said, in a shop just like this, "and you had the makings of a receding hairline—only ordered the *nocciolo*. There was a strange neighbor with an outdoor *forno* in his courtyard. And each time he fed the fire, he wandered over through the hedge with the meat dripping off the fork to show you what he was roasting. The smells were heavenly."

"I was scarcely sane." He made a mental register of how truly lovely her pale skin, soulful eyes, and almost oversize features were. "Thought it an accomplishment if I knew the years and names of wines."

"The poor man who gave his cloak to a beggar."

"It had a bum zipper," he said. "Hardly a gift."

"You had refused your family allowance, Will, and ate canned sardines and lentils."

"I became an expat because I was sensually deprived."

He stopped before a toy shop. The window display had a red plastic deep-sea explorer, with a turbo propeller, rotating lights, and arms with claws. Battery operated. Exactly like one he remembered drawing as a kid.

"And why is it that eccentricity corresponds to tragedy?" he asked. They poked around the shop. The owner was grumpy. The toys rarefied. "And often tragedy transfigures to genius. Dalí, in his fur-lined bathtub, talked on one of his lobster telephones."

"One sold in sterling at Christie's for two hundred and fifty thousand," Lisbet said.

"A curvaceous base waits for the receiver's life-size lobster claws to grab its hips and fuck it."

"It's the perfect George gift, Will."

He hadn't thought of his brother all morning.

"It ain't happening." He wanted to hear the tone made by a child-size upright piano, then played the F major scale. "I'll have to ask him if he ever had his fortune told or joined a pub crawl."

They bought nine marble Easter eggs. In vividly dyed tones and pastels, too, too cute to pass on.

"Da Vinci's family life fell apart as a teen exiled from his mother," Lisbet said.

"Dalí was sixteen when he lost his."

"If everyone got what they needed as a child, we'd all be okay," she said.

They were a couple standing in a shaded corner, banked with wisteria, holding a shopping bag of toys.

"Dalí called his mother his *soul revealer* or something similar," she said.

"Eggs for Dalí." William peered into the tissue-stuffed bag. "Hope and love. Sunflowers and a rhino. Why pay for dinner when a drawing on a check will do?"

"One of the three pilgrimages you actually pulled off, Dalí, da Vinci, and Vermeer."

"Clearly we're not obsessed by chastity," he said. "But we could still have the glass floor, and you could walk around naked during the day."

"I'd like to be so liberated."

"You already are," he said.

How many stories proceed with logical precision? he thought. Multiple planes of reality existed at any one time. He couldn't explain his attitude toward being—any attempt sacrificed the experience. The phenomenon of a relationship evaporated the moment one tried to put in words the fantastical aspects. Try to catch a butterfly without a net.

They arrived at the Vespa, its wheels and helmets locked. Elisabetta's legs straddling his thighs made him long for her as they merged into the kinetic whirl of Roman traffic. There'd be a cool verdant garden to stroll in at the Galleria Borghese before viewing Antonio Canova's *Venus Victrix*.

"Canova waxed her surface and lit candles for exhibitions." He moved by the open window. Another world existed in the Borghese Gardens, which many tourists missed. "A mechanism installed in the base allowed her to rotate seductively. The bright bulb loses something."

They moved room to room languidly, and a low shaft of sunlight fell across the floor, lengthening their footsteps. They stopped before Gian Lorenzo Bernini's *Apollo and Daphne*.

"What's significant," Lisbet said, her eyes resting on Will, "is Bernini chose to depict the exact moment when, inches from

Apollo's embrace, her toes rooted and her hair sprouted leaves. She asked her father to rescue her, but does she convey alarm or hope?"

He felt the sting but brushed it off, clasping the back of his neck with one hand.

"For me, her right leg reaching backward says, 'Catch me,' and her head tipped over her shoulder is a nod, too, perhaps, to expectancy as much as fear. What we witness is rule-imposed mayhem. This is the Borghese collection, tracing mythological ancestry to Venus. I expect an ambiguous representation of love."

She looked so fetching in her white pencil skirt. As far away from his own mendacity as one could get. With her, the magical elements in life made a point about reality. That was the game, after all, he thought, to lose the highly detailed, realistic life and meet something too strange and good to believe—to be more broadly descriptive rather than critically rigorous. All within the element of their differing cultures.

"Ovid wrote that Apollo placed his hand where her breast had been," she said, "and through the bark, her heart beat. It's the story of remorse. Regret is in her face. Daphne asked for more than she bargained for, but they were victims of playful gods."

Elisabetta's eyes glinted. She appeared agitated, keenly tuned, with a hopeless resigned expression.

"What are you getting at, Lisbet?"

"You could say it, but you haven't."

"I didn't want to hurt you."

"You flirt with realism and then reject it," she said. "Who did you take to TEFAF?"

Will hesitated. *You had to have known*, he told himself.

"A college roommate. Isabel Summers."

"*Essato.* I expected as much." She stared steadily into his face. "Why are you so obtuse? You're obsessed with sex, railing on about trains going through tunnels."

"I thought only of you."

She grew so angry she could have hit him.

"How base, anyone can pay a visit to a lover. You are a classic example of privilege gone wrong. I will not be *la Donna Italiana* for you, *la Mama*, or *la Madonna*. I will not be your disciplinarian, confessor, and pardoner in one."

His chin resting on the palm of his fist, Will stood parked on one of the thousand arched marble bridges in Venice, contemplating his upbraiding. *So I will wait.*

As a mistral blew cold from the northwest, the channeled wakes of passing motorboats churned the Grand Canal, and the shimmering Venetian atmosphere of La Serenissima, with a host of murky peripheral figures, made barely any sense at all.

CHAPTER SIXTEEN

Fergus

We seldom know why one or another person moves us, yet we fearlessly step into their worlds. I haven't examined the dynamic because there is no way to separate the sensation from the memory or the desire. I say things like "He sang to me," or "I'm tuned in," "Turned up." Tweet it, "RT" it, like a bird. But sing I do. Change is scary because you're left exposed.

When Ava tells me she is in pain, I feel empathy. I offer her a frozen bag of peas for a sprain, yield my shoulder for support as she hobbles, yet in the back of my mind, as I place a pillow beneath her ankle, a small part of me says: Is she milking it; could it hurt that bad? The distance between pain and the expression of suffering, love and the materialization of longing, occurs in a vacuum. It's a miracle we understand each other at all. The trick in life is knowing what you would have liked, even if you didn't have a clue.

PERTHSHIRE, NOVEMBER 2018

Owen said the ruin of a kirk would be visible on the rise long before they reached the old farm road. Margot leaned lightly for a moment on his arm before entering the cab of the truck. The two were headed out that Sunday to visit a garden in a hidden village. The remnants of a church's spire loomed in the distance as a border collie crossing on the A1 caused them to sit in their truck for a spell for sheep.

"A Scottish Blackface shepherd—my flock is reduced to six," Owen said. "He knows where the sheep will be when it's windy and wet. No one teaches you that."

"And to think you live down the road a piece."

His fingers rhythmically tapped the wheel. "For a spell I had three working dogs. One severe winter, I watched my lead ewe, Oreo, use a stick held in her mouth to scrape away the snow."

"I wish I'd seen that."

"There's a homing instinct we call 'hefting' in some sheep breeds; an ewe will go to the same part of the hill and look after their patch for life." He was, as ever, moved by the melodious sound of her voice. The awkwardness he'd felt left, and the day crept back into focus. He pulled off the road to park. Then he helped Wren out of the cab, appreciating the excuse to place his hands around Margot's waist as he helped her down. "We hike along the fern road to the village. Watch your step. Puddles happen on the south side of the track."

"What's the meaning of the big stone in Wyndham's village square?" she asked. "All Alistair would tell me was that a giant had placed it there for me to sit on."

"Heroic, but absurd." He slowed his step to match hers, dizzy from the rush of time imploding around them. "It's a 'manhood stone' or Atlas stone. A village square always had one, or it was found a ways off down a farm road, as if plucked from the sky. And might have been called a Saint's stone. You picked it up to prove to the chieftain that you were a man, and so it remains today."

"And did you?" she asked.

"Once when I was young, I rose to the test of nerve," he said.

They smiled about nothing and laughed—so much laughter. She stooped to let Wren off the leash. *Ancient skies, ancient trees, swooping swallows, hares in open fields, ancient love,* he thought.

"If a man carries the Mingus stone," he continued, "spheres of smoothness are they, glass-like—so it's a tricky carry—if he carries that beast ten paces, he wears an eagle tail in his hat the rest of his days. Scots have a fascination with the difficult."

Rye and Wren ran ahead on a medieval road headed north.

"I hid an inscription in Latin to us in a painting I did at seventeen," she said quietly. "The lettering climbed the branch of a bush."

"I love surprises."

"*Nunc et sempre.*"

He walked with his head bent in thought and watched as Rye ran straight out, then circled back to stand beside his leg. "Now and forever." He had always intended to love her.

They passed an unwalled graveyard in silence, compelled by the restless tension, as though each held the life of the other in their hands.

"Wren pees like a girl," Owen said.

"He doesn't know that." She picked a white clover and sucked on the petals. "How many people live here?"

"Nary a handful. Hardy types who live without regret. Those who listen to the lure of history and don't mind if mail is fetched once a quarter on the far side of a cold, rugged mountain. It's something to envy—having no debt to the world but enjoyment."

After the fern road, they skirted along a network of foot and bridle paths past species-rich hedgerows. They already inhabited the landscape. He turned, took her face tenderly in his hands, rubbed his thumb across her lips, and kissed her softly on the mouth. No stopping now. They hungrily, hurriedly, pulled each other down on the overgrown grass.

He pulled a strand of wheat from her blouse. They each fumbled to tidy and straighten up the other, in an expression of longing, not happy necessarily, but filled with promise and apprehension, a mix of exhaustion and euphoria.

"We will be thoughtful and kind and not rash," she said.

"Too late for that."

"Fergus is a horn carver and fiddle-maker. He makes practical things, too, like walking sticks. I'm interested in his wattle fences and gates."

"We should have known better."

They walked in silence. Their shoulders touching and fingers entwined, they passed stone dwellings, more a pile of rubble ruins on a knoll. One had a thatch roof in need of repair and a wooden wheelbarrow parked out front with hazel shafts laid. They approached the house with a stag's head mounted over a black door and still more antlers decorating the end wall, where a hand-worked sign read HORN CARVER—CROOKS, EGGS, WALKING STICKS, AND PORRIDGE SPOONS. An old man with a ruddy face and hands, his head a shock of thick white, as white as the snow of one night, and eyebrows to match, smiled in the doorway. He held one of his walking sticks and wore blue bib overalls. To the east was an open shelter filled with hay and slag.

"Fergus Macalister, this is Margot Reid of Otyrburn."

"My pleasure."

"Fergus is on the other side of ninety and still maintains *two* gardens," Owen said proudly, as if the accomplishments were his own.

His shaving horse sat out in the open. The workbench only made sense to Fergus: a clutter of tools, carving gouges and blades, spokeshaves, and drawknives. Horn buttons, shoehorns, whistles and buckles, pitch hayforks, garden rakes, and more, all crafted from sheep or cow horn and some of wood. The dusty window ledge with peeled paint displayed Fergus's miniatures of carved Scottish animals that marched and flew head to toe.

"Go on, Fergus, tell Margot your favorite story."

"I sat whittling on my stoop with my Scottie, my head bent in concentration. It was a day just so—a bright sky. The carefully placed tap of heels crossed the pebbles, and I lifted my eyes, and there she was in all her finery, the Queen Mum. And I said to myself, 'All the country will hear of it, and Rob the tinker's dog too.'" He lifted his cap with a flourish. "She walked the last stretch to my door alone and said, 'I came for one of your best ram's horn crooks, Fergus Macalister.' And so, I made her a cup of tea. And when she left, she toted her *cromach*."

"Choose one, Fergus," Margot said. "No, make that a pair. One to keep and one to give."

And he did: he selected two of his best on hazel shafts. Owen made a faint whistling sound and handed off a scrap of cookie from his pocket to Wallace, Rye, and Wren.

He guided them over the swale to his apiary, sheltered within the bower of tangled tree boughs and vines grown tightly together. Handyman and gardener for many years, Fergus constructed bee skep of twisted straw woven into dome-shaped hives, which became medieval creations.

From there, they passed beside an herbaceous border of unruly cottage flowers and set the white Embden geese to squawk, and one tom turkey, who was strangely peaceful and serene.

"I let the goose alone," Fergus said, "and then the freezer holds a new one."

They landed at a grassy sward of trimmed green grass, where Fergus stopped and the plump tom turkey that trailed him obediently stopped beside him.

"He's going in the icebox too," Fergus said.

But Owen gave Margot a look to say, "No, he ain't."

From this vantage, their view included Fergus's small knot garden, composed of aromatic plants and kitchen herbs set within gravel paths. The art of pleached trees planted in a quincunx, a geometric pattern of five apple trees—a "cross in a square," like the five-spot on a six-sided dice—had taught Fergus patience. He had pruned, woven, and tied together the overhead branches, clearing some until what remained of the crowns of five trunks had grown into eight arches. Fergus had drawn balance, order, and unity out of a living folly of organic matter and nothing more.

Owen turned a wooden rake over in his hand. "Fergus told me when last I visited that Thomas Edison had the quincunx pattern tattooed on his forearm."

"Aye, one man outstanding in a field of his own." Fergus nodded.

The expert wattle fence wove the perimeter of the knot garden with gates at the four directions. Buff Orpingtons pecked between the plantings. Seasons this far north began late and finished early. When Owen returned from the truck, he toted a basket of jam, marmalades, shortbread rounds wearing petticoat edges, and shortbread rectangles cut with edges that resembled the sun. And on top perched a bottle of whisky for Fergus.

"I have to take you home, Margot, though I don't want to," Owen said.

He turned the key and lifted his eyes to land in hers, entirely in his skin, their kisses soft and heady. It didn't matter what they said.

"I hear my heart, regular and strong," Margot said, "but my legs wobble and my body shivers like when I was a kid and climbed the maple too high and couldn't get back down."

"You climbed trees when we met."

In the timber-filled pub, the two sat at the bar. His tobacco smoke warmed the air between them. She waved it away. He let it go out. They might get it right this time around—wherever they were meant to be, she thought.

"Was it moments or hours that we made love?" she asked.

With the evening light diffused, the sea appeared purple on the way home. The night had a fissure that they'd walked through. Mostly silent, they'd driven with two dogs curled between them. She had the house to herself. When George worked in New York, the setting at Otyrburn quelled her tension. She couldn't stay inside. That night she slept alone outside in the orchard.

CHAPTER SEVENTEEN

Dinner with ~~Andre~~ George

*S*ometimes this old house creaks so in a strong Atlantic wind that I swear it's grown old solely to accommodate me. The howl in the chimney stirs my mind awake, and like Dorothy, I land in the morning somewhere else altogether, perhaps at rest in the exosphere. We all live in a bubble. The seven layers comprising the atmosphere that blankets Earth are only so thin. Like my mother, I have "environmental melancholia," and Ava is no different. Emotional intelligence is a genome that we women invented.

Ava started life as a runty pup. If her family had been captured for relocation from its den in farthest Canada, she would have been overlooked. Luckily, I got there first. My small gray pup grew, matured, and eventually became a pack leader. Her philosophy of respecting the wilderness ensured her survival. Ava will not become a fossil slave

to the environment of consumption, injustice, prejudice, hate, or her
partner's distance. The millennials were born elastic and flexible in
a time of change, reading the "book of why." She is a member of hu-
man kindness striving to escape the impulse society she inherited: fifty
ways to wear a scarf, with jaunty illustrations to confuse and con-
found the enemy. In the devastation left by unchecked man, born of
his "illusion of self," the wolf, once again, rises to domination.

NEW YORK CITY, NOVEMBER 2018

"Another?" Johnny lifted his glass off an end table in the comfort of his home. The mood was a fluid give-and-take between old
friends. He placed a birch log in the fire basket.

George grumped less when in New York, Johnny thought,
where a multitude of distractions energized him. There was always something new.

"The old man who unlocks Saint Patrick's at 8:00 a.m. still
takes lunch, weather permitting, on the bench outside." George
tucked his chair closer to the flickering flames and crossed his
long legs. "And the two gangly brothers who cross at Eighty-Sixth
Street and Central Park West have grown strong and tall."

"Yes. You mentioned one has braces."

The papery bark spit back with the hiss of a snake in the puck-
erbush. Johnny's living room doubled as a private study. Bookcas-
es of unfinished aged knotty pine boards wrapped three walls,
the fourth opening to the tree-lined street below. The skull of a
walrus; a rug from Odesa; two nudes, painted in oil by one of a
sultan's wives; a framed letter from someone on a Shackleton expedition; and a spirit mask with Arctic tern feathers, the export of
since banned. The shelves broke at Doric repeating columns, interrupted by the fireplace at the center, composed of square blocks
of ivory limestone, where a copper water bucket held kindling on

the hearth laid with antique dragonhead andirons. His "companion chair," a wing chair upholstered in moss velvet adorned with ochre palms in mandorla characteristic of the Renaissance period. To the right of the hearth hung a small gilded frame holding a delicately hand-colored etching of a nude man seated on a large boulder by a riverbank beside a spruce, his arm rested on a bent knee. He gazed penetratingly at the viewer and watched as fish jumped, catching flies, in the foreground.

"What are the chances you could secure for me another?" Johnny asked, glancing at the German print. He noted George looked exhausted.

"Just ask and it shall be granted."

"An expansive Alpine vista with a river again," Johnny clarified.

George pulled a small writing pad from the inside pocket of his sport coat and made a note. "Altdorfer produced only nine landscapes, and Doña Maria de Trujillo y Merlo knows the provenance of each one."

"Did you two meet at one of Olga's dinner parties?" Johnny asked. George had a generous circle of acquaintances Johnny had not met. It was as though sworn and guarded.

"Maria is absolutely relentless. Her portfolio is hard to match. She began art school at fifteen; now her foundation manages her collection, as well as organizing her annual exhibits. She's influenced collectors from Bogotá to Jerusalem."

"But what is she like?"

"Both of her parents nurtured her interest in the art world," George said. "Maria is alchemical, a little witchlike, expressive and colorful, a spiritual being."

"Few defined contours, and literary art groups since birth," Johnny pushed a long dark bang off his forehead. "The worst kind."

"Exactly," George said. "I love the work. I dread her next phone call." He extended his arm to take Johnny's glass. "Here, let me get the refills. Are you quite sure you two haven't met?"

"Quite," Johnny replied. George's reaction had been most strange. He had widened his eyes. "Alternative worlds where the imagination fuses with reality, I'd remember."

"Something like that."

"I go through my day in the city, pushing through road wars and standing on overcrowded corners, and in my mind, I'm dropping pebbles in the lake at twelve."

"Experience, expertise, and eternal enthusiasm, what is it actually for?" George asked. "Who's the hero and who's the villain? My work isn't a luxury but a vital contribution to the life of the museum." He drew a handkerchief from his trouser pocket, excused himself, and blew his nose. "You photograph places that have been demolished to make way for a car park. Someone has to not only value the intrinsic qualities of a piece of art, or a place, but also be its advocate."

"You sound on the defensive," Johnny said.

"Perhaps I am, entrenched politics, the machinations of power, the personality culture clash—none of it escapes the museum. It's all so terribly tiresome. There's nothing to be done."

"Nothing to be done about what?" Johnny had caught a worried glance.

"Watching the wretched upper echelon of the museum's select board tear each other to pieces, then administer the poison."

"We don't go to work in the morning expecting praise and flattery."

"Who is right, and who is wrong," George asked, "when all are mistaken?"

Johnny pushed a dry log deeper within the searing flames, dwelling on George's last comment. "There's a Frost-edged poet in everyone."

"I don't believe that, not for a minute." George laughed, shadowing his old friend to the kitchen. "You and Margot, 'inextricably linked to nature.'"

"There are many ways to promote an unfamiliar perspective in this life."

Johnny walked with a limp from going out straight on the tennis court in the afternoon. Open shelving painted an eggshell blue, more black than blue, held artichoke spread, harissa paste, sage salt, and flavored oils on either side of the range. A wide molded cornice ran the length of the wall above, and on it sat a pair of identical wooden gilt frames that depicted red-chalk drawings of sixteenth-century Dutch village life.

"The attack of the killer tomato." George nodded and smiled.

"My first year, stationed in Buenos Aires, the tomatoes I tweaked off the last of the vine, this late in the fall, sustained me. In fifteen minutes, we'll sample truth."

Johnny scattered anise seeds in a small frying pan, dry-roasting them until they popped, then ground them coarsely in a mortar and pestle. He added balsamic, lemon juice and zest, and extra-virgin olive oil. He crushed two cloves of garlic, preparing basil chiffonade, using kitchen scissors to cut the basil into thin, delicate strips, and added this to the vinaigrette. All the while, Maria Callas sang "Quando m'en vo" from Puccini's *La Bohème*. He joined her with baritone bellows between prep work, breaking the buffalo mozzarella roughly with his hands into chunks he brushed with the vinaigrette, topped with the tomato and a twist of fresh pepper, and served on a perfectly grilled piece of sourdough.

"Geez, Johnny, you should retire early and become somebody's personal chef."

Johnny set plates on the mahogany counter and pulled his stool beside George's.

"Cooking teaches you that happiness might be included but isn't inherent. It's trial and error."

"What's happening in your love life?" George asked. "By the way, this is delicious."

"I'll bring a date to the party, and yes, George, I'm still enchanted and frustrated by the nature of the women I date."

"Cézanne painted in an approaching storm," George said, "not any storm, a crackerjack, or in Scots Gaelic, a *rumballiach* raging storm. He was sixty-seven. When asked to come inside, he said, 'No, I won't go in. I can do this.' The next day he came down with pneumonia. 'I'll go out tomorrow and finish it,' he said, but he died that day."

"Happiness exists, George, entirely in being content with yourself. Everyone would be a better lover or friend if they took a sabbatical alone."

George wiped his oily lips and fingers with a cotton napkin and reached for a second before he pushed his tortoiseshell glasses onto the high bridge of his nose.

"And I have a press release to write in the year 2018, one month to the Symposium on the Art of the Hellenistic Kingdom, and the exhibition catalog proof is due this week." He paused to ask if there was anything he could do to help, and the reply was no. "Data visualization. That's my job description. Wading through tide pools as a kid, I made a study of mollusks. And now I clamber through cataloged 'Cabinets of Curiosities.' Did you know you'd be a journalist at twelve?"

"I wanted to be my paternal grandfather," Johnny said, "but two summers at the *New York Times* bored the heck out of me. I made a detour. I wanted to be the guy at the mouth of the river, not a collecting eddy downstream. How about you?"

"It happened to me the first time I entered the butterfly room at the American Museum of Natural History. The fact that someone had painstakingly collected geological specimens of Amazonian swallowtails lit all my buttons. I wanted to be the 'keeper.' Realizing my collection would never be a princely one but modest, I entered the museum. The Germans have multilayered words for everything. We fail to describe. *Wunderkammer*, the 'wonder room,' or *Kunstkammer*, the 'art room,' was the precursor to the Met. Originally, it was a collector's own Memory Theater. And now a goddamn 'man cave' is a temple. Sir Hans Sloan has cringed and died a thousand slow deaths."

I work for a weekly news organization, Johnny thought. *I could die, and no one would know I'd gone missing.* He showed George the latest addition to his photo collection, a black-and-white of a lunch counter sit-in on May 28, 1969, in Jackson, Mississippi, which had touched off mass demonstrations.

CHAPTER EIGHTEEN

A Tale of Three Cities

*W*hy do injured butterflies walk onto my palm and refuse to leave? True friends have easy smiles and soft eyes. What does a butterfly smile look like, or that of a kissing gourami?

Though Archie became my only lover who refused to toy with my name, he never had any idea what to call me. My last defense, anonymity, I'll save for an emergency. His eyes had unspoken names for me.

I will come straight to the point—if we could change places, you and I, I would know why you give me the eye, or stare at me with roving eyes, with hot love eyes, with pizza-in-the-sky eyes, and with your bird's-eye view of the matter, feast your eyes on me as if I were the apple of your eye, when I know for a matter of fact, without batting an eye, that you don't have stars in your eyes when you look at

*me—you have eyes in the back of your head; someone else has caught
your eye! I won't cry my eyes out; eagle-eye Violet has hit the bull's-
eye. We friends must understand, poetry is for everyone, and beauty
is in the eye of the beholder.* Yo soy tú. *I am you. Archie's eyes were
smoke gray.*

*The young, who are pretty and springlike, pliant and green, are
a step forward in time. Though bees feed on the young plants' pollen
and the old, if you were walking along a lit street, I promise you, you
would stop at Ruby or Will's apartment first.*

PARIS, LATE NOVEMBER 2018

In the midst of a personal crisis, Will had let his hair grow long.
Ruby will give me grief, he thought, on his way to greet her, *about
how it folds over the edge of my collar—hippie-like.* L'Tardiff sat on a
street corner. The favorable Parisian location meant that in early
November, two sides of the building were fitted with awning windows opening onto the street. Diners at l'Tardiff people-watched.

"Chef Ruby, what do you recommend?"

"The caramelized fennel with goat cheese, herbed sea bass
and potatoes in rosemary green broth, hedgehog terrine, nutty
endive with Roquefort, and we'll split the Puy lentil galette as
an opener."

"I'll pass on the hedgehog," Will said.

"Dead." Ruby laughed.

Their waitress, who had dyed her hair steel gray, though not
much older than Ruby, had clipped it back with shiny multicol-
ored plastic butterfly clips. She looked the part of a Versailles
courtesan.

"*Une bouteille de champagne, merci,*" Will said, then ordered.
"French is pleasing, but old Italian is better. The closest to Vulgar
Latin; everything is pronounced."

"French is so soft, you don't need to whisper," she whispered, "and nobody does denouement like the French novelists."

Ruby wore a black caftan with tan embroidery and had managed to arrange her golden-chestnut hair on the top of her head and still encourage the ends to stick out every which way. Will noticed, lovingly, once again, her "only-Americans-have-teeth-like-that" smile.

"Remember when you were only eight years old, Ruby, and I had babysat, and you asked if we could watch the documentary on Abraham Lincoln?"

"Like no kid said ever. Last week, when I lifted my stemmed water goblet, there in the foot, floated William Shakespeare." She leaned her vivacious eyes across the table into his. "A tiny image, albeit, his face remained there as I drank. How's that for weird? On the third try, he disappeared."

"Long may the strange and wonderful reign," William said.

"Your side part makes you look old." Ruby ran her finger around the rim of her glass. "It instantly says you have a 401(k)."

"And is that a bad thing?"

"Just saying." She tucked her phone into her purse. "You and Lisbet were the couple people stopped to ask, 'Are you newlyweds?'"

"The Italians are the most self-deprecating of all Europeans."

"You froze when asked to melt, Uncle Will."

"Ouch."

"I need a Viggo Mortensen of the senses," Ruby said, "riding into the woods, carrying his pup tent, two dogs—his and mine—a chef's stove, a case of Pinot Noir, one emulsifying blender, tart pans in seven sizes, soufflé molds, my complete DVD foreign-language movie collection—about three hundred and forty, give or take—and our organic wool and latex mattress."

"And I, an inflatable dinghy; then I could float silently along the canal and sing beneath Lisbet's window."

"That's so *simp*. William Lowell, the Venetian wall lizard. Sorry, not sorry."

"I'm *hella confused*," he teased, watching from their table as pedestrians navigated Paris streets in the fall. "What's so simp?"

"You singing to her from the canal when you can't sing for shit," Ruby said, "just because you hope you'll get laid. A guy who messages first—he's simping for her."

"Right, and the guy who speaks highly of his girlfriend—I suppose he's 'such a simp'? Ruby, that's just absurd."

She spread black olive tapenade on warm french bread. "*Yaaas.* I can't even. Find me an older guy—a decade of dignity, not years. Don't tell me you love me and leave me languishing with startups. Guys who need a kick-start fundraiser to get their ass into first gear. No more lovey-dovey, cheating, baby men for me. Nice try, Hunty."

All had gone to hell, but he wasn't telling all. Not to his niece. A man has his pride. A young boy approached the table selling single stem roses. Will stood and handed him a crisp dollar bill. Then he put his arm around Ruby's shoulders.

"What would you like for dessert, sweetheart?"

"Let's head home and take Onyx for a walk. I made a vegan dessert, nuts, more nuts, and nuts again, dates, lemon, or alternately, carob, and one miserly teaspoon of honey." She squeezed his hand. "No, I made tarte tatin."

He paid their bill and they stood. "I don't know much, Ruby." They walked, arms linked, down Quai Voltaire along the bank of the Seine Rive Gauche. "My life's been a series of pot-boiling-over women, types who, at the end of the day, haven't accomplished anything but killing the pilot light on imagination. With Elisabetta, everything moves together, and her steps have a purpose."

"Break the internet."

"When next we meet, we'll be a full house at Otyrburn for New Year's. Ruby, when was the last time you were at your great-grandparents' house? How fucking cold will it be in Scotland in December?"

"I don't want to think about it."

VENICE, NOVEMBER 30, 2018

Will's flight home was beset by turbulence, but he felt grounded by Ruby's youthful optimism. The human spirit is fragile. *Hanging around Ruby is like reading a pop-up book with interactive flaps,* he thought. The question always the same: Was he ready to *hear all about it?*

"Our dinner was lit," he said later that week as Ruby smiled on FaceTime from Paris, he in his office in Venice.

"I gotta bounce, Uncle Will. Invite Lisbet over to Netflix and chill."

Ruby was his one chance at playing a paternal figure. He did his share of doting. Though each had had their usual double espresso and dipped-chocolate croissant that morning, one in Paris, the other in Venice, she had begun the conversation by stating that his caffeine and sugar rush obviously had not yet taken effect.

"Hang on a minute." They were locked eye to eye on the screen. "Ruby, do you agree there has to be an essential sense of weirdness in life and art?"

"Because, duh. I get it from you or Mother. Father expects things to be easily discernable. Art and people."

"How old are you in June? If I have children in my old age, I'll have just one, the precocious wunderkind model that gave George you, twenty-three years ago."

"I'd like a cousin."

PARIS, NOVEMBER 30, 2018

There was more of Will in her than her father and mother combined. *He has never shushed me*, Ruby thought. *When my life begins to change, he's always there for me.* She clipped Onyx's leash to his black leather collar. His nails needed a trim, a job for the weekend. Tuesday was the farmers' market. She craved a dandelion salad. Ruby's daily contact with meticulously arranged greens felt significant. Dandelion was out of season, but a hydroponic greenhouse outside Paris in Annecy extended the tonic through fall.

Ruby alternated her regime of cleanses in the fruitful months between *dents de lion*, "teeth of the lion," and blue-green leeks in the lean. A history major, she saw a story far and wide. Leeks had seen a promotion to cult status. Emperor Nero ate large quantities of leeks in the belief they improved his voice when he sang. Romans nicknamed him "Porrophagus," or the "leek-eater." The Welsh king Cadwaladr of Gwynedd, in an AD 640 battle, made his men wear leeks in their hats to distinguish them from the Saxons. Jean de Poitou leeks were the French woman's secret. "*Mais oui*," her Parisian friends had insisted, "you must take the leek fast for one weekend each quarter, without fail." One day Ruby would have a garden. Leeks got five Michelin stars.

PERTHSHIRE, NOVEMBER 30, 2018

It began decades ago, Margot thought, peeling a butternut squash at the farmhouse sink, *almost imperceptible entropy, but the year that Archie died, the state of the relationship became acute and unde-*

niable. In the museum's catalog annex, when first they met, she had hoped they'd make love, but they hadn't. Calm and collected, they'd strolled through the gallery, and he'd asked what she saw in Bronzino's *Portrait of a Young Man*, circa 1530. The carved furniture held hidden faces, and the sitter turned over his shoulder with one eye while he penetrated the future. A walk in the park past swans. The greens and pinks at rest in clouds. How nice it would be to have a farm by the sea in Maine—to get out of this city. She had given herself something to be moored to. Then there were three.

"We've filled five bedrooms. We could use Will's dressing room in a pinch. Anyone you'd like to see, George?" Margot asked, organizing the kitchen drawer that housed the baking paper, tinfoil, rubber bands, recycled plastic bags, and the "If You Care" no-paraffin-wax sandwich bags.

George had strolled through the kitchen with a shot of espresso in hand. "No, I say leave a spot at the table for the mystery guest, and then they might appear."

By paying small attentions and lending a willing ear, she thought, *he's won people's confidence, though he may well have loathed them. They helped him make his way.*

"I spoke to Robbie about the caterer," she said. "I haven't spoken to Owen about horses."

"Isn't Otyrburn a bit much, Margot—are you sure?" George asked. He bit into a green apple. "Of all the places we could be."

"And if it were your second home in Rancho Mirage on the Palm Springs golf course—all's well."

"We make decisions together."

"And 285 Park Place, Brooklyn?" she asked; it was as easy to fall short of the truth as it was to overshoot it. "Archie's wedding present. I said it was too much. That was my inheritance."

He was silent. It was a convenient way of avoiding questions he wasn't ready to answer.

"Scots are fascinated by the difficult, and we're in Scotland, George."

"William spent the weekend with Ruby," he said. "Lisbet left Will's clothes out to dry on the balcony—possibly indefinitely. And Ruby gave *that boy* the fare-thee-well. What was his name? It must have been quite the wry dinner."

Marriage was a miracle of persistence, a preoccupation with commitment, boundaries, and satisfaction, and at that moment, Margot was profoundly dissatisfied with something about him. He'd forgotten to ask her essential questions and missed much of what she'd said.

VENICE, NOVEMBER 30, 2018

Three weeks progressed, and Will and Lisbet's paths had crossed once. At the two-week mark, they had bumped into each other crossing the Ponte Della Costituzione. A feather rode the mercato del vento—fall's trade winds—to transport new ideas. "I love you," he'd pleaded. He'd spoken too loud. Blinded by the flash of a tour group's camera, she'd revered the many Venetian lovers linked at twilight.

Three hundred and ninety-one bridges—and William had wanted to have dinner. "You need to get your shit together," Lisbet had said, "something like a renaissance." He had tried to kiss her. Her finger held pressed against his lips stayed his progress.

She sat on a stone bench in the *campi*. Pigeons pecked, and honeybees alighted on oleander; both could differentiate between a Picasso and a Monet. *Most humans would be hard-pressed to do the same*, she thought. Where Venice once held 135 fields, it now had intimate piazzas. She should be having her midday nap, but instead, during *riposa*, she held pale golden arancini balls wrapped in crisp tissue paper. *"Assagi,* taste it," her grandmother had begged her as a child. The arborio rice in saffron, with a nugget of cheese at the center, fried in extra-virgin olive oil—Italian comfort food.

Maybe he is writing again, she thought. *Was his single life a distant dream, or when he spoke, had his elusive passivity shone through, and his reluctant return from his remote thoughts?*

Where the seller sold religious images on the corner, she watched as Roma children begged on the curb, propelled by ambition. *I love a man without resolve,* she thought. *He usually entrenches himself when reality confirms his worst fears.* He would do almost anything for those he loved, but how much of the expenditure was a hard battle between duty and convenience? Lisbet's *telefonini* rang in her suede coat pocket. Tonight she had tickets to Monteverdi's *L'Orfeo* at Teatro la Fenice.

A wrong turn after the show, and Lisbet had covered the long, narrow pedestrian street, until she ended up at a blank wall—characteristic of the labyrinth called Venice. *Now, have your wicked way,* she thought, recalling how William often teased her when they made love, in deference to the city's bizarre urban planning. Where lovers hid, not far off, Italians used dead ends on multiple fronts, as a neighborly way of pummeling truths out of reluctant souls.

By week four, he had looked noticeably thinner; no doubt he played Bach nonstop. She'd heard from a mutual friend that he'd made some hard-nosed sales between a client visit in Berlin and a wedding in Biarritz. It wasn't bound to happen again. The tangle of waterways and footpaths meant it wasn't feasible.

CHAPTER NINETEEN

Ever So Close

*H*onesty is the only expression of love. That's why I love my dogs *so much; they don't know how to lie. There are no shining mar- tyrs in the show ring. My collie Galaxy told time. Rhyme, then Ring Side Riot, Ode, and now Whimsy—a dog never casts a black shadow. The rain is full of tears, which feed the garden and fill the dog's water bowl too. The galaxy is a ringside riot, oh so elegantly, of ode, and rhyme, and whimsy. Which lie was worse? The one Margot hid from George, or the one she told herself?*

PERTHSHIRE, DECEMBER 2018

Every day since seeing Owen, Margot walked through the green bower, recapturing memories of summers, *a vast library.* Ever so close, he labored at work in a saturated meadow where he straightened lines, planted by habitat, and wiped sweat off his brow with the back of his hand. He'd readied the dahlia tubers to overwinter in Edwina's greenhouse. Pruned fruit trees scaled to harvest from a tripod apple ladder, not basket or pole. And again, in old Scots, the *bourtree* and *leamhars* were planted, the elder and the elm. They had laughed. There were koi in the Iris Pool. A special corner of the greenhouse to please her, called the Kids Corner. For here, winter long, she would pluck armfuls of microgreens: arugula, spinach, sorrel, nasturtium, thin as a matchstick. Then Margot and George would dine on witty quips she'd heard before and pithy commentaries on topics like food, travel, Europe, and most important, living life to its "fullest."

Hard at work on his farm, Fergus crafted wattle fence and gate. Everything organic had rhythm and fell together. They hadn't met privately since the visit to Fergus. When last they spoke, they still disputed how big the greensward should be that unfolded between the house and orchard and whether to bed the entirety with Scotland's bluebell, the tissue-sheer powder-blue Harebell with five-petaled pendulous bells. *What exactly was left behind by the tragedy? Is human connection more important than even the truth?* She was the girl who wouldn't be. *How often had Archie repeated, "so nothing can harm you," when all faces were not equal?*

Owen had left off and cut wood. The sound righted her. He tolled over the knock, at work in the small upland valley edge enclosed at the back by the ridgeline; he gathered and piled logs high, cherry prunings and cedar, added to the apple and pear collecting at the orchard gate. Owen had taught her to be a connoisseur of fires.

A dew pond sat low in the southern pasture, a natural water hole for livestock, stagnant in summer and rich in algae. He'd lifted a newt and placed the delicate creature into her palm. "To be so lucky to grow new limbs, organs, and eyes."

A red-breasted sparrow hawk swept in to surprise songbirds at feeders. A swath of field led to sunflowers, and "charms" of goldfinch alighted on the moon-shaped seeded heads. He had drafted her universe since they'd arrived.

Keep my eye out for the red kite. The aviator with a forked tail saved from extinction. He might pick over her compost for scraps. She distinguished the green and white of cow parsley in the shaded hedgerow. The bracken slopes for miles around in summer were lit by the tall, pink, and sometimes white, waving bells of foxglove, held aloft on lance-tipped stems. *Fairy wands. But beware, there's poison there, the death-making brew of a sinister novel.* His laugh rang when he chastised himself over a shabby job— "This isn't right; it's just middling"—then spoke of bands of color beside moments of warmth. But she knew all this.

While Margot harvested secrets, Sybil had returned from Navdanya, where she'd tackled ecological threats to the mythological bee, having strolled through fields rich in two hundred varieties of wheat and sixty different types of millet. When Sybil answered her phone, it had been a while since the old friends spoke.

"I bought our tickets. Let's hope a nor'easter doesn't hit."

"Sybil, am I invested in Otyrburn out of responsibility, curiosity, or necessity? It was a visceral response. I loved the place so when I was a child, I never wanted to leave."

"That's good enough reason."

"I kept it partly to stop somebody from spending a million, mucking it up, and ruining everything."

Wren barked as a delivery truck parked in the drive. Margot closed her eyes, overwhelmed with the enormity of it all, with the possibility of explaining it. Karmic ties, souls who have been together for a lot of lifetimes . . .

"And from the memory of when we didn't have to lock our doors day or night," Sybil said.

"Owen Fowler was my first love."

"I remember. I don't envy you."

"He's a widower."

There was a prolonged silence. "Are you still there?" Margot asked, her hand at rest on the window sash lock. Her concentration traced commonplace forms in the courtyard. She couldn't see Sybil, but she knew that she was right there with her; as long as the conversation didn't shift in her direction; then she would find something to distract the pair with a pleasing diversion.

"Of course."

"We delved into anthropic cosmology, the oscillation of a hummingbird's wings, and fractals found in nature, all before lunch. I've spent a lot of time on my own."

"Are you rationalizing cheating on George?" Sybil asked.

Margot was disappointed that Sybil didn't seem to understand.

"Until you stumble on something real, you have no measure. I gave up on experiencing magic—call it what you will—with George early on, and believed that was okay."

"You mean where emotional and intellectual intelligence verge. In youth, we are attracted by novelty. In old age, by the ordinary."

"Sybil. Tell you the truth? It's tangled and complex. Dimensions layer and add years, and different things demand attention."

"You took a vow."

"There's hindsight, there's the day I stopped growing at fourteen, and then there's always a point where if you did even one thing differently, you would have had a different outcome." Wren lay curled in a ball, asleep at Margot's feet. "George and I look past one another."

"How many of us will end up expats in the Azores, Margot, and how many in nursing homes, both ruminating one long past?"

"Writing the letter you promised to write before you died to the one that got away."

It was hard for Margot to hide her taciturn responses to George. Things she'd marked on the calendar and had anticipated—Casa Malca, Mexico, spring 2019—no longer mattered and appeared as vapid dribble and illegible blotches. She tied her hair in a red bandanna and headed for the dusty cellars of the lower ground floor. *"Because, because," nothing is as I dreamed*, she told herself.

She'd asked Owen to fell a group of willows before winter; the Eeyore-like Sasquatch of the arboreal world, droopy, forlorn, and whiny; eager to be someplace else; and related to something, anything, other than death. The tree that swallowed whole landscapes and, on its slow march, was coming for you, or so she believed as a child. *You can't see through me, and maybe there's a reason why you don't want to?*

Five cellar rooms spiraled off a central hall at Otyrburn. The second room stored Alistair's rustic wooden wine and whisky rack; his empty stout crates remained stacked as he had left them. She made a mental count of how many bottles the rack held. Edwina's canning supplies in cellar three, Herbert blueberry planting stakes, Ruby's rusted Tonka truck and painted watering can, then the boiler room.

Georgian by design, Otyrburn's central hall ran front to back, with exterior entrances opposite at either end. Four principal rooms, each with a fireplace, comprised the ground floor: drawing room or the Blue Room, sitting room two, library, and dining room. The first floor in Europe was the second floor in the States. The kitchen, pantry, larder, and utility room were at the back, with a separate flight of stairs. The two front bedrooms shared a Jack and Jill bathroom. Ruby's room was above the pantry, with a remote designated stair run to the kitchen. Edwina's packed library divided the front bedrooms of the main from Ruby's room at the back.

George came to find her. The classic English gentleman wore his sweater-vest and tie. Margot only had to squint, and seamlessly, he morphed into Turner's canvas, *Mortlake Terrace: Early Summer Morning*, 1826, and a strolling flaneur, waterside, sported a straw boater, in a spotless natural linen suit while the gardener worked. He became figure number three at rest on the wall— gentleman at leisure. His lanky form had disappeared, dissolved.

"George, you could hide a hoard down here."

"A disciple of Sir John Soane? Don't unleash that thought. Antiques and antiquities are increasingly hard to place." He rifled through an apple crate of Alistair's tools, with a childlike vision. "Though Parian marble from the Aegean island of Paros produces such restrained sublimeness."

George perpetually outlined the cracks in surfaces, and did so adeptly, but repaired them with little recognition. He held up an old, as yet unopened, whisky bottle beneath the bare bulb. "Sludge."

They climbed stairs. He carried a Keuffel & Esser New York slide ruler. Something he'd found at the back of a drawer in Alistair's workbench. "Collector's items now."

"The man with the curio shop of expertly edited items."

"In the dining room mural you've begun," he held the planked cellar door open for his wife, and they entered the warm kitchen, "it's hard to tell if Alistair and Edwina are mythical, divine, or mortal. Alistair driving the processional in a wagon-cum-chariot is a riot."

"He was mad, in a good way." Margot wiped a cobweb off the sleeve of her sweater. "Help me figure the bar."

"*Pffaah*, when in Scotland, your man is Robbie." George's parsimonious nature dissolved over art and parties but fought temporal gratifications. "What puts a thorn in my side, M, is the lost advancement in the *right places* in life. Instead, augmented reality and the computer voice interface rises into focus."

George embodied Turner's paintings. Pick one, foggy and shifting marvel of a landscape, and like his favorite artist, relaxation included large bodies of water and fishing.

CHAPTER TWENTY

The Undoing

*L*et's get down to the real meat behind lies. In the end, each one is revealed, one way or another. You see my point.

I think, but don't quote me, that Ava was seventeen when she said, "You ruined my life." It was when the snow falls. I had thought that things between us were rolling along fine. I always get caught off guard. I had mentioned something in an off-handed way about group wedding ceremonies "being so '60s."

"You did what?" Ava cried.

(Again, there was snow, perhaps a bona fide blizzard. It was hard to see two feet ahead. Let alone ancient history. So humor me.)

"About twenty of us, give or take, probably an even number," I said; damn it was biting cold—too cold for a walk. "But back then anything flew."

"*What exactly am I supposed to remember about a Hog Farm group wedding, Mom?*"

(I do remember that she had her mittened hands on her hips at that point in the exchange. She always looks so cute like that. Like an angry June Cleaver.)

"*We made a circle with garlands in our hair, both sexes, holding hands around an old-growth tree, no white tulle, Juliet caps, or seed pearls.*" I shivered. "*We chanted and danced barefoot and did peyote; that's about the gist of it. Birdwatching in the afternoon.*"

I tried to catch a snowflake on my tongue.

"*That delightful day, I wore a fur-trimmed white minidress with go-go boots.*"

"*Who was he?*" Ava screamed, her hot breath making a bubble around her head. "*Not my father, anything but that.*"

"*Oh God no, what do you take me for? He was a sweet boy who made kites from hand-dyed silk. When he told me he didn't like the way I'd styled my hair—well, that finished it. I was eighteen, out on a whim, feeling the moment—for a total of, give or take, ninety days.*"

Ava had stamped her feet in a circle beneath her boots, made a well in the collecting snow.

"*Feeling groovy,*" she fumed. "*I don't have any pictures of my father. Why couldn't you have grabbed a guy off the street and jumped in a photo booth just once and, with all your literary expertise, told a good story?*"

"*Love is always complicated,*" I said. "*I just ask that you do your own thing.*"

VENICE, NOVEMBER 2018

Sunday morning in the privacy of his office, Will was grumpy. Earlier by phone, Ruby had said that he sounded "salty," which added a sting to his bad mood. *Lisbet is like a bird sighting, an avian beauty,* he thought, *no wings or binoculars required.*

Sundays, his secretary managed the floor. The tourist stream increased after four. He'd receive a text with a thumbs-up emoji if she had a potential buyer who merited a personal introduction. One well-placed sale could initiate a lifetime collection that delivered, though rarely, the patron who, in the end, wanted to know how they could benefit a museum.

He grabbed his jacket and headed out the door. He turned past I Frari, the Gothic church where three of his favorite Venetians lay buried, the painter Titian in 1396, the composer Claudio Monteverdi in 1643, and the sculptor Antonio Canova in 1822. The cenotaph, or monumental pyramid erected within and dedicated to Canova, took his breath away. He couldn't get over the feeling of vulnerability the immense void left in him. He'd made a habit, since the loss of Lisbet, to stand before the white marble pyramid made bright by the backwash of pink brickwork. Unlike Rodin's *Gates of Hell* or an Egyptian tomb, its door was half-open—an invitation of welcome and terror. The central figure *Sculpture,* cloaked and veiled, carried an urn that contained the sculptor's heart, and behind her walked the mournful figure of *Painting* and one of *Architecture. Genius,* who reclined, searching for integrity, dispensed daydreams.

A member of the committee "Venice in Peril," Will documented the sinking ground below them as it gave way to rising water and the ravages of damp. Venice, the complete and total edifice of watery ambivalence, was in desperate need of desalination. How to save his beloved adopted city? *We're the couple in the drifting canoe,* Will thought, *okay—a gondola. Fuck the autumn-hued nostalgia.* He could watch the puzzle pieces come together or leave it unassembled. Any successful endeavor accepted that what they planned seldom happened; the unexpected materialized. A gallery owner earned the respect of artists by being cognizant of their resentment at being corralled into conceptual interpretation.

He had hired a courier, an Italian boy with eyes of jet and a dimple shaped like a Sicilian almond. His mother baked the ultimate pistachio biscotti. Week one, Beppe delivered to Elisabetta's apartment, *numero* 7, Via Priuli, a Roman jasper vase they'd admired when touring Florence.

Week two, Beppe had placed one dozen white roses in her arms, the same week Will and she had mystifyingly met on the bridge. Week three, Beppe rode his bicycle with a charcoal hatching drawing of a whooping swan strapped in the saddlebag. Week four, he left with implicit instructions.

"Wait politely, Beppe, for a quiet moment in the Prada shop," Will said, aware that if not encouraged to slow down, Beppe would trip through his words like a chattering acorn. "Then read the title slowly—break for dramatic effect, count to three, continue reciting, and hand it to her."

"Tell me what you read in her expression, Beppe."

It went on like this, a box of oranges from the fertile slopes of Vesuvius; a Tuscan sheepskin vest; a miniature figurine he'd molded and fired, meant to resemble her, poised, seated on earth, an arm across a dog's back, *their dog*. One set of antique silver spoons. And *The New Yorker* cover from the week they had first met presented in a gilded frame.

Will entered the small shop of an early-string-instrument maker to appraise the progress on a swan-necked Baroque lute copied after Sebastian Schelle's eighteenth-century creation. Hers would be worked in figured curly maple with a rosewood back. Will had the rear panel of the pegbox carved and pierced like the original.

WIND OF DREAMS

I could paint your portrait,
like a household god,
your laughter reigns with liberty,
the love that came to me,
I have looked upon her smile,
like one who holds
in his palm a sonnet.

—W. W. Lowell

CHAPTER TWENTY-ONE

Eduardo's Bar

*A*rchie and I met walking our dogs. He had rented the O'Toole house in July. In the same summer of 1985, he taught me how to make ghee and a dynamite curry sauce, a recipe he had learned in the California ashram that one year in his early twenties. Fast-forward, and there he was, a middle-aged banker, on my island, with his cruising sailboat, Drifter's Escape, anchored. The feel of flesh, the way the wind whistled when the air grew cooler. Buddha-like and metahuman, we were each an expat to our souls.

"Is that your daughter in the library on Thursdays?" I had asked.

"What was she reading?" He spoke casually, with an instantly recognizable sailor's sun-bleached tan.

"I did look. Great American Dog Stories."

"Tearjerkers. Anything pathos-filled."

I got the drift that he wasn't a gabber. There's nothing worse than being stuck in a cockpit with someone who won't stop talking. "She has a lot of poise for one so young."

"An only child doesn't resonate solely within the thoughts of their own generation." *He had smiled quietly, casually, with one raised eyebrow.* "If they do so at all."

I was thirty-five the year I met Archie, and what a gift Ava was. My writing faults, my own, what of our loyalties and wonders? I loaded each sentence, this life, with more than the paper could hold.

And Ava, water collecting between her toes, both of us barefoot, inches deep in sand. "Little toothpick legs," *I called, prodding her along at four years old. Years later, when it seemed to her that even the purple sea urchins refused her smile and the dolphins just kept on swimming away somewhere important, I'd remind her that she was born in May when the whales return to feed, just twenty miles off the Maine coast.* #familyiseverything. #everythingmatters. #nothingisordinary.

Last week, Ava had opened a book in the comfort of her winter home and read that the Buddha had said: "Three things that cannot be hidden: the sun, the moon, the truth." *Then she texted me to say that in spring last year, when she'd stayed in a motel in Mendocino, enthralled, she'd viewed a stream of whales migrating north.*

PERTHSHIRE, DECEMBER 2018

Owen trailed a single-track road beneath the already-dark sky. The going was flat to the dead-end cove. Incoming foul weather presented in advance. He crossed the undisturbed sand, broken by occasional lichen-strewn rock outcrops. *The more light, the more lichen.* Out along the cove's fringe wove the brown dune grass of December. Bairn's Beach seldom had visitors. The legend was that a babe had been found on its shore, carried there by brown seals that frequented the long, fingerlike stretch of the rock formation. Free-roaming long-horned Highland cattle stretched out on the heated bed of glass-like granules, members of the oldest registered fold that had existed in the Highlands and Western Islands since Neolithic man. Ruins of the stone open shelters, which Owen called *kyloes* in Scots, dotted the surrounding landscape. The cattle grazed their dun-and-red backs.

He stripped, wrapped himself in lengths of seaweed, and strode the shoreline—something he did every so often—for the "beneficial effect" of sea bathing like an otter. The sea lashed the shore rhythmically. He opened his battered old rucksack and withdrew a viewing glass made from an old thermos, then sat with his arms folded over his bent knees, drenched in sharp sea waves, and peered at the sandy bottom. His lips purple, his breath fell in and out. He closed his eyes, and the darkness only made him recall the sensation of entering her.

How she trembles. How we laugh, he thought. *How time rolls back, wavelike, to expose us, and neither of us runs.*

A rotting boat blighted the pristine coast. Whenever Owen encountered lines in shambles, he bent to coil them. A smashed hull, the bench seat torn asunder, spindly weeds thrust through the splintered bottom—a sailor never left lines uncoiled.

Rye scouted and sniffed through kelp and bladder wrack beds threaded with sea urchins. The strata of millennia ringed in quartz around a pebble. Rye had picked up the scent of those same seals that lounged on purple rocks. Until now, Owen had lived life with no need for apology. He'd mapped it so.

Time swept grains of sand under his skin and salt spray into his eyes. Far out at sea, seagulls and crows forecast a falling tide. He should get Rye home. A man was only as good as his dog. He dug his toes into the sand. The steeper the face of a wave, the steeper the gradient, and the deeper the water, between the dark and light on the water ripples formed. He called to Rye in Gaelic—*Trobhad*, "come"—and the two strode back over the beach, which was no different on the return.

If you look far enough out at sea, you can't see racism or white supremacy because it no longer exists. George Lowell was a good enough swimmer but not in a hurricane. A dog whistle blows before a cyclone touches down.

New York City, December 2018

George stood on the second floor of the Met at the entrance to the Tisch Galleries. His straight silver hair swept effortlessly off his high brow. Today, in haste, he had shaved and missed a corner of his lower-left jawbone and was chagrined to discover it belatedly at noon. *I do notice,* he thought, *actually, quite a bit. How art interacts with other art. How short explanations get turned into massive appendixes, here and at home.*

Lovers whispered together before a sculpture, their shoulders touching, as they strolled from figure to figure. When had he and Margot last had nothing to do for a day but play art critic and challenge each other to find the bon mot that expressed the exuberance of a brushstroke or chisel? He sighed, mildly exasperated by the wash of life. *A productive life is the "jewel in the crown,"* he thought, *and we thrive on ambition.* An opinionated couple honored the need for respect. He paraphrased from *An Arcane View of Time*, "Time passes slower the faster you move. Time passes faster for your face than your feet. The closer you are to the center of the earth, the slower time goes." He glanced at his watch—drinks with Johnny after work at Eduardo's Bar. Johnny would cruise past the museum steps at 6:30 p.m. sharp.

In an astonishing array of wealthy kingdoms, from a myrtle wreath hammered from gold to the mortal clash between man and marauding Amazons, the emotionalism of life and death in art coalesced around George on any given day at the museum. It spanned three centuries between Alexander the Great and Cleopatra. George stopped before *Lo Spinario*, the near-perfect form of a boy bent in concentration as he removed a thorn from his foot, his right leg lost. Life zoomed into sharp focus every working day of his life. After-hours, his fingers had crossed the sculpted edge of carved marble that fused a perfect pair of lips. George was paid well to interpret expression, and yet, he had a million questions. The Met's headless female figures had never bothered George. It had always been Margot who fed the silken serpent that climbed her legs to eat in her lap and, again, opened the ivory-and-bronze-wrapped Pandora's box. What compelled her to peer inside? Doubtful, but maybe he hadn't asked?

He dismissed the thought with a brush off his Hebridean brown Harris tweed cuff where a leather button was loose. He'd ask his tailor to fix it. True happiness didn't need quantifying. He grabbed his coat and headed out the door, pleased with himself—perfect timing, Johnny's Porsche 911 Carrera had just pulled up to the granite curb.

"Ready to trade quips over a beer, relinquish life, and watch it on a screen?" Johnny asked, switching lanes. He wore the silver ring fixed in his ear. Cervantes's Don Quixote sported a brown suede coat with horn buttons.

"Hell yeah."

"Real Madrid versus Barcelona tonight," Johnny said. "I'll have my eye on the goalie Munci, a giant with size-twelve-and-a-half cleats that fire like lightning. How was your day?"

"Grueling. There's no method to the madness at the museum. The executive director resigned. Too many tweets about 'revolutionary zealots prepared to loot tombs,' and the useless pricks canceled an exhibition on police violence." George rolled down the window, letting a brace of cold air hit him in the face. "Blow by him. You'll miss the kickoff."

"I like the badass you. Suffer some more."

"Go faster, and we'll be younger when we get there."

Johnny pushed the throttle into third and let the turbo wind up to the red light at Madison—secretly proud of the spectacle. At the summerhouse, he'd swung with Pilar from a rope tied to the oak tree, out her bedroom window, and into the snow. (That's my idea of a brother figure.)

"It's easy," Johnny said. "We need a billionaire to open the National White Atonement Museum and showcase their myopic worldviews."

They parked and walked a block in a crisp winter breeze. The dusky purple twilight made vibrant the stream of red taillights.

"Cosmic chaos ensues, George; then everything goes to shit, and we're left with nothing—or are we?" Johnny asked.

"Pretty bleak, nihilistic even." George feared his hidden dilemma showed. He cringed at the thought of having to rewrite even the tiniest piece of his personal history to read as less offensive to his future grandchildren. He turned to the waiter. "Two Talisker Scotch on ice, thank you." And then to Johnny; "What did you do today?"

"Two hours, maybe three, spent in the darkroom perfecting surreal images—*Cowboy Smoking a Cigarette*. I met him in Arizona, a hulk of a guy, chaps, six-gun, ten-gallon hat, and full bushy mustache. A Vietnam vet who left the city to drive cattle and became a cowboy and then some."

"A contemplative, hazy black-and-white, no doubt. Goddamn, why can't we light up a Bolivar in here?" *When Margot isn't around*, George thought, *life lightens*.

"You're preaching to the choir. Wednesday nights in the woods at prep school, before life got expensive—all it required was a cigar cutter and extra-long matches. Poor Aunt Sophia didn't have a clue."

"Oh, hell, Sophia was onto you," George countered. "Your sweaters smelled *muy robustos* of coffee beans and caramel."

"Did I show you this beaut?" Johnny reached into his pocket to show George his Italian handmade Rasolino Tagliasigari cigar-cutter pocketknife with a handle made of ox horn. They turned the pointless blade over in their palms in admiration as the light caught the steel's sheen.

George praised a good save by the goalie. "The blade's initialed by the craftsman."

"You're going to meet Anna tonight. My date for the party."

"How will I know when she comes in the door?" George asked.

"Does a tall, thin, fiery redhead give you enough to go on? If not, add mystic stunner."

"Johnny B. Goode. Go Johnny go."

Johnny ate peanuts and George told him not to.

I can't foresee him holding on to someone for long, George thought, *or having a stable retirement. The fanciful side of him spells ruin.*

"We'll have the sweet potato fries with aioli and one side of Yukon Gold with truffle oil," George instructed the waiter.

"Two hundred and fifty thousand refugees entered Greece, mostly the Aegean Isles, this year alone." Johnny sampled fries between outbursts of "Real Madrid, *Alé, Alé!*"

"How many died crossing the Mediterranean?"

"Twenty-five hundred—who's to know? It's internalized on a UN level. It's not a migration issue. It's a refugee issue. I almost forgot. How about Romania in the springtime, where fiddle dance parties last well into the next day? No polka waltz or Linzer torte—just brown bears." He ordered a second scotch. "Boy, these truffle fries are potato porn."

When have I ever heard him swear and let it fly in all directions? George kept at it. *A stranger could follow Johnny, and walk by his side, and he'd feed him his sandwich. We all believe we've done something worthwhile.*

"By European standards, I'm outbound in May to the incomparable isolation of the Carpathian Mountains," Johnny continued. "When's the last time we had a road trip?"

He rose expectantly.

"Anna Cavanaugh—George Lowell."

"A pleasure. Glad you'll join us on the malt whisky trail, but don't expect too much out of your date tonight. Johnny has his eye on the men in tight-fitting striped jerseys with quick rights."

As Anna left to hang her coat, her heels clicking over the floor, George whispered to Johnny, "Shake it, don't break it. Wrap it up, and I'll take it."

CHAPTER TWENTY-TWO

Hang Five

*I*n 1969, LIFE *magazine published a photograph of me doing an out-of-body rain dance at Woodstock in an orange raincoat. Years later, we tried to meditate at the Jack Kerouac School of Disembodied Poetics, but really, we were having fun on the bed. That was the true turning point in my career, not the bed-surfing but being asked to teach.*

At the Summer Writing Program, the faculty each took a name: Moon Fire, Shakes and Sundays, Sold Out, Russian Eyes, and Slingshot. I met Gary Snyder and Ginsberg. There were over sixty of us invited as guest faculty, but you got the essence. Hallucinogenic drugs notwithstanding, we did some fine writing. It was not about drugs; it was about expression.

I don't get how couples run out of something to say. Maybe they never heard each other in the beginning. When you buy a boat, check the hull; when you buy a house, locate the view; when you enter a relationship, connection, connection, connection.

PERTHSHIRE, DECEMBER 2018

Wren yelped when he sighted Rye. An afternoon in the vast Highlands, one figure filled the landscape, and two wrote a story. Margot greeted Owen. *We're a boxed set,* she thought.

"You brought a book." She took his hand. "George is home tomorrow."

"*Follies and Gazebos: I Shall Gaze,*" he said.

"I don't have money for either."

The cold, dry wind blew a cricket to land on the pebbles between them, then disappear quickly in a crevice. They sat at Margot's worktable. She undid the wool scarf that wrapped her neck. "I bought Perkins in town; would you like tea?"

"Nothing but you."

"Kissy-faces are for teenagers, Owen."

"Fancy that. It's a *dreich* day when love is reserved for youth."

"Does cold, damp, and miserable figure into every Scots equation?" she asked.

"Okay—life is a series of 'what-ifs.' A folly is many things. And a gazebo is only one. But it's a useless ornament that invites noise."

"It's a difficult needle to thread," she said.

"Hell, Margot, stop talking, and let's go driving."

"You and I are quite alike."

He left with the dogs. "Bring the book," he hollered, the narrow stairs creaking below him, "and grab the Perkins."

She ran to catch up with him. "In my mind, I'm allowed to try on as many lives as I want. Explore a dream, erase a mistake," she said, breathing heavy.

"It's never too late to begin anew."

"Or to feel out of sync."

"It doesn't have to be a desperate choice, Margot, just a true one."

Not too far from there was a folly ruin copied from one in England. Hidden between Otyrburn and Owen's cottage, he'd tracked upon it one day with Rye. A leaf or two fell on the windshield. The garden ideas book open on her lap to the page that displayed a weathered faux pavilion tent built of wood. Its back to the forest, tall weeds had grown within. Painted blue, with red stripes edging the vertical boards, and a gilded Arthurian ball attached to a carved banner crowned the roof.

"Ruby could be married here." She pressed the page flat on her lap with her palm. "As a child, I always wanted a secret place for my imaginary friend, Bookie, and me."

"Alistair said Edwina mourned yearlong." Owen's low and raspy voice floated over the rumble of the engine.

The heater clanked and whirred. It fired the feet and neglected the body, but today it ran. There was no necessity to describe their position.

"It isn't often, Margot, that a network of tightly tied families endures such a loss on an open pass of Highland road."

"I think about death all the time," she said. "I've avoided a visit to their graves."

Owen reached to hold her hand.

"I haven't told anyone this," she said, "but right before the accident, I fought with Angus in the car. I threw his jacket at him.

We made a hell of a racket." Margot stared out the passenger-side window to the sweeping fields of winter wheat. "The last thing I said to my baby brother was, 'I hate you, Angus.' I've always thought it caused my mother to be distracted. That I caused the accident."

He pulled the truck off the road to give her, as he said, his full attention. "You've held that guilt since you were a child of nine?"

"I wanted nothing more than to tell my father," Margot said, "but was afraid to. When I climbed the stairs to bed, for years after the crash, at the french door at the top of the stairway that led into my bedroom hall, I shook with fear, knowing I might relive the memory in my dreams."

"Let it go," he said. "Your mother had experience with screaming kids in the back seat. It wasn't—in any way, shape, or form—your fault."

"Maybe you'll convince me."

Owen shifted into first gear and pulled up onto the road. "From the old farm road, we can see this one from the car. The going's not worth it this late in the year—it'll be too boggy."

They passed a derelict black house, its roof bright with moss, the white sheep dotted around the long brown grass.

"In my lifetime," Margot said, "I've been a party to the smugness of intact couples when one hears the news that another pair bit the dust. There's euphoria found in 'So glad it isn't us.' It mends the tedious moments of faultfinding and reignites the sense of team building."

"Draw your own conclusions. And don't be a party to small-minded people."

He pulled to the side of the road, again, and found the vantage he sought. Although you wouldn't guess it with the sunshine spilling through the clouds, the temperature was freezing.

"There to the east, the tree sprouting from the loch. Now steady your eye, and follow it to the outline of a crenelated tower. Do you see it?" he asked.

"I do." In the distance, fishing boats rocked side by side in the harbor. "I don't know if there is a privileged relationship with the mother tongue, on my part, but I was raised in an atmosphere of Scottish cultural memories. In the city we were misfits. Archie could be hunting numbers that lined up correctly, and though he didn't carry a rifle, he advanced observing firsthand."

"The disobedience in dissonance," Owen said.

She shook her head once. "No, New England eastern effeteness and repetition."

"I don't know how you knew the right time to tell me your secret," he said. He adjusted the rearview mirror. "The legend goes one brother built the one-hundred-foot length of ruin wall to hide the view from his house of the estranged brother's house on the far side of the loch. He built it out of rubble, the towers and the crowns. Nothing remains of disappointment and discord."

She put her hand on his thigh.

"What if I said that today, I don't give a hoot about history or sadness?"

He got back on the road.

"If I can't kiss you"—he smiled—"hand me one of those ginger cakes."

She shifted in her seat. "I don't believe in magic. Let's go make love in 'Fiona's cottage.'"

"You told me *no*, no, no. Now you want to ravage me at my *wee hoose*. I've never trivialized love."

He put the car in gear, cast his gaze over his shoulder, and pulled out.

"Margot, like any Scots, you headed north to find what you sought. The emotions that don't reside in consciousness."

"Some things can't be appreciated quickly," she said, "and can't be rushed." *He knows this.*

"The ruins bit is fundamentally Scots. What other maniac tries to lift a ring of paired stones that weigh three hundred and thirty-three kilograms? And then go and walk with it?"

"How many pounds is that?" she asked.

"Seven hundred and twenty-seven and one-half, to be precise." He pointed out a solitary red tin hut. "Have you read Yeats's poem 'The Fascination of What's Difficult'?"

"No. Read a bit of *The Good Gray Poet*," Margot said.

"Whitman and his grass. Yeats works a comparison between his ailing colt and the annoyances in everyday life that peeve him, then closes by saying, 'I swear before the dawn comes round again. I'll find the stable and pull out the bolt.' Free and unburdened is a hard thing for a Scots to do."

"A woman is taught to be the fixer."

"I can wait, Margot. I can wait for you till it's my turn."

"Really?"

"Because life gained expression," Owen said. "The gloss of the petals on my peony blinded and the bees came in drones, and those two turtles that appeared beneath the crab apple, out of nowhere, they had something to say too. The northern harrier made eight circles over my chimney before he flew in your direction. Whispers and rumors, hell, the whole world speaks to us."

They laughed exuberantly.

"Are you going to make love to me?" Margot asked.

"If you hand me another one of those Perkins." Owen cracked his broad smile. "Just so you know, the idea excites me enormously."

When he brushed a spray of crumbs off his jacket, the dogs hunted the floor of the cab.

They passed an elderly couple bent on the hill, cutting the peat. The day was a snowy, wet, muddy mess. Yet far beyond lay a small stream being washed by the incoming tide. The heater had retired for the moment.

"They must have run out," he said. "Not a welcome sign in December. In May, cutting begins, and laying up of peat bricks to dry over summer in the wind. It's an unforgiving place for the aged."

"How's it compare to wood?"

"Toasty peat smoke? A croft needs eighteen thousand peats a year. In his youth, that old man out there probably cut one thousand peats a day. In the depths of peat bogs is what remains of a prehistoric Caledonian forest. Highland Perthshire is rich in peat."

"Environmentally?" she asked.

"It's worse than coal. If we leave the bogs alone, they capture and store carbon."

The road into Owen's cottage, riddled with potholes, made him, on reaching the midpoint, straddle one tire on the ridge of the high mound along the center so as not to drag the truck bottom on the crown. Sheep grazed in the open, with white coats, black faces, and curled dark horns.

"Blackfaces are their own keepers," he said, "and so shepherds like them. Independent types, but they come near." He reached through the open window and scratched an ewe's nose. "Did you ever believe you had anything in common with high-society wives?"

"With increasing George's social cachet? You can't be serious," she said.

"We exert our forces in one direction or another. We ruminate on life, love, and death lifelong."

"On what's lost and wanted. False friends. Something unique," Margot said.

"I know you're lonely," he said.

"Loneliness is an easy state to push aside. It doesn't weigh anything."

"A carefully constructed identity crumbles quickly."

"Friendly small talk in a bakery," Margot said, "half an hour of yoga, and I believed my dreams had color again."

"Broken places are the best places to heal."

"I wrestled with how many times you'd had sex, Owen, and with who?"

He turned off the ignition and parked before the sunlit cottage with double chimneys and a thatch roof, tucked tight against the back of a mountain—sheep bleating at the door.

Margot didn't have to look long. "The house hasn't changed."

"It took acquainting myself. The folks still have the sea farm. I was a bit put out about not standing at will by the ocean, but the loch's won me over. It isn't a big mountain, but it has a big presence."

He helped her out of the cab, and the two dogs chased their reflection around the loch.

"That's a 'water dance' of grebes, not ducks," Owen said.

"What's the difference?"

"They have lobed feet, not webbed feet."

"My favorite's a 'wisdom' of owls," she said.

"And mine's a 'murmuration' of starlings. But just by a margin over an 'invisibleness' of ptarmigans."

"A 'skulk' of foxes."

The wooden plank door swung freely over the threshold. The fire within encouraged it to shrink, not stick with wet weather's humid swell.

"I told you," Owen said.

"A hell of a lot of books."

Every square inch fascinated her.

"We've both read forever, it seems," he said.

"I remember. Your mother had you read one hour a day and report back, a family movie Saturday night, and cartoons on Sunday for thirty minutes exactly."

"What a catastrophic waste of time. She was right. We had friends. We went outside to find them. We drank water from the garden hose, not a bottle. No one was able to reach me all day— and I was okay. I figure novels exist to put things we don't have and pursue into life."

"And to escape what we can't change," she said.

"Margot Reid, are we in love with each other or the history between us? Myth binds."

He covered her in tender kisses. And they were down in one, laid out on his creaky bed, beneath the beam that supported a run of books and peeling paper. Her beach-glass-and-shell bracelet jingled—struggling to remove what was in the way of yearning.

"We're getting too damn good, too fast," Owen said.

She was unutterably happy but afraid to say so.

"It was always a point of no return," he said. Freckled from years in the sun, his limbs were long and sinewy. "Quiet. That's where things set right; low-pitched sound travels farther."

"And all shadow is darker at its source."

In bed, they held hands, their fingers caressed. She walked naked over to his painting-things desk, sat on the window seat, and lifted in hand the watercolor paper with the chalk-white workings of a tern.

"I don't have my head in the clouds. My only power lay in my story. A person's unhappiness has a language of its own that a bored gesture can't dismiss."

If he had blocked in the outline of his life in dark strokes and then worked the light over it, it would still be piecemeal, an unfinished sketch. He'd said as much. The intricate composition of a bird in flight performing fancy acrobatics, he'd struggled with it until it suddenly tore at the paper and took flight. The late-day sun cut through the window, rode over the figuring desk, and fell in patterns of gold across their flesh, where it glistened.

"Fairies float on particles of dust," Margot said.

"You got that from Edwina. I've heard it before. Don't let this place fill your head with pixie prattle. Christ, in these parts if it isn't small talk about saints and miracles, its big yarns of water horses and sea serpents, giants and ogres. For the love of God, Scots make a profession of seeing *things*. Tell me this: Why is it that people in Greece tell the same story as those in Scotland? In a different age and terrain."

"Why is it that one summer, not long ago, when standing before the pantry, I muttered, 'Mother of Amon,' under my breath, before I had any idea what I had said. Meshullemeth, mother of Amon of Judah—crowned at twenty-two, the equally awful successor of his father—is mentioned only once, opaquely, in the Bible. Come to think of it, the pantry was made in Jerusalem."

He made Margot an omelet, and they ate fireside. The candles burned out. Then he took her home.

CHAPTER TWENTY-THREE

Heinke

*T*he colors of their stories are bright and fine, as are their faces. It happened before the War of Words came to a head on January 6, 2021, when a pestilence had covered the globe. When a mask both protected us from the virus and bandaged the wound, and hidden were the dark secrets each carried home. Borrowed money and lies are heavy carries. The ultimate famine is not starvation but dishonesty.

Who will reestablish the delicate ecosystem of kindness? The next generation, in a naked room, will conjure the solutions without a key. The Exxon Valdez oil spill happened in Prince William Sound in 1989, the year Ava Blue was three. In 1998, I had to explain Bill Clinton's bullshit affair with Monica Lewinsky to my twelve-year-old and her girlfriends. Summer of 2001, I taught in Vermont at Middlebury's Bread Loaf Writers' Conferences. We were closing

*up the apartment, she and I, which overlooked Otter Creek, when all
hell broke loose. That was Ava's fifteenth year, when bodies had flown
from the sky, freefalling from skyscrapers in Manhattan. The year's
2018 now, and Karma is still barely talking to anyone. And Dharma
remains to be seen. Mothers and daughters should say to each other,
"Don't let me be misunderstood for long."*

VENICE, DECEMBER 24, 2018

Will took his hot chocolate out on his loggia. Chilled, he wore
Irish wool in Venice. The last of the crimson leaves whirled as
he dipped his croissant and watched the steam rise off the moist
ivory-pocketed dough at the close of a bad week. *My engaging
brother, the busy Santa*, Will thought. Heinke Hessel had shown
up at the gallery on Monday, asking for William Lowell.

"*Salve!* Mr. Lowell, finally we meet!"

Though short, Heinke Hessel had filled the threshold when
he spread his arms wide, his chin thrust upward with a generous open smile of greeting. His round belly, softened by the tight
weave of his dark-navy wool sweater, drew the eye cascading
downward to a rather sizable bulge in the crotch of his pleated
trousers. He possessed the markings of an aristocrat. Dark, bushy
eyebrows emphasized his hawklike nose, the paleness of his brow,
and his receding silver hairline.

"What can I do for you?"

"Ah." Heinke sighed, his glance sweeping the gallery. "No
Postimpressionist, passé work, and plenty of abstract expression-
ism. So refreshing! Good job."

"Thank you."

"I read your artistic statement. You studied at all the best: Yale,
the Rhode Island School of Design, and the Royal College of Art
in London. Impressive." He took a step forward, his arms folded

over his chest, shortening the distance between the two men. "I would like to introduce you to a colleague of mine over lunch this week. Her obsession with twenty-first-century art has never been higher. For Maria, art is the food of love."

"I hate to disappoint, but I have a busy schedule."

If a wolf comes while someone's asleep, he sniffs him, Will thought, *but if he pretends to be asleep, he grabs the wolf by the tail and traps him.*

"Let me take a look at my schedule," he said, "being you're a friend of George's and all." He opened his phone's calendar. "Wednesday at 2:00 works."

"Perfect. Doña Maria is in Venice for the week, returning to Ibiza. She has the most wonderful Modigliani."

Two days later they met at the Florian in Piazza San Marco. The fine figure of Doña Maria de Trujillo y Merlo wrote straightforward blank verse, with the minor exception of the delivery of her speech. Will interpreted it as a tightening of a string, as musicians use to tune the instrument. She delivered a fading cadence at the end of each line she spoke. It had a hypnotic effect on Will.

Tea was served. Between the blooming tea leaves, the masterpiece of form in Doña Maria's fine features, and the olfactory power of her cologne, William struggled with alertness. He ordered a cup of the house 100 percent Arabic coffee.

"It may sound irrational," she said, "but at a conference at the Sorbonne, I became intrigued by the mystery that breathes behind things. The porous boundaries between reality and a work of art, when all is said and done."

Will couldn't make out her accent; it was as though a hint of German had crossed the border into Spain. He ordered a club sandwich *al tacchino.*

"I want you to help me in my search for works exhibiting, oh, what shall I call it?" Doña Maria sighed. "A major magic-realist phenomenon—as in metafiction, which challenges the linear aspect of time—textualized on canvas."

"Does the work have to include an implicit criticism of society?" Will asked, egging her on. Quite sure there was a pile of slop behind the Gucci veneer. Heinke had retrieved her napkin off the brown-and-white marble, diamond-patterned floor.

I can't believe George is in bed with these guys, Will queried, *and their half-made societies. Was George drunk when he met these two?*

"Heinke, the issue of numerous crates delivered to my door must be addressed. I simply don't have the room. I'm sorry for any confusion between you and George."

"Old favors are not soon forgotten in my world." Heinke beamed. "Consider the correction made."

Let me tell you that the tea party presented bizarre jumps and amusements. William's mind was richly layered, that afternoon, with the imagery of sacks drowning in profit and callous murders. George, since childhood, had screwed up the simplest tasks in the most catastrophic ways. Devoid of the normative manner that most children have, it was as though he'd heard someone babbling about a fortune, and he'd crawled out of a chrysalis and believed it.

A water taxicab's horn blew; a child called to his friend, who answered. The Venetian teen gang on the corner whistled after pretty skirts, the harmonica played and coins dropped in the beggar's guitar case, and the door slammed in the widower's flat one flight up. William drew an espresso and played with the idea of purifying the apartment by burning sage. For the first time since he was a kid, he enjoyed the heavy wind with snowflakes falling and the crystal ice that formed at the tip of his lashes.

Margot stuck her head in the back bedroom doorway where Ruby slept. *Hilariously irresistible*, she thought, *my own Ramona, without sibling rivalry.* The only way to understand the labyrinth layout of clipped yews was to view it from this bedroom's mullioned window.

"At one time, I slept in this room. I still remember climbing into bed, only to recall I forgot something, the fear of stepping over the stones in the dark to shut in the chickens. Were you warm enough? The few times we celebrated Christmas here, it was so cold winters that my water glass froze overnight. Fires burned continuously, but your great-grandparents seldom turned the radiators on because central heating was too expensive. We'll be no different." Margot moved to the window, afraid her emotions were written all over her face. "Have you worked out anything new in Alistair's hidden message, Ruby? If you figure it out, you've got one on me."

The orchard's bare bones in winter glowed with an icy silver dew.

"Nope. Not since adding a *V* and an *A* to your *H*. It's nice here, warm, cozy, but I couldn't turn off my mind last night, Mom."

"What were you thinking about, sweetie?"

"Sometimes I think they had to go in a way that left me unhappy forever," Ruby said.

"Who?"

"Gramps, Edwina, and Alistair, everyone I ever loved. The ones I never knew. But love somehow anyway."

"One day you'll view your present unhappiness differently," Margot said.

"I doubt it."

Margot kissed her forehead. Would she forgive her? Would she ever grow to view the heartbreak she'd cringed through in the stories that unfolded as a gentle lesson in life? "Archie said that what he most loved and respected about you was that you never asked for anything but his undivided attention."

Ruby was the first arrival at Otyrburn—one dog and a carry-on packed with baking papers, a glass vial of CBD oil, and chocolate-making tools. At rest against the cast-iron radiator, she pulled out an Arturo Pérez-Reverte mystery. The last gusts of December threatened to blow themselves out. Riding horses waited in the stable, and smoked salmon in the pantry.

Don't marry a guy if it's his second marriage; he'll tell you that his first wife made dill pickles. And never, under any condition, try to separate a man from his fishing rod. George's capacious tackle bag was open on the kitchen floor as he sorted through salmon flies, a box of dry Daddies, and a casting manual. In the morning light, he appreciated a nymph with silver beads for eyes before he packed it all away for spring. But George hesitated. In their original boxes, unopened, were his two new acquisitions for "big fish," designed and hand-tied by the champion fisherman from Seattle, Washington. The Dancer and Zonker, with a red flash, if successful next spring, would prove irresistible to grayling, trout, and even salmon. He organized his gems while Ruby stood in the kitchen. She wore a white T-shirt with "Take a NOTE of what I stand in need of," from Julia in Two Gentlemen of Verona, *Act II, scrawled in red lettering across her chest. George liked the idea of surrounding himself with eccentric people.*

"I hate to interrupt your fin-fever." Ruby broke away from cracking eggs on a gray morning and lit an ivory myrrh candle with a label reading *Orati Sancti* Francisci in gold lettering. "Are you sure you wouldn't have preferred a son named Ambrose or Magnus, wading in the loch's reeds, sporting matching tweed and deerstalkers, toting his first trout?"

"Heavens no! Gentle daughter, what's 'Julia' baking today?" George openly admired her drone-at-the-hive dogged busyness, proud he'd played a part.

"Stout cake with whisky caramel and toasted meringue. Two tablespoons of whisky," she mumbled, reading a recipe in *Great American Cakes*, "I'll add three. When does the gang land?"

"They filter in all day tomorrow. A lollapalooza event for nine—twelve when Robbie and his wife, Lily, and Owen join us."

The whisky bottles racked in the cellar, the beeswax candles collected in the sideboard, and the champagne flutes polished, the lavender that sweetened the guests' bureau drawers scented the empty rooms and wafted into the scrubbed hall to mingle with the orange oils that penetrated the worn grain.

When Margot passed through the kitchen, the cake was in the oven, and George remained content to inventory. He had the right equipment, the determination, the committed resources; used the proper bait; understood the process. He was indeed a good fisherman. Good things come to those who wait. Though optimistic and patient, she wagered he did it for bragging rights. "The big one that got away." What did he like best—a baited question? Over the river and through woods, fishing was one thing he and Will did well; summers, they had practically lived in the river or the sea.

Margot strapped on Edwina's wooden backcountry skis and stopped only when she came upon a run of rabbit footprints laced across the new snow. The frantic creature, in an attempt to evade a bird of prey, had woven its plea over the meadow in a mishmash of figure eights, until the line of escape abruptly ended.

PERTHSHIRE, DECEMBER 25, 2018

Owen ate oatmeal fireside after he had added a serving to Rye's bowl. He stoked the fire. For century upon century, a double bowl of oatmeal lasted a man a half day. Scotsmen were larger and brawnier than the English, merely owing to the mighty oat. The long sunlit days were the trade-off for the dark winters. Sixteen hours of darkness each day begged for souls to slip away. His mind ran over their last tryst, his fingers through her auburn hair, the way it laid across her breasts. Sweethearts for privacy, they had bedded, by necessity, out in the deep sea of heather. Headed to the Hill of the Yew Trees, they hadn't made it to the crown.

In the splintered cavity he occupied without her, the neat cottage became a place he barely recognized. He couldn't live without her.

VENICE, DECEMBER 25, 2018

"Lost, restored, and found," Lisbet said, smiling in her doorway, "if given the key to Venus's honeypot, you belong to me."

"Any and all pledges you shall ask me to make, I accept—no, I welcome."

Kissing, they tripped over each other in eagerness and made their peace all across that bed. In a room papered in swirling patterns of peacock tails, they were each other's pupils.

"I tingle to the tip of my spine." She played with the "sun gem" on her finger that fell from the sky. Peridot is often discovered in meteor craters and has been gathered by spacecraft near the sun, as old as the solar system.

"With nature worship"—he rose, returning with a bottle of champagne—"I started praying for your return—me, to God. Visited tombs."

Still tied on the end of a fret dangled a small black velvet box, now empty, threaded by a claret velvet ribbon to one of six tuning pegs. The night was theirs; round two rode the back of round one.

"Sweet Jesus. I couldn't even hike a mile." Will wove his fingers through hers. "Let's stay in bed till the flight tonight. I want to break free from fine art and conservative galleries, follow the sculpture trail in Barcelona. Do something, anything new."

"There's beauty all around us; you take as much as you require."

"I thought a lot about rock pools in childhood, when life was innocent and unthreatened. About how in one summer, there'd be more anemone collecting, and another, sea urchins. Sea change, life change, about how I was no longer a young artist—working things out, finding things by the side of the road."

"We could have an asparagus farm."

"And birds that come into the house."

"After erotic love, the Romans demonstrate their approval by sneezing on the left, then on the right."

"Then sneeze I will. I like a happy household."

CHAPTER TWENTY-FOUR

The Gathered

*I*n my first year of life, I walked how many miles? The annoying side of writing is description. The public side of friendship—is it conscious thought or calculation? Fast friends make slow turtles. How can I gauge a poet's seriousness without proper instructions, or measure the pride in a handknit sweater? You see, the moon is full; it floods its brim and blinds me, momentarily, to the perfection of the stitches right before my eyes. I am at my typewriter, HELLO, and you are here for a story.

On Hopper's Island, where Ava was born, and again in Taos, where she spent her early childhood, I placed her playpen outside in all but the worst weather. As soon as she could speak, Ava could tell you the difference between a typhoon, a haboob, and a nor'easter. Most of the time, in Taos, I managed to get her back inside before her mouth filled with sand. I loved the vastness then, and the wavy lines, compared to New England, where everything was narrow, straight, and tight. Jack Kerouac was the reluctant godfather to the hippie movement. And I, regrettably, was a reluctant mother to anyone.

That brings me to the hotly contested subject of Ava's last name. When I chose to raise her solo, I had openly said to the universe: I have the liberty to do as I wish. I have followed the way of the Tao and "avoided the authorities." Here's my rationale. Kerouac's family, and mine, worked and lived at the textile factories of Lowell, Massachusetts. Both were of French Canadian descent. If I had had my druthers, I would have searched Kerouac out and, quite possibly, married him at eighteen, in 1968, and we'd have had one fine year together before he died at forty-seven. Scribbled secret notebooks, unspeakable visions of Proust sipping tea, and wild, undisciplined composing, what did Jack forget?

"Seriously, Mom, where did you go to—what was inside your head when you picked a last name like Kerouac?" Ava had sighed.

(I'm sure she had wailed. June Cleaver was in rare form again, baking ricotta rum-soaked raisin pies, which I appreciated, and slamming doors, which I didn't. Sweet sixteen going on sinister seventeen.)

At my typewriter, I hit the return key.

"Can you tell me how that makes you feel, sweetie?"

I adjusted the pencil tucked behind my ear and gave her my undivided attention.

"Put yourself in my shoes," she said (she wasn't going anywhere). "Reflect, if you will, on your junior year: American Authors of the Twentieth Century." Her hands went on her hips, classic, with one exacting knee bent, as a glaze settled over her eyes. "The class breaks into the chorus of "On the Road Again," led by your English professor, before you're barraged by classmates asking for writing tips, cheat sheets, and a copy of my father 'Jack's' autograph."

"I thought I was gifting you with a connection to his earthly genius." (My tea was cold.) "Kerouac told the true story of the world, of love, of joy, of spontaneity. The jewel at rest in the center of the individual, Ava."

"How about this," she huffed, then stepped outside, a stone's throw from the beach, "out on a date with the co-captain of varsity soccer, and just before he kisses me, he asks, 'Are you in the flow, Kerouac, freed of any syntactical inhibitions?'"

She picked up a piece of driftwood, angry-like, and heaved it into the sea.

"People's names are based on actual events and people!"

"Wow. That's a lot of baggage, sweetie." I handed her a tissue from my pocket. "Blow as hard as you want. Say what you want from the bottomless well of your heart."

"Don't think I'll ever be happy about this."

Ava was moving away from me now, across the sand and up the hill through the dunes to our house. A buzzard circled low and lazy overhead.

"I bet the Tardifs and Kerouacs are related," I called, "distant cousins for sure. When a tight-knit tribe of the Québécoise left Canada, they did so holding hands. There were only so many Filles de Roi to go around, and not enough trappers to satisfy the choice 'Daughters of the King.'"

"That's disgusting!"

I wasn't all that worried. My father always said, "Gee, I wish there was something that I could give Violet that would make her happy." Instead, many times he never saw me, though I was right there in front of him. I had come back down the back of a mountain that he *had yet to climb. Ava would wander in zigzags if she so chose. And I made a promise: I will see the sweat on her brow when she returns. When Ava Blue Kerouac learns she has gone as far as needed, she will arrive where she was meant to be. When Margot listens to her original self, not the "wife," or "the mother," but the one visionary voice that belongs to only her, she will grow.*

Perthshire, December 26, 2018

A little red sleigh, snow globes, Margot thought, *what did I love about them? The sled held a journey. And when I shook the dome, I was at home in a new world, waiting for magic to happen.*

"Do we have enough whisky? I've stashed eighty-six-proof nectar in thirty-year-old bottles that I'm dying to try. Everyone arrives by seven, right, M?"

George sipped Earl Grey tea in an earthenware mug and snacked on sugar-dusted shortbread from a 1950s round holiday tin decorated with red poinsettias. She hadn't answered his question. He held in his hand an old holiday card to Alistair and Edwina dated 2008.

As your beloved narrator, I admit it was a bad picture of them both. I'm convinced that photography is the "third eye" Hindus speak about, and family videos take it one further, snapping live-action emotions in a time capsule. When Dad rolled the old 35mm on Sundays and the projector's white light bulb cut over the top of my head. I saw love, genuine happiness—if only glimpses. (The film developing cost dearly. Hollywood screen babies, Thomas and Anne-Marie, their generation put out when the camera rolled for posterity.) There was no ~~Delete~~.

"M, did you hear me?" George repeated.

"Yes, that's right. Robbie won't let us go dry."

Margot listened with half an ear as others tasked with half a shoulder. She could, on any given topic, predict his reply. It ran like a news crawl: events, weather, politics, and infrastructure. Each presented without any original commentary. The fractals were missing. The veins that feed and run through everything.

"What do you think Ruby keeps in her mysterious makeup kit anyway?" he asked.

"She's a full-blown Francophile, George."

Seated at the kitchen table, she held in hand a natural wood pencil, with a no-good eraser end that only smudged red. Margot turned the page in her calendar diary.

"The schedule's taped to the cupboard door. The hunting party on the grouse moors is Monday to Tuesday."

"We should get to Isle of Skye in the spring, astounding geology, world-class surfing, and bottlenose dolphins."

(I'll relate the meat and potatoes, which is actually interesting.) Dolphins make love for the fun of it, and not solely when in their estrous cycle, Greek delphis, *also including the porpoise, which meant, more or less, "fish with a womb." From old French* dauphin, *which led George full circle to the Roman playwright Terence and* Adelphi, *the tale of two persons that came from the same womb—brothers.* Reading glasses to the top of her head. "Everything that you want? What about what I want, George?"

"You live as if cushioned by a dream." He said the sentence slowly, casually, goading her to react. This device was typical of him.

"A party we can't afford, your need to keep up appearances?" She slammed her hands down on the counter.

"Oh God, here it comes."

"You're boring me."

George was among those people who only make safe investments. Caution is a sign of prudence but also of shrewdness, and
they both got that.

"You're emotionally fractured."

"Give it up."

The heap of wet boots left at the door grew before Margot's eyes.
A storm had dumped fresh snow across the Perthshire Highlands.
Copper tubs of clementines studded with cloves perfumed rooms
already redolent with white roses and evergreen swags. Few lo-
cations would have afforded an easier refuge from everyday life.
"Everything for us," she thought, *George's rendition alone. My father
backed him.*

Sybil and Max Mowbray entered the kitchen in matching Fair
Isle sweaters.

"Check out my sweater." Max pulled the lower hem beyond
his belly. "Industrially made in Shetland for one-third the price
of a bespoke model Sybil fancied, hand-knit on Fair Isle by one
of only two hand knitters left in a population of fifty-four. One
has a wait list of ninety, and the other has closed her order-taking
book indefinitely, the starting price—six hundred and fifty dollars. *Ching-ching!* A sweater is a sweater—or a 'jumper' here in the
old country." He put his hands on his hips. "Do we have time for
a pub run before dinner, George?"

The men left, leaving three women home to greet two more
parties' arrival. Sybil and Max had unpacked in the front bedroom, where they'd share the Jack and Jill bath with George and
Margot. Will and Lisbet would sleep surrounded by walls papered

in white lilacs at the top of the stairs. And opposite, Johnny and Anna would share the bedroom suite with a dressing room. All but Ruby had a working fireplace.

Margot moved to adjust a mercury glass bird ornament on the pine-cone wreath.

"I googled him over the years. And of course, found nothing." Margot held Onyx and rubbed the velvet underside of his ear slowly between her fingers, ruminating. "Owen on Facebook would be a parody of himself." She let the dogs out, and then her face clouded. "The first time, we got off the property and were alone together—in the back of his truck."

"Be careful what you promise." Sybil looked at her and gave a slight sigh. "In any relationship, you don't get a preview. You survive or not and are not consulted."

The raspberry tartan silk drapes reflected candlelight from half a dozen mismatched candelabrum sconces in the green dining room, where a pair of "termes," or sons of Jupiter, flanked the sides of the marble fire surround. The mythological guardians are portrayed without legs, so they can't flee and shirk their duties. Portraits of strangers softhearted Alistair had adopted at auction for a song and named "Mr. Can Do" and "Mrs. Did It Already." The Regency mahogany table, on its last legs, seated twelve, and the guests had gathered, with Blood and Sand cocktails in hand.

Agatha and Grace from the Slow Food movement would cook for the week. Tonight they'd serve British beer-battered fish and chips to their tired guests. *What will I remember after the ribbons and bows?* Margot thought. *Not the literary luminaries I read over the year, maybe the Yule log cake, seeing that I gave it away last year without a forkful myself. I'll remember a feeling of emptiness or one of fullness.*

"To the first of many," George greeted from the head of the table, dressed in wool flannel. He lifted and swirled his Blood and Sand cocktail, with a tilt of the cut-crystal bottom. "To the raggle-taggle of life, when pelted with snowballs."

"A warming winter tipple among a circle of incestuous friends," Max said.

"The best-laid plans," George said. "The drink's named after the 1922 silent film in which Rudolph Valentino played a bull-fighter in a destructive affair with a wealthy widow. A Sicilian blood orange is the secret."

"Try to talk on the phone in the midst of a love affair," Johnny said. "It's like sucking an orange through a straw."

The Persian carpet in hues of rust and rose absorbed the clanking of glasses, silver on earthenware, and the laughter of friends together after a prolonged absence.

"I've never had better chippy." Max wiped hemstitched linen over his lips. "Pass the vinegar."

Max admittedly remains a "gourmand." And a self-described "stout-ish man." Why? "Because it makes being pudgy more fun."

"And the venison and peppered pear salad—outrageous," he continued. "The green pea soup with bacon had a splash of hidden whisky. You'll have to heave us out the door, Margot."

"The monarchy may think they own fish and chips," Sybil said, "but it was the Sephardic Jews in sixteenth-century England who cooked their fish on Friday and returned to enjoy it on the Sabbath."

Will rose and banged his chair on the table in true Scots fashion. "Lisbet and I are engaged."

The unpredictable cocktail party had overflowed with congratulations into dinner.

I'm happy for them, Margot thought, *how celebratory, new love, ushered in with exuberance. And love that's born out of step, greeted by squabbles, like the play of fractious children. The fox with hen's eggs is behind the barn. Owen and I have everything and nowhere to go.*

"She's writing a play," Will said.

"All alone, he experienced the Stendhal, or Florence, syndrome."

"I took many shortcuts through cloisters and sat before stone images like one of the damned."

"It takes one glimpse of the statue of David or Botticelli's *Primavera,*" George said, "and Florentine tourists drop like flies and are carted off to the Santa Maria Nuova hospital." He salted his plate. "So you pulled on your windcheater and entered the storm."

George rolls effusive over marble relics of lost love and ambition but is stymied over self-expression, Margot thought, listening as the steam in the radiator hissed and someone cleared their throat. *He's a bookend who props up others' thoughts without writing any.* Will was an extrovert, but he was also the guy watching, writing it down, and taking it in.

"What will you write about, Lisbet?" Ruby swallowed a bite. "It needs a fistful of mint."

"The American transcendentalist movement. The challenge, to be brutally honest with each other."

"The Sage of Concord and the Judge address the struggle in everything," George mused.

"If love has touched you, end of the story," Johnny said, resting his knife on the edge of his hand-painted plate.

Margot noticed he studied her portrait of Ruby wearing Edwina's jade necklace, her brown eyes taking on the viewer without apology.

"May the roof above never fall in, and may we below never fall out," Anna said.

In his absence that night, the burning boughs Owen had cut in the fall filled the sitting room with the fragrance of pear and eucalyptus. Margot pushed the pair of large Delft urns into the corners of the deep window ledge with a shove. Spying Wren's deer antler tucked beneath the sofa skirt, she handed it off to him.

"What's on the agenda tomorrow?" Sybil asked, standing after dinner beside an ample wicker basket heaped with logs.

"Kilt fittings at 10:00 a.m. in the drawing room—a gift from George and me—when in Scotland, a few more knobby knees. The tailor will have them ready for New Year's Eve."

"As intimate as the pot and the ladle," Anna said, her hand lightly on Johnny's thigh; they were seated together on a worn Peking blue love seat woven with ribbon stripes. "There was a short period at eighteen when I wore nothing under my skirt, traipsing around Chelsea. Senior year's refusal to comply with the nuns."

"The perfect complement to a sporran and Glengarry bonnet," George said.

"That's aggressive," Ruby said, then adjusted the swivel arm on a brass reading floor lamp with a black wooden post. "Gramp's sporran held a silver dollar for Mom."

"Something for social media?" Johnny asked. Ruby was surfing.

"I am aware it's a trend that will pass like powdered wigs and big hair." She occupied one of a pair of birch armchairs. Leaning forward, with her arms folded across her knees, revealing the gilt-wood leaf carving on a blackened oval back.

"Secret pacts and irrevocable challenges," Max said. "Bring out the good stuff, George."

"Tomorrow we ride to the mouth of the Bull River," he said, then began to pour glasses from a mahogany secretary, with nicks in the veneer along the channeled legs. Margot thought his hand shook. "Robbie taught me to add a splash of water first to 'release the serpent.' Let it sit, no ice."

"The gardener's gone, and the rabbits have run wild at the world's end," Johnny said.

"When I did a summer service program as a teen in Ecuador, we ate guinea pigs," Will said. "The adorable family pet lives in the house."

"God, no," Ruby said.

"Were you at Exeter with George?" Anna asked Will.

"I went to public. Ruby, I didn't want to leave Ecuador."

"He was the only one initiated into the tribe," Lisbet added.

"We dug ditches for their new water system."

"Gave away the things he'd carried into the jungle, scared off the wild dogs keen on the overly gregarious city girls, and be-friended at least three locals on social media for two years, while the rest of the kids held back with disdain over the community's impoverishment. Afraid to mingle."

"The Quichua believe we retain a piece of the earth's pow-er when we live with respect," Will said, headed off to bed with Lisbet.

Brothers by engineering only, Margot thought.

Lisbet hummed sleepily at her bath before bed. The steamy sky-light above the clawfoot tub framed the constellation Perseus. A brass towel warmer clanked in the corner.

Will lit a pillar candle. "An Italian quarry owner in Carrara, Italy, once told me to choose the marble the seller refuses because it doesn't read the same as the rest, those blocks with accentuated veining near the outcrop, the blocks Michelangelo would have chosen—not just marble."

"If you're talking about *if*, then you're talking about human choice," she said.

"I want to buy a house, somewhere, and call it Priceless Friend, and fill it with little ones."

"There are no children left in Venice," she said. "Just cats. I want them to know childhood. I love you, Will."

"I couldn't have told you so." Sybil wiped toothpaste off her face in the Jack and Jill bathroom at the head of the hall. "I figured you and George had created the ideal marriage."

"Why couldn't Owen have been happily married?"

They brushed their teeth together as Max and George, the last to leave, finished swigging golden smoky peat down below, fire-side. Sybil sat on the sheepskin-covered stool, her electric brush humming. The window, draped in swags of white cotton gauze, framed the ambient light of the moon.

CHAPTER TWENTY-FIVE

Electric Kool-Aid

*D*ear Ava, my daughter who studies words with Greek origins that landed in Webster's Dictionary only yesterday, kyriarchy: "how identity shapes our experiences by overlapping and compounding systems of disadvantage." The "matrix of domination," isn't that what you called it?

Does anyone remember Penelope in the Odyssey, and that she smelled of sea air when she unpacked her Hermes typewriter? I predict you'll name my granddaughter after a volcano, and she'll be born swimming and meditating at the same time in the freedom of words.

You will finish your dissertation, "Where Worldviews Diverge," and, in the process, find your way into a new understanding of home and family. Education frees you to be who you were meant to be.

A force of nature, you have an appetite for unconventionality. The sovereignty of a mountain and of the sea—no one can make you do a damn thing! How do your multiple identities intermingle? I have ideas, Ava, but really, I don't have a clue. I read in your introduction "different kinds of prejudice can be amplified in different ways when combined together." Change is both cyclical and fundamental. Yours and Margot's stories happen in the space between your steps. The ground that can't be photographed, daresay recorded.

PERTHSHIRE, DECEMBER 27, 2018

Ava had entered the kitchen at Otyrburn with Margot and Sybil, fresh from their walk. Agatha and Grace had long since finished whipping together chard and saffron omelets without being bothered by a pair of dogs underfoot or by the prospect of another mouth to feed at lunch. Ava saw six cakes under glass on the baker's rack, and a lively full house. She shook her head. *Bad timing. What bum luck to crash a party . . .* She then exchanged a brisk nod of hello with George, who had hailed her from across the room, where she stood, hanging her wet coat. He then motioned Margot directly into the pantry.

"Archie dies just shy of eighteen months ago," George said, "and your 'sister' appears unannounced. I'm not buying it."

"I saw the photo of him with her mother," Margot said. "Why are you so paranoid? A two-hundred-year-old money pit isn't on everybody's to-do list."

George glanced back over his shoulder to the crowded room. "Offer her lunch—and send her on her way."

"She has my nose."

"Thirty-seven secluded acres of arable, fertile soil, clean air, and abundant clean water rights?"

"You need meditation tips," Margot said.

"You've got a snippet of scant information and a stranger in the house. For all you know, she's lived 'feral.'"

"Do you think I'm not asking questions too?" she said.

"Okay, Margot. You've just opened a reality-blurring novel, and you can't stop reading it. Admit it."

"Why is it one of us always ends up in the crosshairs?" she asked. "And why is it you're so quick to believe that all is not well?"

"Where's the heavy hardship, Margot?"

Their patience strained, they broke as Owen arrived at 11:00 a.m. in his tartan, Rye tight on his heels, while the weekend party lingered in the kitchen, sipping Bloody Marys. Lavender and sage strung from the rafters above their heads.

The morning's news first: Met Director—Under Investigation on Intent to Deceive. *The bulletin had arrived in Johnny's newsfeed stream at 5:30 a.m. in the privacy of his bedroom. Downstairs, the* International Herald Tribune *lay undisturbed on the kitchen table. His efforts to snag George from his teeth brushing had worked to no avail. (Note to myself: insert question mark.)*

"I only put this on for encouragement," Owen teased Anna, as Malcolm, the tailor, strung his measuring tape around her waist. "The MacGregor's, Red and Black, is the easiest set to weave. It ran up and down hills before tartans became fashion. Unlike other clans, we don't do dress, undress, dress down, fancy dress, and hunting when one tartan will do. On exception, the lassies will wear a dance tartan of green and white to appease the competition-minded."

Had the effort to invoke the memory of these people whom she hadn't known stressed too much importance on the endeavor, as if that were the end game? Ava thought. *The imagination is typically better than reality.*

At the edge of the room, Will set his glass down and glanced over the morning paper in hand. "Can Fragile Cities Cope with an Influx of Climate Refugees?"; "Magnetic Induction Cooking Could Cut Your Carbon Footprint"; "Met Director Inserts More Than 1,000 Fake Etruscan Sculptures." Ava noted his face grew pallid. He folded the paper under an arm and left the room in a hurry.

"One thing to bear in mind when considering tartan," Malcolm injected into the rolling room, "is wear it for genuine tradition-al reasons, not on a whim. If you don't belong to a clan, choose what suits."

"Owen wears his mother's clan tartan." Margot wore the kilt Archie had given her in high school. "In the Highlands, Fowler takes a back seat to MacGregor."

Owen had made a "wee joke" with Anna, about making her an honorary Scot because she could care less about airs and graces. "Fowler is Anglo-Saxon, from *Fugelere* in the early thirteenth cen-tury, or 'bird-catcher.' MacGregors, though, are legendary. Rob Roy rode the ridge shouting, 'Royal is my race.' Margot's, Clan Donnachaidh, or Clan Robertson, is the oldest clan in Scotland and the only one able to trace its origin directly to the feet of the Celtic Earl of Atholl."

Anna placed her arms in the air, with a shrug, and a nod to Owen, as Malcolm moved his tape down and over her hips. "An Irish woman plays no part in her betrayal. My ancestors bird-dog and, in one leap, cross the North Channel, raised daggers in hand."

Ava compared weaves on bolts with the guests, catching William take the back kitchen stairs two at a time. Everyone was dog-eared and dazed. Nothing matched the image in her mind.

The house was too big, her sudden appearance too comical, more than one face dour, and the sky a hazy gray. This was her astonishing odyssey home.

William had raced to cut off George in the upstairs hall.

"Are you depraved?" he asked, winded.

Handed the morning paper, George, unruffled, read the headline. "I will explain everything."

"How much fucking money do you need? This is going to kill Margot." He ran his hand through his hair. "Tell me you didn't."

"A catalog of dubious origins was acquired under false assumptions by the museum itself," George said. "No more, no less."

"Fakes are designed to challenge the expert. You're supposed to be the expert!"

George slipped his phone out of his pocket, only to replace it. "There must be a museum insider. I'm wrongly accused."

"I know it all too well, 'the authenticity of art is of utmost importance,'" William said.

"The Italian government authorized the excavations—the chemical composition of the black Bucchero wares had proved sound."

"If there is egg on your face," Will said, "wipe it off and join the party. Today's paper goes in the fire. And for the love of God, spare Margot."

"My efforts are well done—my job, my marriage, my doubled investments and property values. The collection on display has existed without dispute for over a decade." He crossed his arms over his chest. "Get off my back, will you?"

They broke and rejoined the party.

The youth hired to assist with prep work ran the compost bucket outside.

"There was a day, fifty years past, when the richness of an acre of land supported above and below as much teeming life as the weight of a cow," Owen said.

The ring of dishes being stacked in the pantry sounded in the sprawling canyon of a room.

"I left Hopper's Island because the soil was too rocky," Ava said. "In Camden, I have the best of both worlds, the sea and the earth."

Sybil is a bit stuffy, apparently conservative and tighter than the bark on a tree, she thought. *And Ruby demonstrates an intellectual astuteness—though these folks are genuine flatlanders.*

"So Violet's still alive," Margot said. "Archie met Violet my twelfth summer on Hopper's Island. Ava was born mid-May, 1986."

"I attended a tailgate party in Maine once after a lobster festival," Max said as the kitchen flooded with late-morning light.

"Mainers do have a hard time trying to figure out when the tide is high next and then low." Ava smiled generously. "But I've never made a corn-husk doll."

"I've only been to Maine a few times," Johnny said as the kettle sent a plume of moist steam into the dry winter kitchen. "Do you have a favorite spot on Hopper's Island, Ava?"

"At Dixie Bull Bluff, the wind rises up, no matter which way it's blowing, right off the sea."

Johnny offered Ava a chair, joining the seated half of the group. She was petite, a dark brunette with unsettling blue eyes.

Ava peered out the window, full face like a child. Margot was her sister? It was more than plausible. It was highly probable. *Margot and Archie had the connection to Hopper's Island, after all.*

Margot strolled over to stand beside Will at the edge of the room by the marble pastry board.

"Are you somewhere in the middle of that maelstrom's vortex?" he asked.

"Yes, with my mind and matter cleaved down the middle," Margot said.

"She's chatty," Will observed, "though I'm not overly qualified. No tools in my bag."

"My 'sister'—a childhood dream. Nothing much happens."

"Ava is an instance of 'all space is filled with matter in motion,'" he said quietly. "Beware the rule of three."

"Don't sound so primal," Margot said. "Why do you say that?"

"The New Year is a tabula rasa—hold on to that."

Max joined them and aborted any further private discussion.

"*Clan* is the Gaelic word for 'children,'" Malcolm the tailor said, "but a tartan tied to clans is an invented tradition of the nineteenth century."

"A bloody moneymaking scheme of wool merchants," Owen said. "A clansman wore any tartan woven. The color of the ribbon in your bonnet told your clan allegiance. That or the sprig of a plant."

The worn kitchen worktable fit ten in a pinch, crowded shoulder to shoulder. By noon, the party—sized, and the tartans selected—had moved from one meal to the next without noticing. They sat for a luncheon of cauliflower and cheddar cheese soup with pan-fried partridge.

"There's whisky in the soup again," Max roared. "I'm never getting off this mountain." He paused to fill Ava's water glass and his. "Kerouac, now that's an opener."

"I don't even need to be in the room." Ava grinned, seated at George's right, confident that, at the very least, George was one of those gathered who thought that entertainment in Maine was giving somebody the wrong directions. "Violet is a living work of art."

"I want to meet her," Max said.

"She's a bit of a recluse who has hardly enough time for her dog. My mother's a writer."

"What does she write?" Lisbet asked.

"About her life. She has mottos she lives by: Conventionality conceals the weakness of conceit. Then she'll tell me that once she was someone's 'hummingbird,' and then someone's 'slide rule.' Or that if you live for the faults of another, you forfeit your own truths." She sipped red wine. "I had endless reminders not to be bummed out by the rigidity of upper-middle-class confines. She studied and taught at the Jack Kerouac School of Disembodied Poetics, which ties into my name, and she's still asked to teach there occasionally. She met Ginsberg's guru, Rinpoche, Corso, and Burroughs. Straightlaced isn't in Violet's vocabulary. I think she may have had an affair with the band Eric Burdon and the Animals."

"All of them?" Ruby asked, her soup spoon held aloft in midair.

"She hems and haws on that one," Ava said. "Then there was the affair with Richard Brautigan. For years she handed out copies of *Trout Fishing in America* for Christmas, birthday, and house-warming gifts. I think there might be a stash of letters between those two, and come to think of it, her and Ferlinghetti. Though older, he sympathized with, and fostered, many of the Beat poets."

"City Lights, on Columbus Avenue," Anna said. "Is she a poet as well?"

"To the end. The more indecent, the better."

"You have quite the knack for reinventing yourself, Ava," George said, seemingly intrigued. "A stint as a cook on a frigate in the Antarctic, a nanny in London, the Alaska Fellows Program in Juneau, and now an application pending for a Thomas J. Watson Fellowship."

"I generally see what I want in life and try to get it."

"What's your concentration?" Lisbet asked.

"Intersectional feminism," Ava said.

"And what exactly do you mean by that?" George asked, breaking bread.

"Discrimination doesn't exist in a bubble."

He not only thought that I had been pregnant at thirteen but also that I was illiterate, Ava thought. *If a tie to Margot means I inherit George, as it stands now, I may regret this decision.*

"The other night I had a dream," Anna said. "I was an American Indian woman with five clay bowls at my feet, and beneath my skirt, a cock between my legs. I'll tell you, Ava, it wasn't hard becoming an 'outsider.'"

"Anything can do it," Ava said. "I pull into towns—my destinations are set in advance—and I interview women. We cover a lot of topics. I met an elderly rancher in Kalispell who said to me, 'You're always going to be the mother that they love but want distance from, as in—I'll never be like her. We're related only by a fraction.' Only days prior to the interview, the 'horse killer' had put down her favorite, Nomad. And she had asked the vet for his advice." Ava noticed that Ruby had a dimple in her chin too. "I think the saddest woman I met was the one in Rhode Island who told me she never sang, not a day in her life, after the age of eight, when a music teacher told her to stop singing because her voice was 'that terrible.'"

"Are you married, Ava?" Lisbet asked.

"No, single, and I like it that way."

"That sounds like Gramps." Ruby had left the table. She flipped the top card from the shuffled deck laid at the center in her "sundial," then set down the Queen of Hearts at the eleventh position on her clock solitaire. "Good God! I did it!" She'd won the near-to-impossible hand by completing all other four-of-a-kind sets before the fourth king was revealed.

The three dogs gnawed happily at antler bones on the mud rug at the back door. Ava surveyed the kitchen, looking for Archie clues. *He spent his childhood here,* she thought, *here in a far-reaching landscape hemmed in by mountains, not the sea.* She made a note to herself to, before leaving, study a portrait of a young boy in an orchard—a young boy with red hair and a dimple in his chin.

After lunch, Margot, albeit reluctantly, saw Ava off, having exchanged contacts, with plans for her to join them for dinner later in the week, along with the name of her favorite taxi company.

CHAPTER TWENTY-SIX

The Bull River Ride

Words that part curtains—you can never tell when they're going to happen. Lorca couldn't either, but spring they do, pouncing from the periphery. The archaeological digs that reveal how man lived and what he treasured. The montage on the fridge displaying baby's first bunting, first tooth, first birthday wish, tucked in the frame of a backpack on Daddy's back, secured with a jeweled magnet. What is an immobilized man, albeit woman, to do? Coffee in hand, already late for work, another day, another year, and yet, he hesitates before the contemporary exhibit of his efforts. He isn't hungry; cheese wouldn't suffice if he were. Full of wounds, he kisses a holy relic and dreams of inkwells and wet paintbrushes; the tools that command his silence don't weep. Here he lies in the eyes of the world. Along the lake he whispered. Along the Appalachian Trail, he sold his industry, *where the sky brushed the roofs of houses, and he extracted gold from his castaway longings at the round table with three friends. "Because of us," he said, "sleepless people stagger at four in the afternoon and collect themselves before the dawn."*

PERTHSHIRE, DECEMBER 27, 2018

Ten riders made rounds in the stable yard before the late-afternoon ride, choosing their mounts from native breeds flicking their tails. The white plumes of the horses' breath rode over the frozen vapors on grass and limb. Where a crystalline kingdom had emerged, the frozen river's blue veins ran down the naked mountain flanks.

Before the sun set at 4:00 p.m., on blanketed snow, the party gathered to patch together smoked haddock and cheese and snack on broken biscuit cake. The last riders tied reins to bramble. Owen found himself beside Margot. They were lucky to get into the mountains, as the roads had started closing behind them. A meter of snow lay where the flakes still fell.

"You're wallowing," he whispered over her shoulder.

"Today I have a sister. Yesterday I did not."

"Maybe," he said.

The snow, polished by wind, glistened in spotty patches. Margot blew on her gloved hands. "I've lived a half life."

The icy bits pinged against their oiled jackets.

"I'm sorry about that," Owen said. "The rule of three: a person can live three minutes without air, three hours without shelter if the weather's severe, three days without water, and three weeks without food. And yet, whole lifetimes pass without enough love."

"Beware the rule of three. What gives today?" Margot looked him square in the face. "When I was little, I accepted that love was a boat that would sail straight to happily ever after. But that was a long time ago."

"We are who we were as a child," he said, "until someone, or something, tells us we are not."

They joined the group, fueling the fire to a roar, battling the determined wet flakes.

Looted antiquities, Johnny thought, *deluded collectors, duplicitous public officials, and crooked dealers in bed with George?*

"We're comfortable down below," Owen said, "but the wind reaches one hundred and seventy-three miles per hour at the peak."

"The cold grows hardy types," Max said. "Out of sight, out of mind."

"Perthshire Highlands abut the Cairngorms but were included only recently in the Cairngorms National Park range," George said.

It was letting up a bit. The sky and the earth were one gray wash.

"I packed a birding book." Through any given day, Sybil, moved by her observations in nature, exhibited a range of listlessness and joy. Like her singing bees, flying over the hills and far away, the rich tone of her voice added passion to her speech; a rhythm by which even the ignoble and ugly gained new meaning. "The snow bunting is the only songbird to winter this far north. And the only birds ever sighted at the North Pole—four thousand or so songbirds, and one as small as the sparrow survives to sing through the extremes."

George circled the fire and passed the mustard knife to Johnny. "Start a 'Sybil Says' ledger. You'll fill it quickly."

"It takes one to know one," she said.

Johnny gave George a glance that said. "We have to talk."

George had immediately brushed it off, Johnny thought, as if he were vilified and most maligned. His "If anything shows in a museum long enough, it becomes real" bullshit. Headlines that would read surreal for most, George had channeled into an afternoon's fancy that floated down creeks, rivers, and valleys. He had, in the truest sense, gone fishing.

"I picture Violet with flowers in her hair," Will said.

"I would have had an affair with Jefferson Airplane," Lisbet said. "I like people who evade an easy definition."

Johnny spoke over the hiss of the fire over a moist log. Over the trepidation he felt about the FBI, Interpol, and Italian police. "Me too—not the affair with Jefferson Airplane—but sometimes you get just the opposite of what you expected." He stretched out a kink in his neck and tilted his gaze at the sky. "George and I take the last train to Romania this spring. Did you hear, Margot?"

"I did; George can't refuse."

"'Off to church, Mother,' my father's calling when heading out the door." Owen laughed, refusing the sausage pâté. "Anytime he has his shotgun or fishing pole in hand—dragging one of us along to scout rivers for the proverbial lump of gold the size of a horse's head found here in these hills in the 1800s."

"Just yesterday," Margot said, "I opened *The Still-Hunter* in Edwina's library and read her dedication to Alistair: 'To the Hunter for good luck, from the Hunter's Widow.' Christmas 1940. Why didn't I ask?"

"We forget that the elderly had passionate love lives of their own," Lisbet said.

William brushed an ashen ember off his down-filled jacket sleeve with a gloved hand.

"We are taught not to ask 'unnecessary' questions. Today's a case in point, at Margot's expense."

"Or maybe her good fortune," Sybil said. "Ava had a dimple in her chin; that much was true."

"All bolts are loose at the end of the year," Will said. "A homeward-looking stranger at the door."

"And not so long ago," Owen said, "people placed unwanted bairns in the crook of an oak and accepted that fairies would find them and turn them into a changeling."

"What do people do in Maine?" Ruby asked. "Chop wood, stack wood, haul wood, then sit on the porch and stare at the log pile."

George, with the late sun on his back, seated beside a bright spot of pretty white snow, pulled his Smythson diary from his coat pocket and unclipped his classic rollerball pen to fix on Saturday's entry: "Cairngorm rises 1,244 meters above sea level" and "Perthshire hills are the perfect secret place for panning for gold." Then he double-checked that he'd put Romania on the calendar. One whole year recorded in handsome leather, twenty years stacked in his office. He couldn't survive without his ledger—important colloquies, great meals, and great wines, it was all in there.

George watched a squirrel on a tree. "We're at the mercy of a few sane people. The fall of Rome aligns with the fall of civic duty and morality."

Ruby rolled her eyes.

Even the mountains were purple. When it came to leisure pursuits, the evening would work for those who worked lucrative day jobs and the stay-at-home alike—for the mysterious and untamed in all of us. The sky flashed pink, then orange to stop a roller coaster in its tracks.

Johnny pointed out the barely visible, serrated lines of snow-filled crags along the farthest peak that chased down the windswept mountains.

"Europe is a wax museum," Max said, then yawned.

"Archie opened holiday dinners with a toast to the Reid motto—'Glory is the reward of valor,'" George said, closest to the fire. *Archie Reid*, he thought, *bigger than life, even when dead. "Daddy's girl."* "Can't you hear him, Margot?"

"Yes, like he stood in the clothes he last wore. He was a hugger."

"Apparently," Max said. "British people are insane."

"Three members of the most powerful clans in Scotland are serenely posed around one fire, and neither historically has a gripe with the other," Owen said. "In Margot and Ruby, you see the ancient Picts who made the stone circles."

"Did Archie ever remarry?" Anna asked.

"No. But wherever we stayed long enough, there was a woman who thought I was 'cute.' 'Margot, this is my friend Genevieve.'"

The fire burst as a dry log caught. The sun's low-rayed fingers made one last attempt to stretch across frozen lakes.

"Archie was another irascible Scots lost in the mist," Will said. "And yes, evidently, anything but monogamous."

"A Renaissance man—history, lit, and the arts," George added. *Loyal to which family?* "And a mean son of a bitch."

"Take it back, George," Margot said. "Sometimes, I had the impression that he resented my intrusion." Her voice had shifted to a heartbroken tone. "That peace with me, after Mother's death, had brought some sacrifice."

"That's generous of you, considering," Sybil said. They shared a blanket.

"Yeah, Dad, own your ugly," Ruby said, then tossed a packed snowball for Wren to chase. "Why isn't anybody asking me how I feel about a ready-made aunt? No, don't ask me tonight. It would feel like a kindergarten circle sharing time." She tucked the loose ends of her long chestnut hair down the back of her jacket. "You visited Hopper's Island summers, Mom. That was supposed to be your special time."

"Once I thought that your grandfather struggled with how to keep his sense of joy alive." The sky broke blue before it began to slowly darken. "But after tonight, I'm not so sure." Margot took Ruby's hand after she'd plopped down beside her. "I hated his urge to put a dollar sign next to everything, but in some respect, he was trying to let his truths seep through the cracks."

"A dollar and cents sign," George corrected. "You survived." *She's never grown up*, he thought.

"I remember a good deal," Margot said, "but I can never remember how a song starts until someone plays the first three notes."

George saw Owen's glance linger briefly again on Margot. *So be it.* The party collected, they headed home damp, in the bleak reach at the close of the day.

Ruby squirmed in her saddle, and it creaked. "Owen, will you help me, please?"

"I jigged it a bit." He handed her the reins.

Shortly, the other horses dug into the soft snow, and the air rang alive with the jangle of stirrups and the snorting of mares and geldings. The last lights came on in Otyrburn as they entered the hay-filled stable, and the wind rattled in the distance.

"Dinner at eight," George announced—desperate for un-cluttered space, desperate for revenge, desperate to squelch any voice of dissent fired in his direction or intrusion into his private affairs. *Life deserved to be indulged, then washed down with interesting discussion.*

Johnny and George left the tack room last, which was organized with antique tack hooks made out of old railroad spikes—Alistair had cleverly hung pairs of old horseshoes at a ninety-degree angle to each other. The Wellies hung upside down by slipping the heel into the open ring.

"I will brook no insults," George said distractedly.

"Why bother?" Johnny closed the barn door on the night sky. "Then you didn't see the *International Herald Tribune* this morning?"

"Do you remember freshman year when we studied semiotics?" George asked.

Johnny removed his wool cap. "Vaguely."

"We studied how meaning is made, how words and signs make meaning. Art is in the eye of the beholder." George latched the stall door, having finished his evening chore. "Do you have any idea what's relegated to the 'trash bin' in the basement at the museum?"

"Do you need a lawyer?" Johnny asked.

"Certainly not. I'll straighten this out after the holidays."

"Listen, George, last I heard, if the FBI opens an investigation, it takes more than a phone call."

"A good lawyer, a few hours of paperwork, and back to business as usual."

"The last thing you want to do is turn this or any other parts of your life into the boorish performance you loathe."

"Agreed, though Lady Chatterley has swapped out an English gamekeeper for a Scots gardener." George hung the tack on the wall. "I've decided what to give Will and Lisbet as a wedding present."

"What's that?"

"Picture Rembrandt's *The Jewish Bride*. I'd like you to capture the middle section of the portrait, Lisbet's midriff, with their arms and hands crossed together over her wedding dress. Nothing more. Then blow it up. History will discern who Rembrandt's couple is, or if it's, in fact, Rembrandt's son. And then there are those in the Isaac and Rebecca camps who claim the painting is a *portrait histoiré*." George grabbed his gloves to leave, headed to the house. "The profound delicacy of her fingers laid over his hand."

Johnny watched with experience as George's attention shifted off topic. He had taken a left at the rhododendron and was lost as he roamed in vestiges from the Holy Land on an art quest.

"Three hundred paintings," George continued, "about fourteen hundred drawings, thirty-one etchings—each, may I add, highlighting a deep reverence for the vigor of chiaroscuro—more than ninety self-portraits. How did Rembrandt accomplish so much?"

George swung through the highs and lows in life quicker than most, and whether plagued by financial trouble or personal strife, his work didn't suffer long the dank and gray. He lived in a sharply defined outer and inner world and passed between the two with impressive ease, like an athlete confident in his regimen, spoiled by consistency, and when he crashed and broke a leg, it would be difficult to mend.

CHAPTER TWENTY-SEVEN

Dead of Night

How much does free verse cost? Do they charge less on the Sabbath for bursts of perception in one common world?

As the snow fell and a thick blanket of crystals collected outside the window sash, the party sat in the Blue Room, sipping and chatting. An animated discussion was underway that evening about the numerical importance, historically, of the number seven. Some even compared the conjuring of "seven" to working with alchemy. The majority associated its transformative properties with mysticism.

Bees, among Earth's oldest inhabitants, number twenty-five thousand varieties, yet only seven produce honey. And according to the Talmud, the universe has seven heavens. In Christianity, Judaism, and Islam, God resides above the seventh. And the modern Jewish bride circles the groom seven times. Hallelujah. Shalom.

Some things, relationships included, have to be hurtled through space and fired at upon entry. Perhaps the number seven is a little like that.

PERTHSHIRE, DECEMBER 27, 2018

Johnny had dedicated the better part of the early morning to focusing on George, and here he was, back at it after dinner. *What was the deal between George and the Spanish publishing heiress, or his slippery Dutch dealer, Heinke Hessel? How deep was George's taste for adventure?*

George passed Owen on his way out of the room to let Agatha know it was time to serve dessert. Johnny eyed the two. He could see how Margot might be attracted to him.

His calm demeanor, quick and fresh—I'd say lively, he thought, *contrasted with George's increasingly heightened elitism, his twenty-first-century stiff upper lip.*

"How long have we known each other, George?" Max asked. "Since we wore short pants together. A researcher uses spring rainfall to predict algae bloom, 'hallowed be my wife's name,' yet I can't get inside the head of an old friend."

"Isn't it enough to contend with our own madness, Max?" George said.

Johnny registered his behavior as edgy. George had a habit of sizing up the situation with the necessary objectivity.

Robbie had closed the pub and was settled in a snug seat of plain-cut thick mohair, his arm wrapped around his wife, Lily. "The lairds know better. They ask few questions and lead from the front with a slice of pie and a bottle of Brown Robin."

Max accepted his plate, spread his napkin over his lap, inched his butt to the rear of the deep-welled armchair, and folded his arms contentedly across his chest. "Feed and ply the guests with drink while you work your interrogations. It's one of the oldest tricks in the book."

Ruby rested her feet on an embroidered Moroccan leather cushion. Onyx stirred from sleep, rose, circled her lap once, and plopped down, exactly as before.

George couldn't have done anything to hurt Ruby, Johnny thought. He had googled the Spanish publishing heiress earlier that morning. She now lived in Mexico City. Doña Maria de Trujillo y Merlo had been charged with six counts of forgery for signing documents for a fraudulent purpose. The more Johnny learned, the more he began to catch on that perhaps George and his cast of eccentric characters weren't as smart as they pretended to be. *There's some dangerous, if not interesting, resonance going on with George's idea that there's safety in numbers*, he humored himself, listening as the wind howled in the chimney.

Only indoors could you calculate how frosty it was outside. "When a bird flies low, the air is set heavy, and the wind is coming," Owen told me once. "When they fly high and light, there is no wind." Then, as if he'd spelled a sequence in the mystery called life, he'd added, "It must have something to do with it. Like an esoteric coding."

Margot looked around the room. *Without permission, life had grown larger.* The moon-dial clock clicked on the half hour.

"In the 1990s," she began, "when the Bosnians relocated to Scotland, the folk in Perthshire looked through them. 'The Bosnians' wouldn't stay long, they said, but Owen said hello."

"That's my late wife, Uma. Stories from her world were a mystery tour. 'Some people are like clouds,' she'd say, 'when they disappear, the day becomes more cheerful.'"

"Archie always said I had more Frenchman in me than Scots."
Margot airily waved her hand. "That my voice, even in youth,
was not distinctly an American voice. After I lost my mother,
he said I was like a frozen child; neither handmade blanket nor
Edwina's pie consoled me. He was forever telling me to speak a
little louder, watching me standing by the window, asking where
I was. In the end, I was either too European, or too cosmopolitan
in New York."

The night he told Owen to stop hanging around, she thought, *no
daughter of his was entertaining a shepherd. And he only had one.
The way I smiled at Owen,* "small and flirty as a bird." *And stub-
born, I was mulish and had turned sixteen solely to adopt Owen's language, his mannerisms, and his Highland customs, when my father's
annoyed me. Archie was jealous. Even then, when I was just a child,
when Owen came along, he had no patience left in his heart.*

"The rabbi's daughter, that's what my father called me." Sybil
held a copy of *Sexism in Monarchy, Past and Present* in hand. "'My
daughter, the good little mensch.' I was like a tiger, hidden in
twigs, shadows, and light, shattering illusions. 'Oy vey, goodness
knows. Sybil, you ask too many questions; leave your father in
peace.'"

"Entering sixth grade, you spoke all at once of the insects, the
opera, and then demanded the definition of *gestalt, miscreant,* and
a *Potemkin village* in one week's time," Margot recalled.

Stealing and giving timeshares of myself; enough, no more, she
thought. *A child's inner world is lively.*

"Time changes nothing," Sybil said. "Dad's ninety-two and
still jokes. 'Ply me all you will, you may not use my violin strings
in your experiments!' My most recent birthday card said, 'PS: A
'punchinello' is a fat little Italian clown, i.e., 'absurd person.'"

"I prayed at night," Anna said, "so that I did not go to hell. I flattened a kid when he called me a 'cat-lick potato masher.'"

"The Ruttenbergs all finished Hebrew school, and I punched a kid at public school in the shoulder for calling me a 'dirty Jew.'" Sybil admired Edwina's collection of arboreal-themed paintings, drawings, and illustrations. "What's the difference between dialect and slang? And why are there three different sizes of hyphens?"

"When my mother and I left Ireland for good," Anna continued, "we slipped through a door that offered good pay, and we didn't look back. Grandma O'Sullivan prized the idea of America, a place where people who spoke different languages nevertheless understood one another. My mother left her behind there. I never quite forgave her. A letter left by the postmaster was the closest Grandma ever got to the States."

There was a set of three marble containers on the mantel, a vase, a smaller vase, and a butter box with a lid. Above the mantel, a pair of hand-hammered brass wall sconces with arms for two candles in each. The polished-steel pierced and engraved fire fender had leaping dogs entwined within vines. Ruby questioned why it was called the Blue Room when the decorative elements were all green.

William stepped aside to check his messages. Something from his secretary: Another package for George, a four-foot cube. Should I have refused it? He poked through a small wooden box on a writing desk that held a collection of art museum greeting cards.

"George lived in a houseboat his junior year in Amsterdam." He flipped a card over to read the artist and the museum that had acquired the piece. "He'd told Huxley that in Europe, they did things 'differently.'"

"Students found their own housing," George said. "The en-tire campus consisted of a run of elegant single and double-wide gabled townhouses." He adjusted a pair of leather bookends. "It seemed natural enough to do my PhD in London."

"The family visited Holland over the holidays," Will contin-ued. "Picture George with long hair and a goatee, dressed col-orfully. The pungent scorched-grasslike smell of sweet Mary Jane wafted over the rails of the boat. While his classmates were studying Rubens, George was hobnobbing with the next gen-eration of the rich and famous. The elite aristocrats of storied European families armed with wads of party money and winter and summer castles."

How old was he, Will thought, *when he sold that small oil he'd acquired at a flea market to Lady Courtenay, his "benefactress"? Was everything about George a grand gesture of artifice? He had been chas-ing Aphrodite since he was a kid.*

Will peered out the window; on the opposite knoll, over the garden wall, the hills had altered their course to intersect, and at the low tip where they met, the faint lights of Wyndham traced across the sky.

"How long had you been missing, George?" he asked. "There was no sign of life after that storm the summer of 1986. Huxley's ranting, 'What idiot sailing instructor takes a class of fifteen-year-olds out in a hurricane?' And Mother's face is gray, and her emotions as mercurial as the Atlantic. The rings on her hand holding mine cut off my circulation. Huxley's ferocious scowls, and scathing scolding, three inches from the face of the 'world-class' sailor from Hawaii. The world was coming to an end. *Then*, they found you. Afraid to venture out, you'd hidden in the storage building. No one had noticed you weren't aboard the nineteen-foot *Lightning*."

"I forgot my life preserver." In spite of the seriousness of the situation, George almost laughed. He stood by the curtains, as if seized by a private thought. Quickly dismissed it and picked up the Edinburgh paper's Sunday edition on the table.

Where's his social consciousness? Will thought. *With what I know, I wouldn't even let George mind my gallery. He's an unapologetic proponent of nothing.*

"Big brother, little brother, eldest daughter, vindictive neighbors, and small-town gossip. Irish folklore says the seventh son of a seventh son has magical healing power," Anna said, and in the soft light, stirred a lump of brown sugar into her Earl Grey tea. "I'm an avid seer of symbols and omens."

"The seventh-son bit depends on where he's born," Robbie said. "In Romania, he becomes a vampire. In English folklore, he turns into a werewolf."

"In terms of reason, something is strange only because you find it so," Owen said as George paced by the window in his winter attire. "*Gang aft agley*, 'things often go awry.'"

Ruby, propped with determination on her elbows and belly in the circle made by the reclining friends, valiantly tried hard to stay awake, Onyx snoring rhythmically beside her. Even the noise of the party seemed to fade. Will was thinking of none other— they were two dogs on the fire fender, locked in mortal combat. George's face, as ever, expressionless, the explanation never given fully. Will's eyes rested in the darkest corner of the room. George's memories of an event and the true account repeatedly differed. And George, always so convivial, in a conspiratorial way; it was difficult to tell who was doing whom a favor.

"Remember, Mother, when I stuffed an acorn up my nose in Auntie Sybil's garden? And Edwina heard the story and said I was 'inhaling nature.'"

"She said you got that idea reading *Charlotte's Web.* Edwina outfitted her day for tasking and not much else. Daydreaming, and there was a whispering behind you, and you had bought the words of Anna's seer, or waited on a prophet."

"In Edwina's world," Owen added, "a garden alone didn't forget the sweat you poured into it, or the lack thereof."

"Everything you love and know can wash away," Johnny said after a moment. "Words of kindness are remembered for a long time, and expressions of empathy change the course of history."

Ruby had finished a french braid in Lisbet's hair by gently crossing one hand over another. She was speaking quickly. "Disaffected high school students will spell the end of the bourgeois family structure, and the anger of women asking to be legitimized will become a manifesto society no longer ignores."

"Your device is overheating." Max nibbled on an almond sablé. "What did you feed her when she was a little pup?"

"Social media is a platform for bragging rights," Ruby added, adjusting the red suede strap on her shearling slippers, more like Birkenstocks. "All the people who are too happy to be interesting live there."

"I'm glad you kept the house, Margot," Sybil said. "Archie would say that you, Margot Gaylord Reid, have grown into the value of your voice."

"Why, Sybil, that's so sweet."

"'Meghalaya,'" Sybil said, "'the abode above the clouds.' It's quite a lovely sentiment. I've toured the northeastern state in India. The Holocene commenced eleven thousand seven hundred years ago, with the end of the last ice age. We're in the 'Meghalayan' now, triggered by a two-hundred-year mega-drought."

"In the nineteenth century," Robbie said, "Wyndham had twelve pubs, with names like the Reading Room and Let's Away, and the distance door to door was six miles. The distance a horse could go. Now we have one. A time past, and almost forgotten, when neighbors set up spare cribs in neighbors' houses on receiving the news that family was arriving from out of town." He passed pints of ale around. "If we're all foam, no beer, we need reinforcements. Bottoms up—there's a pork chop in every bottle."

"Let's rustle up some grub," Max called. "A decent tin of tuna—the ever-ready snacking standby—a little red onion, olive oil, lemon juice, salt and pepper, and if we want to get fancy, Pepe Havarro roasted chickpeas."

But everybody blew by him. It was time for bed. Poor Max. No one gave a hoot if he'd reached the zenith of his "food is music, and music is love" frontier. Imaginative, perhaps even eccentric, he was among the happiest in the crowd.

Owen rose and headed out with the dogs on his heels. Margot tagged along. Coats on, their breath hung in the cold. In the wintry night air, the ivy-twined branches on the gate beside them had long since frozen over.

"When you and I met, I came empty-handed; I was just a kid. Not so anymore." He looked at her hard. "My sheep aren't scattered over the field. I need only a roof over my head, a fire, and you. I know as much about George as you do, for Christ's sake, and I've only just met him."

"Is Ruby asking if something's afoot between you and me?" She regretted the question and hoped to change the subject. Margot didn't like talking very much about herself, and yet there she was, though, revising certain immutable principles.

"While George is sipping the tea?" He blew his hot breath over her cupped hands. "My melancholy Margot, I would rather you didn't continue down that particular road. Some light should shine on you. I wouldn't call your marriage lighthearted, more like light-sensitive, light-deprived, in the dark."

"I believed myself safe from the follies of my youth and too old to consider seriously making any changes in my way of thinking. I've spent my whole life defending a certain idea of myself."

"All the sounds of contentment you make. I know them now," he whispered.

"Please, Owen . . ."

He turned up his felted wool collar and shuddered before he let his breath out slowly.

Their fingers brushed and clasped briefly. He pressed a letter into her palm and turned, parting. As she entered the house, her cheeks had flushed; even as a redheaded child, a snowy night would do that to her. The conversations drifted as guests parted. Margot read his words, perched on the edge of the cast-iron tub. Her life would never be the same.

Lovely bird—

I am roused. Here it is dead of winter, and I'm already taking a walk with you when the gorse is in full bloom. I hear you cutting me off—saying there are obstacles. But you and I, though we learn lessons from stone we aren't made of it—though our people's kingship rests on the Stone of Destiny. The rock is a symbol of resolve, not abandonment. Our ancestors domesticated and honored wolves, revered the dead, and read signs in watery places. The Celt in you and me carries the story of "lack *of place" for propulsion, not stagnation, and tales of "lost memories" for connectivity, not absence. History massacred our people, young, old, women in childbirth, herded off their lands and out of their homes like sheep, and yet they thrive and fight for succession to this day. Are you still going to try and convince me there are barriers? My love, I'll steal you away.*

—Owen

CHAPTER TWENTY-EIGHT

Ricochet

In my experience, a farmer has dirt on his mind. A banker has rolled-up sleeves and money. A sailor hears a crowing cock back on that strip of land he so desperately wanted to be rid of. A runner has shoe-goo he can't be parted from. The poet who left Penelope on the rocks glanced over his shoulder.

In my youth, I swore I dreamed too much, but that isn't so. Tacos are good eaten cold the next morning. One day, a young Ava Blue bicycled to the bluffs and sat in a cave. There was a tiny swallow that had fallen out of its nest. She fed him ice cream and orange drink, and he survived and flew away.

"While we're on the subject of truth, Ava," I said, "there's something I forgot to tell you."

"I'm listening," she said.

We held glasses of cold green tea with fresh-cut mint leaves, in high summer, out on the wraparound porch. I looked at my twentysomething pretty little darling. This was going to blow her day.

"This isn't an excuse, but as a writer, one who is open to everything in life, sometimes, and it only happens occasionally, but sometimes, because I'm repeatedly running through interior monologues in my head—I can't be sure if I've told you something already or not."

I looked away from her for a moment and gave the toad that'd recently lost a leg (and was living in a terrarium on the porch) a dead cricket, then continued.

"Recollections bring amazement, and sketching the flow acts like a movie in my mind."

"And?" she asked.

"For a while, a brief span of time, I was on an FBI watch list."

"What the fuck, Mom."

"The Weather Underground," I said.

"Have you no shame or sense of guilt?"

Children's voices rang at play along the stretch of beach.

"That's unfair, Ava. Sometimes I think you're too serious for your own good."

"And you're a winged wild thing."

"That's not you speaking. You would have been right at home at the Monterey Pop Festival, alternately, the Fantasy Fair and Magic Mountain Music Festival—that one rocked. I heard Jimi Hendrix play for the first time in Marin County; we all did."

"Probably not."

"We believed, for right or wrong, that if we did nothing and let the war continue, the government had achieved its materialistic purchase of our lives, and that we had participated in the violence."

"You don't think I know that? I'm your daughter!"

"Remember how in 1967, I ran away with an older guy who was a poet? We drove that Buick from Maine to New York City, picked up friends, and hauled cross-country to Haight-Ashbury. That was the Summer of Love. In the spring of 1969, I was a freshman at Cornell opposing the Vietnam War. It all began when the SDS collapsed. That's when the Weathermen recruited those of us Students for a Democratic Society who had demonstrated and sat in. But they took it too far when they kicked ass. I didn't go to Cuba or North Vietnam. I was part of a small early Cornell collective. Black Lives Matter was born then. I was into organizing the masses toward peace, not "days of rages." So I got out, Ruby. I got out. Never had a fake identity or lit a bomb. When the WUO declared war on the US government, I had flown."

"Thank God," Ava said, "you had a smattering of common sense available."

"The goal wasn't to intimidate but educate."

"I've heard that before."

"What was right and what was wrong wasn't clearly delineated during Vietnam."

"Did you spend time in jail?"

"Three nights."

"What did you think about?"

"I thought about the people who weren't going to get out. I thought about the freedom in a sky."

Margot and George had reached the stretch in their relationship when each acted in one-upmanship. Had already had "the call" from Ruby, heard "the news" from William first. Though George had many regrets, within the freedom and benefits of a marriage, he hadn't addressed any. Move the pile of dirt that blocks your clear border with yourself.

Midmorning, Will and Lisbet hadn't left their empire bed but had named the four brass head finials: Bonnie Parker, Isadora Duncan, Bettie Page, and Colette. *How did one ever truly know anyone?* Will thought.

"Am I imagining it, or has your censorious brother backed off on his caustic bites?" Lisbet said.

"Live lifelong with a brother, with a lover, with a parent, and then what? One day discover a shocking, disturbing truth that blows the whole equation out of the fucking park. Maybe my morally sound father, whom I mistook for a Quaker, liked porn a bit too much, and one day my mother stumbled upon it, which is why she took a lover in England while working on her master's in art history; or one day, one of my children might be raped and not even tell me."

"Talk like that, and why do we take anything seriously!"

In reply, Will started to hum.

"He's in deep shit."

"And?"

"There's an investigation underway."

"Our George? Is *The Sitting Leo* map that he sold us suspect?" Lisbet asked.

"One of the peaks of seventeenth-century cartography. It better be authentic."

"Isn't it strange; you never know even the people closest to you," she said.

Energized, Will poked about, rekindling the fire.

Edwina, like her mother before her, had dressed the sleeping chamber with a gilded bed corona, and so it remained. The baldachin draped with white linen was a storied piece. The carved crown, circled by acorns and oak leaves, was topped by a perched swan, its wings spreading over the center, its feet gripping a delicate bar capped again by acorns. Let the rest of the party jump out of bed. Lovers know better.

Will fondled her hair between his fingers, then trailed them along the lower curve of her backbone to trace her hipbone and cup her buttocks. Nothing was on the lovers' schedule until the evening's bonfire.

"What's the deal with Ava?" he asked.

"She reminds me of a serious child who pouted over the gravitas of having her hair cut."

"The one who left the party game to visit a hydrangea and turned to chase a bee."

"A bit like Margot," Lisbet said.

"With less innocence."

"Why do you say that?" she asked.

"Margot's not as squarely in this world as Ava appears to be." *Margot, beautiful Margot,* he rattled to himself.

"'A certain distance' rests between her and George," he continued. Lisbet drew closer to him. The glow from the morning's sun lit up her chin and the corner of her mouth. "She's hinted at that for decades."

"We all experience that void in a relationship on different levels."

"Determined to make a good impression, George gets in his own way." He removed his watch from his wrist and checked the time: one minute to ten. I caught him in his bedroom at fourteen jerking off. He tried to bamboozle me by calling it 'onanism.'"

"You weren't both born with a dictionary in your mouth."

"And he thought I was deaf and dumb. 'Hold on just a minute, Will. I was practicing a form of Taoism.'"

"What were you, eleven? Able to read the dictionary too."

"And so on. He backs me against the closet, with a cuff on my ear. Then charms the folks in the kitchen with platitudes five minutes before dinner."

Crows landed on the branches covered with hoarfrost.

"Don't lag behind," Owen called outside, the sound of early night owls ricocheting through the woods tight against dusk. "A spooked horse is dangerous. If yours goes off a bit, keep the *heid*: 'stay calm, and don't get upset.' They'll be tranquil together. Don't spur a willing horse. Remember, use your heels gently, if at all; lead with your thighs." He questioned whether George had heard him.

And I see it like that, Owen thought, *the way George talks like a car salesman. Words hover over him when he isn't talking, even in Scotland, a land without any whitewash.*

The wind blew out of a cloud, and the first stars dispelled the tedium of dark days and bad weather. The one-hour traverse began along a wide trail to the plateau, where, earlier in the morning, Owen had laid the bonfire, which was being tended as they rode.

His thoughts traveled backward to the lessons of his father. *He had taught us boys, in no uncertain terms, to knuckle down when doing something we'd rather not, to get bloody on with it. "Use your loaf!" When Margot went away to university, and when she hadn't written, I had long since forgotten the name of the sea chanty she sang. But if I hear a snippet, I'll know.*

In the center of the entourage was Robbie, overdressed, a visible bead of sweat rolling down his forehead and across his leathery skin. His fleshy knuckles had turned rosy. Reined beside Will and Lisbet, the Scotsman began to sing in Gaelic.

"*It's a braw bricht moonlit nicht the nicht*—It's a brilliant bright moonlight night tonight."

And before the second stanza, the party saw the flames on the knoll of the Warrior's Head, four long and boggy miles off, pinpointed by a small village to the west. Moonlight bathed the riders' bodies in a blue haze and transformed them into divinely robed Renaissance pilgrims. In the caravan of simple souls with many cares, each carried a single sorry remembrance, and in a whimsical frame of mind, each hoped with lighthearted nonchalance to part with something.

"Forget the Scots versus the English." A towering personality in or out of the saddle, Robbie chatted animatedly, riding with Johnny. "Remember the Jacobites versus Redcoats? People get that all wrong. Jacobites fought to put the rightful royals in place—the Stuarts. And those Redcoats were made up mostly of English and Scots Lowlanders. Remember two years, 1715 and 1745, the years of rebellion. And mark that the Highlander is the jack of all trades."

"'A horse, a horse! My kingdom for a horse!' A Highlander doesn't need a horse," Owen added. "His legs do the running over the peaks and down."

"Aye," Robbie joined, "it's the Lowlanders. I'll give you that wuss Richard III, walking around on wobbly knees. Owen's dad, Rhys, was the only Highland trainer who let his horses out every day."

"When my mother wasn't planting a garden or burying a dog, my father was sweet-talking a foal when she passed through the stable in search of her twine." Owen asked if anyone needed a saddle blanket over their lap. "Park the Jacobites. Remember Queen Victoria and John Brown? Jesse, her favorite mare, carried her on Highland traverses, no different, when she wasn't out walking the heather for four hours a day. John Brown loved her so, he'd jump out of his saddle to pick her a sprig of heather." *And I've done no less for my Margot.*

"Hey, Owen," Ruby called, positioned about three riders behind him. "I figured out who you remind me of." She waited for him to turn back over his shoulder. "Ivanhoe."

"I'd argue with you about that," he called. "But if we do, we'll turn to stone and reach a divide."

Cute as her mother, he thought, *and just as bright.*

"In the summer, when you see the white heather lying out on the heid, Ruby, it's there for a reason—it marks the graves of fairy folk. All other heather is purple, stained with the blood of Highland warriors fallen where they had lain."

And I hope you could hear that one, George, he sang to himself.

Robbie reached into his bulky sheepskin jacket pocket, shook his shoulders as a tree weighted by snow unloaded, and pulled a bottle of Jameson out of a brown bag. His body heat fluctuated so; his fingers now were bluish with the cold.

"Take off a load and pass the hard stuff," Max called.

The stars made a riot of the sky. Groups of people were lying here and there, scattered beneath the ring of firelight. Johnny and Will broke macaroons at the edge of the circle and blew their warm breath over their fingers.

"Did you visit George in Amsterdam junior year?" Will asked in a hushed voice.

"No, I didn't have the money."

"The lavish lifestyle of 'Lady Courtenay,'" Will continued, "a child prodigy, international violin soloist, may have been funded by works from the permanent collection at the Met that turned up at auction blocks."

"If you stop, you'll be caught in a lie," Johnny said.

"Say it ain't so." William thought of the caviar and crème fraîche tartlets with chilled lemonade his parents had served on the lawn at Sag Harbor. "My parents are to blame. Their elitist and rude behavior—many of my girlfriends didn't get a hello from my well-coiffed mother. The folks were a little cold."

"How did you survive?"

"I just chalked it up to another day in the Arctic," Will said, and smiled.

"The women of the Castilian House of Ivrea did not sit on the porch with the men. Tennis whites and swimmers' bodies in sheer cotton dresses. The servants at my grandparents' home were Amerindians."

"And your parents?" Will asked.

"They grew their own food and cooked in solar ovens on three acres in Long Island. Hippies raised me, prominent leftist academics. Gabriela Ivrea and Santiago Franco had targets on their backs in Argentina. Human Rights Watch advocates constantly in the wake of a disaster."

How many times can you debate what constitutes Ovidian art? Will thought. *George is a closet blue-blood snob too.*

"How much did you buy from him?" Johnny asked.

"A map—in the sky, a cherub named *Zeghan*, 'blessing,' doles out 'wealth,' 'safe time,' 'art and science,' an allegorical figure of 'Sleeping Mars,' in the foreground."

Johnny kicked his heel into the snow. "To deceive oneself is easy."

"How's the weather there in Argentina?"

"It smells like jasmine."

"I had the pleasure of a luncheon with Heinke Hessel and Doña Maria de Trujillo y Merlo about a month ago; as though from nowhere, he appeared." Will scanned the landscape by fire-light to place George. "Then I googled the pair of them. Made a few phone calls. 'Drop the sack under the ice and run,' that's what a detective friend advised. A federal judge has spent the last decade attempting to pin Hessel down, but he's a slippery eel. Changes description, and location, like a butterfly."

"People like that always seem to know where their pursuers have gone," Johnny said.

"Is George blinded? What a mess he's made, what a Russian folktale."

Johnny nodded. "There are people who live under despotic oppression and near-slavery, their lives instilled with a fatalistic hopelessness—but George isn't one of them."

They joined those gathered.

Margot shivered and snuggled with Ruby beneath a Stewart tartan blanket. Within minutes, Ruby complained about being overheated and threw her half off.

My little piggy, Margot thought, *lovingly affable and liked by all. Where does innocence leave off and guilt begin? We were virgins together. The orchard was our home. The nettles had been painful. He should have known. Or the time we disturbed an adder. But the midges were by far the worst, thicker than the blackflies in Maine.*

"Mother, what was Hopper's Island like?"

"I was mysteriously happy there. My bedroom window framed an apple tree. We rented the same house each summer, white with a western porch, perfect for waiting on a hurricane. It was decorated with small oil paintings in unfinished pine frames, of alpine skiers, abandoned lobster traps in marshes, and exposed boats rotting at low tide. When old enough, my twelfth or thirteenth year, I went to a girls' summer camp, and Archie lived on his boat. More reform camp than s'mores and macramé, but Archie was oblivious. There was a girl from the sixteenth arrondissement. Another whose father was a lawyer for the EU lived in Brussels. Both wore diamond studs and were headed to an extra year of school in Switzerland—the 'thirteenth year.' They laughed at my naivete. Sex, drugs, and petty theft. Names weren't important, Ruby, on Hopper's Island, but faces were. At times, and only there, I thought your grandfather had come to rely on me."

"Sybil was a wildcat, a few shades beyond blonde," Max said.

"I ran with two scrappy older brothers."

"I couldn't have a car in Maine, Scotland, or Switzerland," Margot added. "Archie's 'insurance policy.'"

"A good idea." Owen took his hat off—the edge was salt-crusted—popped it back on, and gave the dogs a chase around the fire ring.

Margot watched him run. "I didn't think so," she called. Then thought, *My father shut it down—what I wanted.*

He was a bit out of breath; the dogs were faster. "My first lurcher, Breeze, was the runt of the litter. She was a braw bird dog until she got me in the doghouse. Brazen by day, the smart-ass pilfered everything man put on the counter. All my dogs do. And then, when night fell, she made her nocturnal incursions onto other people's land. The only way to get her in the house was to shut off all the lights. Then wait for her fearful whimper at the door."

"Awww, *the wee laddie and his dug*," Robbie teased around midnight, sounding like he'd smoked a pack of cigarettes and drunk a pint of bourbon. "I bet you were a braw pair and charming to boot. But my dog's better than yours. Ringo won first place at the Canine Spelling Bee with 'Portuguese Sardines.'"

"The tie between a boy and his dog is hallowed," Anna said.

"Which dog is the pick of the litter: the pup who runs the farthest or the one with a keen sense of smell?" Johnny asked. "Neither, the one who listens."

Margot sensed George was uptight whenever he intently studied his cuticles. The flames of the fire danced higher.

"Nobody painted light like Turner," he said. "In *Snow Storm*, at sixty-seven years old, he lashed himself like Odysseus to the mast, in the face of a full-blown storm for four hours, so that he could get it right." He shivered. "Is anybody else cold?"

"'Soapsuds and whitewash' was said of it," Will said.

"And a burger in Denmark costs one hundred and fifty kroner—seventy dollars. Google it."

Ruby rolled over on her back, gazing at the heavens. "There's Ursa Major, Owen."

"Bears record what they hear in the woods—better be careful," he said.

"Saint Hildegard von Bingen said, 'Bear meat turns people into spinning wheels of lust.'" Anna grinned.

"You've bared your soul, Anna," George said, then complained that the seat of his pants had dampened to the point of discomfort.

But how he guards his interior life, Margot thought, his philosophical musings on the spirit of love. George lives with a door sealed up.

"Are we a hunting party in the morning?" Owen asked. "Two stay together when crossing a fjord."

"We won't get into a bar fight on the way home," Will called.

"*Yer oot yer face*," Owen hollered after Will.

"I beg your pardon."

"You're drunk," Robbie clarified.

"We'll not get out of this scot-free. Tomorrow, Agatha will rescue us with the hair of the dog. Lucky George, no need to curb Wren tonight." Max reached into his parka pocket to warm his fingers, delightedly tearing the wrapper off a caramel Stroopwafel. "Lo and behold. Don't mind if I do, United. The snack you sneak into your bag for later—eat your hearts out."

"I'll take Delta's Biscoff cookie any day," Anna said.

Three sheets to the wind, with a nip in the air, aquiver with eerie wails and staccato barks, the party bit the bullet. The ground darkening and softening beneath them, pelted by snow, they let out. Rye pounced, again and again. He'd stirred up a mouse by starlight, and then, defeated, he gave chase to the riders.

The woodland nymphs and satyrs had bedded in the high silver wood hours ago, nestled under rocky crags, dark and grizzled. Far-off lights flickered in unspoiled, unvisited cottages, where, if one thought about it, one was surprised to find them dotted across the sea of snow.

An owl soared, its flying soundless, a silent *whoosh*, as it passed by the party, and then the prolonged barking, the equal of a medium-size dog, of a great horned owl, *hoo-h'Hoo-hoo-hoo*. And they knew it wasn't a dog only because it was overhead. Margot envisioned the reach that exists between others and ourselves and how, at his best, Owen lifted and carried her a distance, then set her down somewhere new.

CHAPTER TWENTY-NINE

The Idle Ridge

I f there are thirty-six civilizations in the Milky Way, as scientists
in Nottingham suggest, and I am rigorously honest enough to dismiss any wayward acts of my father, and descriptions in textbooks
alike, what remains is innovative and ~~liberative~~ action. I stand corrected. When freed or released from ownership or obligation, I wake
again, with the same elbow patch on my shirt, but see a multitude of
beings before me, and in the ocean that birthed them, pink and blue
and violet shining gems ride the surface of the undulating shoreline.

The stillness of Scotland haunted and sang. The second son, the
eldest daughter—Anna nailed it—none of it mattered. The place of
the Gaels, mountains of snow and ice, the steepest gullies, maybe with
a wee bit less snow.

PERTHSHIRE, DECEMBER 29, 2018

The house was quiet the next morning. The dishwasher too full the night before, Will hand-washed mugs at the sink, and Johnny dried at the drainboard. Sybil pulled out a chair at the breakfast nook set for three. They sat together at Otyrburn, sampling cheese that Owen had left.

"Not a bland cheese," she said, "it has a nutlike, buttery tang." Rhona wrapped her wheels in linen and added a spruce-bark band. "Margot said that Owen's task over summers, when they were kids, was fertilizing the orchard. For one month or two, his flock pastured here."

Will stood and parted the linen curtains to the outside edges of the window. *The holiday I got engaged—and embroiled in a police investigation.*

"Have you seen a news crawl since we arrived, Sybil?"

"My phone gets less than no reception."

Johnny nodded at Sybil, his dark eyes near. "Keep her away from the news."

"George isn't the kind to break into a sweat and moan, 'Oh no.'" They were stumbling around in the dark. A cloud passed overhead. Will switched on a lamp.

"He's in a jam at the museum," Johnny clarified. "What other red flags? The three Dutch etchings in my kitchen had seemed an exorbitant gift at the time, which George had pooh-poohed. 'An emblematic trinket of admiration for the friendship.' What exactly had he meant by 'the messy parts of museum life'?"

"He always seemed so conscientious." Sybil had picked up a pencil and begun scribbling on the back of a sheet.

"If we side with George," Will said, taking off his sweater and placing it on the bench, "in the name of goodwill and brotherhood, he has to tell us the truth."

"The whole thing could be a fabrication."

"It's possible."

"He does like beautiful, valuable things."

Sybil looked afar across the snow-swept, sleeping garden, its brilliance blinding. "It's a sunny day. Some awfully nice women are making dumplings, and we're going to shoot some birds. That'll keep her occupied." She scratched the back of her blonde head. "I won't mention our huddle."

In the garret, in Edwina's library with a multitude of books tucked haphazardly in alcoves, from world literature to quirky stuff, Margot moved rapidly over the shelves, reading spines. Pulled a copy of A. S. Byatt's *A Whistling Woman* off the shelf and read on the inside cover an alchemical message in Edwina's script: *A laurel branch will float, and a wooden spoon sink.*

Randomly rummaging around, she rifled through an over-stuffed drawer in a library desk and found a small brass key labeled "safe deposit box." She began writing to Owen, and when finished, she dressed for the hunt and joined her guests.

Sybil and Ruby wore jodhpurs. Ruby, socks, no boots, and, Sybil noted, restless.

"*C'est une folle journée.* Mother, I'm done with the mistletoe."

"Why is it a crazy day?"

How strange life is, Sybil thought. *When a dog can teach you life-changing lessons—what the hell had happened to George? In a close-knit community, in an idyllic setting, winter hikers were lost routinely and perished just steps from this door.*

"I don't have to give an explanation." Ruby swept crumbs off the breadboard and into her hand, then checked the hour on the round, brass wall clock that hung above the range, 10:50 a.m.

"Ah, the ancien régime. Rubbing of noses, sniffing, and licking—everyone's kissing, so I will too." Max chuckled, then kissed Sybil.

Engrossed beyond the ordinary, for George, nothing could have been more seductive than food, wrapped up by disseminating the right and the wrong way to record history. Greek, kynien, "to kiss." Ovid had made the whole of Italy the holy grail of love. In his ancient Rome, to be betrothed, all one had to do was kiss passionately in front of a group of people.

When Owen entered the kitchen midway into George's explanation, Sybil stood near the door, where the mistletoe remained, mumbling to herself absentmindedly, lost in the intricacies of lacing her boots. Owen's dark, coarse hair was in disarray. He wore gray tweed, a tattersall shirt, and a flying-pheasants game-bird necktie—his formal hunting attire. He admitted that he was rumpled and out of sorts on being deprived of his morning coffee. He took his coffee black.

"Who's riding with me?" he asked.

"I am," Sybil answered, pushing her disheveled hair out of her face. "Parasitic hitchhiker."

"What was that, Auntie Sybil?" Ruby asked.

"*Viscum album*, or your mistletoe, is an angiosperm that obtains its nutrients on the back of a host plant. Tropical in origin, eighteen thousand years ago, at the close of the last Pleistocene glaciation event, it migrated northward and southward. Mistletoe often grows on oaks. A few infections cause no harm; many on a vigorous tree may stunt the growth and even kill it outright."

"No one's ever going to say she has an intellect rivaled only by garden tools," Max said, stuffing his multilayered self into his jacket. "*Cheiloproclitic*, 'attracted to a person's lips or mouth.' And that ideal ratio: Sybil's Cupid's bow, one to one between the upper and lower lip."

Men with secrets, Sybil thought, *looting the goodness out from under their wives. I'd like to get my hands on George's small black notebook. See who's second in command. And in whose residences the goods are displayed. This lavish country estate is probably owned by his henchmen. Frickin' asshole. Margot will have to sell in a forced sale at a fraction of the value.*

Someone stood, yawned, and put the kettle back on. Max removed his jacket. Sybil observed Margot, loyal pup Wren asleep at her chair—he had aged with her. *I'll leave a goodly amount to the Art Loss Register,* she thought, *in Margot's name when I die. An intimacy exists between women that men do not share.*

"Sybil sleeps with one eye open and only half her brain asleep," Margot said. "Dinner at Sybil's is a long meal, with plenty of hard truths."

"Treat a wound with raw honey."

Margot lugged her duffel—they'd spend the night at the lodge—the brass buckle clanking annoyingly.

"The first car's leaving," Owen said softly.

The party broke and began hauling bags and picnic baskets while Will and Ruby hung back and visited for a spell in the "Green Room." Affectionately tucked against her uncle's shoulder, Ruby shared a club chair. There were many things she could discuss only with him.

"Scotland is literally the worst," she said. "Who buys bread at the supermarket? I can't even."

"The place has a dark side," Will said, "and things have a life of their own."

Instinctually, he would guard her from whatever George had concocted.

"Eff outta here—*Excessivement terre-à-terre.*"

"Down to earth, yes, Ruby." He removed a throw pillow from the chair they occupied to free up space. "A unique sense of humor, Scotland is a cosmic tree that sat in the cradle of independence too long, refused to budge, grew fangs, and became afraid of nothing."

"Sus." She leaned into him.

"And you mean?"

"Duh, *someone's* acting shady or suspicious," Ruby said.

"Your mother is a bit like a nun."

"She likes things just so."

A soft smile flashed over his face. "Granted, your mother is diva-esque."

"And now a sister?"

"We have no idea about Ms. Ava Kerouac."

"Did she seem self-absorbed to you?" Ruby asked.

"Not in the least. She's assertive." He glanced at his watch.

"How is it that sex becomes a matter of complete indifference?" She stared at the cracks in the beams of the old ceiling.

"Sex builds like an architectural structure. The goal is positioning the keystone. Painting the trim gets old."

The horn honked five times.

"I gotta bounce. See ya later, Ruby."

She planted a kiss, then called to his retreating form, "I sure love family picnics, *said no one ever.*"

It was December, and Ruby was right, no one wanted to hike in the snow, but they did so anyway because, well, to not let down old friends, and besides, George had promised a chocolate mint on each pillow for the party of ten later in the lodge.

Owen drove his heels into hard earth, framed by the stark cliffs of the Idle Ridge sliding into the clouds. The red wool tassels on his socks blew in the wind over the tops of his green Wellies. His pants were gray-and-oxblood tweed to match his jacket.

"A newcomer may find the practices confusing, though the etiquette of sporting shooting circles doesn't go ignored. Today, I'll be your Shoot Captain out on the game field. I'll cry, 'Don't shoot,' if an owl, a hawk, a songbird, or protected species gets up. We're on a driven shoot, which means two men we'll call the 'beaters' will walk with sticks sporting white flags, flushing out the game from six sites we'll visit. Safety is the priority, and respect. If you don't aim to eat your kill, then please don't shoot. If we're all in for dinner tonight, we'll bring home five cocks and dine at the lodge on my mother's recipe, roast wild pheasant with Swiss chard, wild mushrooms, and sweet potato—vanilla puree."

"Do we have to?" Margot asked.

"If it makes it any easier for those qualmish about the hunt," he continued, eyeing her, "pheasants are ferocious to each other, committing murder and gang rape. In the seventeenth century, birds were shot while on the ground or perched. They may have netted and hunted with hawks. In the eighteenth century, when shotguns improved, they were shot in flight. *Driven* means 'shooting up,' and there you have it: the double-barreled breech-loading gun brought the emergence of the driven hunt."

Margot stood with her head tilted skyward and her mouth open, catching falling snowflakes as an overloaded branch of snow let loose beside her.

"Aye, that's right," Owen called to her. "Only go for the *skelf*, not the *spitters*."

"The 'large snowflakes,' not the 'small driving snow,'" Robbie clarified. "At last count, there were four hundred and twenty-one words for snow in bonny Scotland."

"I wouldn't do that if I were you," Sybil warned.

"Pen ready," George interrupted, then snapped a photo of the party with his cell phone.

"Among various sundry things, that laced net of lovely crystals holds sulfates, nitrates, formaldehyde, or mercury. And when in New York City, the gasoline exhaust adds benzene, toluene, and xylenes."

"No loafing allowed," Max said. "It used to be. 'Don't eat the yellow snow'; now my cryophilic darling says, 'Beware the green, orange, pink, and black.'"

"The high pheasants and partridge would prefer, nonetheless, to walk in that snow if they could, rather than fly." Robbie stood among dried brown ferns, their tops drooped, weighted by snow crystals, with his fox terrier, Ringo, at his side, at the ready.

Owen had the oft-repeated impression that Robbie's shock of thick white hair threatened to drive off his cap. Rye set up a howl. A brace of pheasants got up in front, making quite a commotion, crossed to the other side of the clearing to no avail, and took a devious exit into the dense cover formed against the dramatic cliff face. But not before the party caught the bright plumage and blue heads crowned by a red eye patch worn by the cock.

"It's got two bloody triggers!" Owen cried after a failed shot by Johnny. "Aye, the birds are high and challenging when they're coming at you—fieldcraft pays. The low birds should not be shot at but left to fly."

George and Margot were in the same field, he observed, but their recognition of each other was the equivalent of a handshake. Owen thought about how a couple's mutual efforts to assert themselves and exercise control led them to contend with each other through distorting maneuvers and power plays.

Ten minutes passed with no action, then another five, before a clutch flew and the blistering sound ran; one bird turned upside down and gracefully plummeted, whisp over whisp, to the earth. Rye and Ringo ran through the brush, retrieving, returning with the wet-dog scent of a wolf.

"Roll over, play dead, get off my leg. Good dog, Ringo," Robbie teased, patting his wiry head. "He likes to be sworn at. But I adore him and place his eiderdown bed by the radio for his favorite Sunday quiz show. Don't mind his ears; they prick up at the slightest provocation." He rested his 16-bore shotgun over his shoulder to accept the prize, placing it in his side bag. "Aye, it's a good time to stop for a sharpener."

"The drinks are on the guy behind me," Max said.

Robbie opened a dovetailed wooden box that held small glass bottles and offered around individual nips of whisky. "How that blue-teal came in at one hundred and twenty miles an hour!"

"There's an idiosyncratic character to the Highlands," Max said, cuffing his orange earmuffs about his neck. "It prefers to stand alone."

"I like the pastoral you," Sybil said.

"Color in the Highlands is a way of penetrating the stone," Margot said, openly eager to get off the field.

Owen noted George looked perturbed and oblivious.

"A Highlander, even down on his or her luck, is a little more go-lucky than the rest," Robbie said. The soft ground melting below his size-eleven boots muddied the earth with the rising heat of the day. "Scots have an extra mile to run. You'll only lose the birds that you felt sure of killing, those that were covered with deliberate, calculated accuracy."

The hunt continued to weave its way over the moor till noon shone and plank tables were erected, featuring meat pies in pastry, leek and potato soup, marzipan dates, and flutes of rosé champagne. Then high noon crossed over into late afternoon, with gully climbs below soaring ridges, as Owen scoured the snowbound hills to find her, to lock eyes.

Before 4:00 p.m., the group headed to the lodge, set in an elevated position within the Cairngorms National Park. The eighteenth-century Struthan Beag, "Little Stream," had strong historical connections to the Jacobite rebellion.

At the entrance, a short-eared owl perched on its thick white legs atop a fence post, and the puppylike bark rang, *voo-hoo-hoo-hoo-hoo,* uttered like a chicken clucking through the foothills by the female of the species, which hunts by day over heather-land and moorland.

"Flying high, voles seem large," Owen said, "but they're small nomadic birds the size of pigeons." As though on cue, she lifted off on the wing, with a beak clack and hiss of annoyance.

CHAPTER THIRTY

Struthan Beag

*W*e did a lot of stone-skipping on Hopper's Island, Ava and I, before and after a sandwich seated in a tide pool. Turkey with cranberry sauce on whole-grain bread tastes best with salty fingers and lips.

Her first job was at a bakery. The old center of Hopper's Island sat at a fork in the road called Clouds Crossing. The entrances to three original structures practically stood in the way of traffic. It was the spot where two old trails converged at the highest peak on the island. Two of the three shingled buildings were empty; the third housed the only on-site bakery, Dulse and Dundee. Each shop front had enormous picture windows out onto the street. While Ava worked, stationed at her worktable in her white chef's coat and baker's hat, rolling dough and decorating cakes, her progress was made visible to passersby.

When she came home dusted in flour and sugar crystals, Ring Side Riot showered her in kisses. Old, gray, and deaf, that dog hadn't lost his sense of smell. At seventeen, she talked about how the sacks of flour were made whole when "the magic of life met the commotion of what it is to make nothing."

Summers, it was hot inside the bakery. Then the demand, with the summer crowd in residence, was the greatest. From either end of the dusty, midge-riddled street, girls and boys came by barefoot, some on bicycles, one pedaling and one riding the bar, to see what she was doing. There were times when even I stood on the porch, my hair flying by the fan in the open window. From Clouds Crossing, the fields of rye stretched toward the sea on either side of us.

PERTHSHIRE, DECEMBER 29, 2018

The paired donkeys sentinel over the sleeping gardens remained undisturbed. Struthan Beag's door was robin's-egg blue, and a soft moss grew on the walls. Ava had accepted Margot's invitation to join the party for dinner. Once, Ava had driven northeast to Machias, Maine, where the sea lay so flat and still that she skipped a stone to Canada. *I'm a long way from home,* she thought.

The wind-lashed party entered through a vestibule into a large foyer. Amid a jumble of barking dogs, they placed their bags, greeted by their host, Ian MacPherson. The sound of a bagpipe-trilling neighbor running through his repertoire emanated from the back hall.

Ian smiled, holding the door ajar to the night air. "Shane walks the length of his mile-long driveway practicing, so it was no trouble asking him to keep walking."

"We survived," Anna said with a sigh, "wild weather, trekking without a mile of packed snow at the side of the road."

"It's warm, good." Sybil looked the place over with a nod to Ian and Ava. "May God help all the homeless wanderers. Be glad you weren't one."

"I kept a cushion toasty," Ava said. The party appeared more down to earth, wet around the corners, their exteriors softened by a day spent in the wilderness.

"Where the weather's dulcet, the beer's lousy. A smoke and a sharpener in the drawing room before dinner, ladies permitting," Robbie called to Ian.

And the entire party did just that—scattered down dark-wood-paneled halls to the comfort of Ian's kilim-strewn library. The deeply fluted and floret-carved ivory marble mantel held a tall red marble plinth column with a brass acanthus capital, where, perched on a ball, sat a bronze griffin. The walls were papered in green velvet. To the left of the hearth, under glass in a small, rect-angular frame of black wood, a watercolor depicted Edward the Black Prince in Garter robes. The darkly lobed leaves of a white orchid shone in the room's low light.

George strolled toward a religious work of art on the wall and gestured at the painting with his glass. "In art, it's always about the details. In art, one has to study history. To understand history, one has to know the facts."

"The struggle is real," Ruby said, and shrugged, visibly tiring of the older crowd.

"Not exactly a barrel of laughs," Lisbet said from her place on the sofa, without raising her eyes.

"Take Bosch's adoration of Madonnas," George continued.

"Bougie," Ruby said flippantly.

"They ate old rye bread, morning, noon, and night."

"Keep it one hundred, Mom."

"In Bosch's world," George continued, unscathed, "let go of reason, and life goes to hell."

"Jesus, George, when are you not enlisting good souls in a brotherhood you've designed?" Will asked. "You could sell a multilayered dreamscape from a kiosk."

"Always with the books, geez." Anna sighed. She bent and smelled the pink roses held in a silver bowl at rest on the open shelf of a writing desk. "I love peeking in people's houses."

The diffused light through the ivory linen shade softened the early wrinkles in Anna's face. Ava read her effort to hide her dismay and surmised that she found George pretentious too. Johnny didn't pick up Anna's glance. He wouldn't be back when they landed in the States.

The exhausted group's effort, after a day spent in constant companionship, left no room for expansion or restoration (despite the homey atmosphere) beyond that afforded by drinks and food. Though everyone had their role to play, they'd be lost without Max.

"George would lose a debate with a doorknob," he said.

"Retweet," Ruby called. She did a high-five in the air.

"William and I took the 'Heaven and Hell Cruise' as teens with the folks," George added.

Ruby opened one of a pair of small wooden chests, the one with iron corners; the other had leather handles. Both had key locks and were set upon a circular table covered with a fringed paisley cloth. Then she picked up an antique pair of opera glasses and peered around the room.

"What did you say your thesis was, Ava?"

"My thesis, basically, is how to return to women their long-lost importance."

"Slay." Ruby clapped.

"Only the queen moves freely in any direction over the chess-board and promises victory." Sybil sipped from her steaming mug. "And the king can only be beaten with the cooperation of the queen."

"What is your mother like, Ava?" Anna asked as she mean-dered through the room. Reaching the large globe on a wooden plinth with scrolled feet, its world map drawn on linen-hued lac-quered parchment, she gave it a spin.

"Violet lives off the grid on Hopper's Island. She has a positive take on life, unlike me."

"Something she would have shared with my mother," Margot said.

"Yes," George said, "but Adela wouldn't have stood butt na-ked, waiting for the rain to take a shower."

"Violet dries off under a rainbow."

"I was lucky during my childhood," Owen said, "hardly a day passed without a heron or egret fishing, or streaking down around the loch."

"If Mom has a sister, then I have an aunt."

"A mitzvah." Sybil smiled.

"And I have a niece." Ava returned the compliment, wonder-ing what Ruby was like as a kid. "Though early in the season for Camden, right before I left, the deer ate the tender top half off the crowns of my new blueberries."

"Burlap wrap," Sybil advised. "Wait till they eat your grapes."

Will leaned back on his chair rails, the stiff oak creaking, and absently clicked his knife shut and slid it into his pocket. Snow blew down beyond the lit window in a horizontal blur.

"What I remember of the Netherlands is pretty girls in short skirts riding bikes," Will continued. "But I was just a kid then, so don't blame me."

"Quiche," Ruby said.

"Lasagna," Max said.

"Hotter than hot," Ruby explained, visibly annoyed. "Uncle Max, I was trying to tease my Uncle Will."

"And whipped-cream peaks you could ski down," Will added. "That trip Mother planned in 1983 was an acid trip on rail, wheel, and wings. Remember the city's killer cream puffs, smothered in rich dark chocolate, George?"

"You ask the Dutch baker for a Bossche bol."

Robbie and Johnny moved to the maple round table and a game of chess, their heads earnestly bent fireside, one ear on the discussion at large and a walnut pawn stepping out two, en passant. Ava stood, watching their moves. She glanced at the books covering the walls and piled up all over the room.

"What one loss, or sadness, expressed by women in your interviews, struck you the most?" Sybil asked.

"About sixty percent of the women in my survey reported that in their relationships, they hungered for attention and wanted to be admired because they felt that was all they had left."

"How many talked about having mystical inclinations?" Sybil leaned back in her armchair.

"Many, from all walks of life. One postmaster who delivered the mail explained her experience as an affinity for nature, and by a love of 'Mother Earth,' as a loved one, or family member, not magic hidden from sight."

"A seed germinates in the dark," Owen said. He had just shared an observation on a collection of fifteen identically framed small watercolor drawings of extinct species on the wall opposite.

"Do you like strawberry picking, Ava?" Ruby asked.

"The down-easterner does, and I had a Maine coon cat once too."

"I love small dogs riding in wicker bike baskets," Ruby said, "Dorothy-me."

"Go to school, pay hard-won money to have a 'Druid' tell you that a tree is beautiful." Owen stood, stretched his legs, and moved by the fire. "In art or nature, you either feel it, or you don't. A child will hug a four-hundred-year-old tree. The two recognize each other, like dredging up a spring in January—a little poking with a stick, and it gurgles upward. A spring will run the same temperature year-round."

"I heard a Himalayan Buddhist, a sublime yak-milk cheese maker, say, 'Life flows between us all like smoke,'" Johnny said.

"Unless, of course, the cheese has slid off the cracker." Max winked.

In the narrow hall, with a lull in the party as people broke and freshened before dinner, splinter groups toured the house. Johnny overheard a harried George on his cell phone in an empty study.

"I know what time it is in Saint Barts, and that you're on board *and* on vacation."

Silence.

"Hand over the package," George continued. "These are take-it-or-leave-it conditions."

And a second punctuated pause.

"It's still a crime of vengeance, polite but insistent."

An even longer break ensued.

"No! Never! I will not negotiate."

Johnny quickened down the hall, in the opposite direction, his oft-whispered suspicions seemingly confirmed. He found Will and Sybil, gathered in the foyer to park sweaters and a bag before being seated, and motioned to them, and they convened in a private sitting parlor.

"The good, the bad, and the obvious." Johnny paused to think. "I don't know how to use any of this information effectively."

"To everything, a purpose." Sybil buttoned her sweater and crossed her arms.

"I overheard too much," he added.

"Sometimes we shovel shit," she said, leaning in close.

"Heinke, George, and Doña Maria, every set of three is not complete." William nervously rose to stand near the doorway, only to return. "If in the wrong, George will invent any excuse to do exactly as he pleases."

They heard their names being called.

Ava surveyed the gala table spread, listening as Sybil asked about the translucent quality of the porcelain collection and its freeness of form; she strummed through images of how her life would read, reworked to include the elusive, vague, and passive forays of fusty academics. Before he served the pheasant, Ian, dressed in a burgundy velvet smoking jacket, a match to George in black velvet, asked that they look out for the random stray shot missed by an otherwise excellent and diligent chef.

"Peppery. Are those juniper berries, Owen?" Sybil, seated on his left, cut into the bird that had soared overhead hours earlier.

"'Life's elixir.' You got the sorry seat by the gardener." He filled her water glass. "The red berries are prolific, and as a child, I'd gather bags full. Did your mother garden?"

"My mother made me promise I'd never marry. Both my parents were Jewish and freethinkers. Dandelions were all she gardened. He played the violin. But I skied between their legs. My grandmother was the only teacher in a Lithuanian one-room schoolhouse for thirty students. Father was a mathematician who always wanted to shoot deep-sea videos in the Dead Sea. He spoke German, went to university in Vienna. 'If the paths are jammed with people, and you have to get to your brother's house, which is five and a half miles away, before the sun sets at seven-thirty, precisely, and the road you're traveling over zigzags, while you fight a wind gusting at thirty knots per hour—how long will it take?' Who has the sorry seat now?"

Owen straightened a leaning taper in the candlestick. "One summer, feeling misunderstood and unhappy, I tangled all the mares' tails and cut the geldings."

"What's the history on Violet's side of the family, Ava?" Anna asked.

"Some of her family sashayed down from French Quebec for the milder Maine winters. But that was a long time ago."

Well, thought Ava, surprisingly, *I'm more optimistic than I've ever been in all my life.* She liked her new circle of friends so well, she contemplated delaying her return. It was as though she had parked her car in front of an old-timey general store, without a list to fill or a care in the world.

"Your mother never mentioned Archie?" George asked.

"I was a child of stardust and sea glass, found on a beach and instantly loved beyond all reason." Ava helped herself to the bowl of butternut squash. "She sprinkled stories across my childhood. My father was a king who lived in a glass castle called Otyrburn. But that was pretty much it."

"A devil-may-care attitude doesn't mean one isn't focused or deliberate about life," Anna said, readjusting the black suede headband in her red hair. "Ask me one of your interview questions."

"Okay. What did a stranger say to you that made you happy?"

"'Redheads are good luck.' Then she pinched me. Blew me a kiss over her shoulder and kept on walking. I was about five."

"*Gonnae no dae that*?" Robbie scolded in the blue stillness of contented diners. "Please stop doing that!"

He held the walnut pepper grinder aloft in his tight fist for all to see.

"Hand the pepper off to a Highlander by setting it on the table before him—not in his hand directly. It's bad luck."

"It sounds pagan, and it is," Owen said wryly.

"Poppycock superstitions," Sybil grumbled under her breath, "and pecking automatons."

"Tell him that evil spirits can't appear as an 'unkindness of ravens,'" Owen added.

"Your maternal grandparents signed documents with the blood of a newt."

"Remember, Ruby, when I told you to cover your eyes during the Bond sex scenes?" Margot laughed, spilling a splash from her water goblet in her eagerness and sprinkling the Irish moss, eucalyptus, and cedar table runner. "That was an implicit invitation to scandal."

"And I did, then spread my fingers, just *ever* so slightly, to catch *every* detail."

"In Sardinia," Anna said, "maggot-riddled cheese is thought to cure sexual lassitude."

"You can call that healthier if you like," Ava said.

Robbie sputtered over a spoonful of his cock-a-leekie soup. "Anna, sweetheart, such vulgarity."

Ava passed Owen the warm bread basket of black buns. He reminded her of someone, someone with an extraordinary sense of physical and mental alignment, someone who didn't care if the days were hot and the nights cold. "Is it rapacious, Owen, to dig up perfectly good plants?"

"I save what I can. Plants should have wheels for feet."

"Mulch-heavy. If you don't like it, pull it out," Sybil said, her plate half-full.

"Monkshood was the 'queen of poison' in ancient Greece," George said, "though I couldn't recognize it if it stared me in the face."

"Growth happens in my garden," Sybil said, "more than compost."

"At first back-breaking to learn, a garden speaks an obscure language," Owen said. "But it seldom disappoints."

"Death and rot in the garden," Max said. "Piss off, the lot of you."

"Another day, another meal." Sybil sighed. "Max has invented his own food pyramid. A cake divided into seven slices."

She set her silverware in the continental resting position. The fork facedown, its handle at seven on the dial, and the knife tip under the tines at the center of her plate.

"What's new at work, George?"

"There's never anything new at the museum," Margot said. "Everything's at least two thousand years old."

"You look tired, George," Sybil added. "Are you getting three to five REM cycles of sleep a night?"

"I do more than lug the long red carpet around for blockbusters." He pushed a morsel of gristle to the edge of his plate. "My work could be deadly boring, but it's not. Things are more open than you think."

"Well, I still say you look a bit pallid." She adjusted the cash-mere wrap sweeping across her back, to rest swung over the crook of her elbows. "You need more root vegetables."

The room at Struthan Beag had arched doorways and retained some early-nineteenth-century pull-down maps. "Africa." An Albrecht Dürer pen and ink, then painted with watercolor and gouache, hung on the wall, weeds, grasses, and earth—a tuft of earth with all of life drawn into the mud.

(In all honesty, I can't be quiet. Margot says that George used to pull people in on a basic level. "He was fun." The end of the rule of gold-mining white men, I say—why would we expect buoyant prose from petrified artifacts? Projections come out of projectors. In a void, or an atmosphere thick with suspicion, loving, quiet, and humble sincerity can't exist. Walk a thousand miles with a struggling young poet and learn more of the life of a shepherd at late afternoon, the brutally violent repression of student protests, and the otherness in even one work of art than if you had unearthed a river of strawberries.

A poor man keeps his cultural identity intact, safeguarding his emotional validity. At any stretch along a highway trip, he is his own prophet. The wealthy, conceited people, I may add, will ask you if you came in contact with any writers and thinkers. They'll want to see your nudes, hear about your purchases, strolling through your garden, dropping Latin names to show you they speak in the language of flowers, before they scatter their semen in the stream. They answer you with feeling that cannot foresee the future.)

William had excused himself from the table, momentarily, to straighten the lower edge of an oil canvas on the wall opposite, taken a step backward to judge his correction, and rejoined those seated. "When Mother gave us wax seals, George minted his coin and sold them throughout the neighborhood."

"That was bothering me too," Ruby said, all smiles. "V cute, Uncle Will. You're like two grandfathers quibbling over who has the bigger zucchini."

"My research leads me to believe that one of those men had a lack of care and concern for someone he swore, he claimed to this day, that he loved," Ava said. *A clear sense of direction forestalls many problems*, she thought.

"Not all anxiety stems from women being both forbidden and desirable," George said casually. The last to finish his sweet potato–vanilla puree, he had slowly moved on to dessert.

"Is that it, Will—I'm verbose? Who cracks chestnuts anyway?"

"*Ataman*, George," Max said.

"Again?" he asked.

"A colloquial term used when 'attaboy' seems contextually inappropriate, often due to age." The staff placed a gold-rimmed plate before him. "Holy cow, here we go again. A behemoth slice of raspberry and whisky cheesecake."

"*Ex nihilo nihil fit*," George consoled. "Or 'from nothing comes nothing.'"

"And raking helps prevent California's forest fires." Sybil grinned.

"In *Orpheus and Greek Religion* by W. K. C. Guthrie," George chatted after dinner, with Anna and Sybil, on the way to the library, "the departed stand with *Totenpässe* on their person. Think of it as a passport for the dead, worn on the neck or forehead, by initiates into Orphic, Dionysiac, and some ancient Egyptian and Semitic religions."

Ava, one step behind, left the room asking herself how the tablet George would tie around her neck would read, made of lead, not gold: *fill this imposter's soul with evil misfortune.* After the curse, the directions would take her on a circuitous route to hell, killing her dog along the way. Then she pondered whether or not she had imbibed too much of the rich holiday spirit.

"Dogs need walking," Owen said, rising and signaling at Wren's wagging butt.

The liquid, velvet night air was cool on their heated flesh, and as the door closed, Owen and Margot heard William calling to Johnny, "You're a whisky nerd." They walked with what felt like an ocean between them before the dogs peeled off, yelping into the blackness.

"Owen, where's the owl?"

CHAPTER THIRTY-ONE

Night Birds

M y father was dying; as a child, how I loved and admired him. Maybe I have a cultural ADD, googling one minute, typing on my Hermes the next, loving him and loathing him—our relationship. I had wanted to hold on to the long-consistent thread of meaning that bound me to Thomas Grey, but it always slipped through my fingers.

In the weeks before his death, I dreamed of him; we were both young and looked almost like twins. Across a crowded room, we had smiled at one another. A big, shit-eating, happy grin that belongs only to youth in their prime, poised to accomplish things. Without disappointment or expectation, if only for an instant, we had recognized one another and communicated through the joy of love.

"I thought the world of you," he said, the white sheets made paler still by his ashen color and blue eyes. He was in his old bedroom at the *family farmhouse. Not surprisingly, the size of the birds on the camellia wallpaper had grown smaller with each passing year.*

"And I of you." I had moved from the edge of the bed to the window. "Though the way I remember it, you said I'd suffer from crippling depression, without a family, a husband." The translucency of the sea in October—Hopper's Island void of tourists, the whale tour boats and fishing boats alike asleep in the harbor. I had swum just hours earlier.

"No one whizzes through an entire opera, Violet." He had trouble lifting his arms. "Is that what this is about? 'Daddy issues'?"

I hadn't seen much of him in ten years.

"In your last letter, you wrote, 'I'm not attending your poetry workshop reading,' then attached a blurb about Ava cutting classes. All my life I've been painfully aware how little you value my education and my work, and now you're assuming the same about Ava."

"We've both been capable of cruel manipulation," he said, "and a lack of plain decency."

"Academics are so sure of the reality of their impressions, myself included." It was hard to hold the door open when trust was gone. "If only I could have made a weaving run, like happy bird chatter, and found you again, but instead, we sat as adults and overthought our moves."

"We're all imperfect humans in an imperfect world." He asked for water. "How many years did I lose out on Ava's childhood?"

"To be a father is a privilege, not inherited, but won." I looked around and met his grave, then gentle eyes.

"It means we divorce ourselves from the traits we find distasteful. Cease trying to control the other's speech. And maybe, Violet, for once, see what identifies us as a cluster unique among all others." He looked old and frail, not in the least bit distant or enigmatic.

"I agree." From the house, his endless equations, my artistic underachievement, his unconscious or deliberate endeavors to detain *my mother at home (in this lovely house), the porous placement of our words, the blurring, the reduction—even now, I still stubbornly hemmed and hawed, and wanted out.*

"So have you found it? Your person who finishes your sentences?"

"Marriage, not a mirage? No, obviously. But I'm happier being an open reservoir, not a preserve."

"Maybe lonely."

"Maybe so." I moved closer, my hand on his. "I love you. I've always loved you, Dad."

"And I you."

He was dead within the week. It was my job to scatter his ashes.

PERTHSHIRE, DECEMBER 29, 2018

Beneath a cover of passing shadows, Owen's and Margot's forms had disappeared into the concealed wildwood. Struthan Beag's flickering glow seemed miles away. The oak near, as their shoulders brushed, he guided her to the tree and pressed her up against the bark. Despite the cumbersome weight of their winter clothes, they managed to find a way. The loose ends of her scarf fluttered between them as he entered her. His voice sank to a whisper.

"If everyone made love like this, no one would ever work."

They both laughed over the wind.

"We're kids behind the barn."

"We already did that."

"It's all silly nonsense." She handed off the folded note she'd written earlier. "Lust is a shade of madness."

"Pen pals with benefits, is that what we are?" he asked. "Lust, that experience falsely known as 'being in love.' It seldom, if ever, lasts." He pocketed her letter. "Whatever happened to the letters I wrote you that summer and asked Edwina to post? I lost your address."

She kissed him and slipped her hands into her sheepskin mittens. "What did they say?"

"More to the point, what didn't they say? Two pages of a yellow legal pad, at a go, scrawled front and back. My brothers said I was nuts. Scottish waters held a lot of pike, and the freshwater shark had six hundred sharp teeth because it came after your lure, only to bite it off."

"It's so foggy."

"I think there's a chance we'll make it back."

"Rye, *trobhad!*"

The dogs came running, with their tongues hanging out. Margot and Owen returned to Struthan Beag, stepped out of their boots and into house shoes, and hung heavy jackets on the pegboard. In their carnal intoxication, the heat of the house was heady and suffocating.

Drink whisky wrong, and you could be damned for all eternity. Will had stretched out on a Turkish kilim; multitasking, he flipped through pages of a bagpipe-making book, learning that African blackwood and boxwood, both strong and tonally precise, were choice.

And there was nothing Max liked more than debauchery. Ava and Sybil had walked off, instinctually, arm in arm, to form a splinter group, as if compelled to have a chat about someone they both knew and missed dearly.

"I do. I absolutely love it there."

"India is one place that keeps appearing hypnotically before me," Ava said.

"It's a life-changing journey." Sybil stooped to view a wooden staircase model and display of Roman bronze sculptures. "All the tears of the world in a single teardrop. But of course, I expected India to be lovely."

"These days, I spend my waking hours in the public library. Liberation from the bondage of rebirth will have to wait."

Ava watched as Johnny occupied a carved oak stool nearby. He had a smile that was cozy and sweet. *The smile of a cubby-bear*, she thought. From the scraps of their interactions, Margot and George were the odd couple. He adored something about her. But for one of them, it was finished. Ava was on the line as to precisely which one.

"Whisky in Scotland isn't an arbitrary endeavor," Johnny said. "Drink whisky neat, be sure to share it, and inhale for a minimum of thirty minutes—before sipping."

"You forgot the humming in your glass and singing right back," Robbie said.

"I'm nauseated by rules," Margot said.

"Gremlin squatters and garden gnomes don't obey the rules," Sybil said.

"My father swore it wasn't a dram of whisky," Owen said, "without dipping his finger in the glass and rolling a drop methodically between his thumb and forefinger. Mother went one further, dabbing a touch of the muse on her temple and wrist, with an aristocratic privilege, as if it were Chanel. And if it was a three-hour-long drinking party, and we were wee lads, she'd put a drop on the end of our noses like she were the pontiff sprinkling fairy dust."

"And a Japanese whisky bar isn't kosher without nine hundred varieties." Robbie looked overheated and mildly irritated. The library thermometer was set too high, and the cast-iron radiators, far too ambitious. "People taking photos and Instagramming their whisky glass—tommyrot. The whole damn world has lost sight of the memory of the people who went before us."

It was a meditative room. Writer and conversationalist alike were at home. The pierced and engraved serpentine fire fender incorporated floral elements, with a pair of hunting dogs facing one another at the center. The pitched and mottled surface of a Gustavian corner cupboard at the far end of the room collected slow shadows cast from the Baroque candle stands, nearly three feet tall, with marble tops supporting pillar candles that burned. Owen had remarked on the powder horn on a stand with a lid of root.

"Did you suffer from 'father hunger,' Ava?" Elisabetta asked.

"I missed being able to kiss my father good night." She bent to pet Rye, quietly at rest at her feet. "My life was one large paradox. Life with a man, with anyone, made my mother feel awkward, ignorant, and imprisoned. Rather than skillful, wise, and free."

"I guess that's better than a helicopter parent," Ruby said. "Most of my friends have stranger-danger anxiety over dating."

"My grandfather Grey's family hailed from Rome. His Roman jurisprudence and severity meant that I would not be subjected to the same. Violet chose voluntary motherhood. But I did not grow up isolated."

"Relativity in all things." Sybil nodded.

"She found her own expression by continually confronting contradictory elements."

"I'd say Violet has a unique take on personal freedom," Will said.

"Yes. She respects the principle of absolute freedom. And pooh-poohs precision for nuance and tone. When she left a relationship, it was more often than not on her own accord."

"Then she is an artist in the truest sense," Johnny said. "Is she published?"

"A collection of short stories. She's always impatient to get back to her work. Though right about now, she's swinging in a hammock, overwintering in Taos with a friend, eating bread, garlic, and chili paste, hoping the monarchs reached central Mexico."

"Monarchs don't travel in pairs." Sybil was seated, as ever, cross-legged on the floor. "But the female lays three thousand eggs, as long as there's milkweed."

"There is an infinite flexibility, a quality to life, that Violet always lived by," Ava said.

"No buying into the rigidity of an established system." Ruby worked away at an iron blacksmith's brainteaser puzzle, held in her lap. "Aesthetic."

"The one thing she told me about my father was that he believed 'if justice isn't strong, strength rules.'"

"That's Archie," Margot said.

What I know and don't know, Ava thought, *is all too apparent. I'm not writing a tender memoir. Maybe laugh-out-loud funny.*

One reached Struthan Beag's library by climbing a twisting run of rustic chestnut stairs with a heavy rope banister. The white plaster walls illuminated the tower room's approach. Crafted entirely from golden birch, it held over one thousand volumes. A chandelier of antler arms woven with large crystal drops hung suspended from the center of the box-beam coffered ceiling, and beneath, a round tilt-top table, also in birch, supported maps and atlases, natural history, and color-plate books from Nuremberg.

Before George entered the library, Johnny pulled him aside, and they stepped into a private room opposite. *He expects me to go all to pieces,* George thought. He picked through a stack of *The London Magazine* and rested on a cover essay, "Autobiographies of Friends: A Unique Genre."

"I overheard you earlier on the phone," Johnny said.

And what of it? The hardened journalist is astonished, George concluded. *He knows well enough that I'm not paying any attention to him.*

"I remain one step removed from the gossip. Furthermore, I am never in the room. I bid by phone. It is a highly unregulated industry."

"You can't be serious."

"You're blowing it all out of proportion."

"Perhaps I know you better than you think."

"When an august twenty years old, Johnny, I learned early on that art, really great art, rarely stays in one place longer than a year. Art hates to be oppressed. It lives a nomadic existence."

"So in your world, George, there's 'everyone' and then the 'educated elite'?"

"An art collection is built upon legitimate and illegitimate means. The impoverished aristocracy, who sell their family heirlooms to the nouveau riche, with tens of millions to spend, and in the middle, the wily dealers."

"Stop being blasé." Johnny shoved his hands into his pockets and drew the distance between their faces to where their eyes had no escape but to see. "Are you a dealer or art adviser?"

"An art adviser tells you what to buy and where to find it. I'm more interested in the mysteries of a masterpiece."

"What in God's name is going on, George? No, I get it. There's a plethora of thieves in the form of experts and connoisseurs."

"When is life not a balance between horror and awe?"

Johnny gave him a sidelong glance.

"Jesus, George, enough. And now you're the tight-lipped elderly bachelor in a Berlin apartment, sitting on a hoard."

"There's a psychology to art collecting. If I'm interested in treasures, it's of a more ethereal nature."

"This is desperately serious. Don't dribble on about delicate and difficult negotiations as if it were a hobby, the sentimental kitsch of the art world."

For a while they were silent. A faint chill traveled down George's spine.

"Van Eyck acted as a spy," he said.

"All significant art has been rescued by a double agent, censored, damaged, looted in three different wars, ransomed, and used in diplomacy."

"There's always somebody else with a closet." George looked away. He admired a pair of sixties Swedish brass sconces with cut-glass shades. *Your first thoughts aren't always your best*, he thought. In his estimation, the house itself was in no way remarkable, but its interior decorations were not only numerous but of the highest quality. Because of the mismatch between the size of Struthan Beag and the degree of finery, he speculated about the lives of Ian and his family. "Besides, I haven't told you the half of it yet."

Johnny said nothing because he had nothing to say. That was, in effect, the end of their conversation before they joined those gathered.

George watched Sybil pause, survey the room, and stride over to a glass cabinet with brass knobs. She opened a well-remembered first volume with a marbled spine and corners of leather.

"When Alexandria was ransacked, a half-million papyrus rolls went up in flames," George said. "Seventy thousand copies of the Hebrew Bible drafted by both men and women."

"Brownies run off if they see someone reading the Bible," Owen said.

"Pic or it didn't happen," Ruby teased. She sat beside him on curly gray sheepskins strewn on the wide board floor, nearest the spruce tree hung sparsely with green and indigo glass balls and topped by a small silver star.

George had tired of narrative conventions and peculiar metaphors long ago. *Archie threatened to bring an end to my way of life*, he thought. *He elongated Margot's childhood and abbreviated her confidence.*

"Ava, does your interview include women my age?" Ruby asked. She thanked a server and selected a sugar cookie Star of David from the silver tray.

"It does."

"Everyone is so spoiled and entitled and thinks they deserve the perfect partner and the perfect life. Millennials, like me, break up over nothing."

I hope she marries somebody with money, George thought. *Cultured, traveled—one of us.*

"With one thousand pictures a day from morning till night and fake edited photos confusing your goals," Johnny said, "who isn't concerned about superficial things?"

"I catch myself looking up in a crowd," Ruby said, the front of her shirt covered with confectioners' sugar, "while hoping to meet someone the old-fashioned way, by accident, and the rest are busy with their phones. How depressing."

"And I'd come to paint in a town, at your age, in my post-hippie America, and be living with a girl I picked up there."

"I didn't know you painted."

Anna had interrupted Johnny, George thought, mildly exasperated by her.

"I don't anymore. But when I painted, I painted with doglike devotion until the next thing came along."

"Collecting pearls in Indra's net." Ava smiled. "With no desire for fame?"

"And limited resourcefulness," he said. "Then I discovered the theater and became increasingly skilled at formulating illusions from baseless places."

"Youth, and the inexhaustible fields of freedom." Max leaned back into the deep cushion. "I can see you in an enormous beat-up Western hat."

"But we aren't twenty anymore," George said, cutting him off.

"What a risk to take, living with unmade beds!"

"Grow older and prostitute your ideals." Sybil practically sang it, rich in tone. "They are not strange words to hear."

"What I get from the millennials I interview, Ruby, is, 'We are the most isolated and miserable lot in history.' Or, 'We are all screwed because of the hook-up culture.' Or that 'the world has gotten *so weird*.'"

"What was considered random conservation with someone is considered weird," Ruby echoed. Her cheeks were burned from the sun's reflection off the snow the past week. "We're fucking doomed."

In the overheated library, Onyx, Rye, and Wren slept as if drugged.

"The extreme ideological siloing has made matters far worse," Lisbet said.

"The two biggest complaints that I hear from women in general are 'He is never there for me,' and 'There isn't enough intimacy.'"

"When anyone dismisses another's feelings, they make a terrible mistake," Lisbet added.

"You need no one's help, Ruby, to have faith in yourself," Ava said.

Margot's perpetually short on faith, George thought. *She has a strange self-awareness of herself.*

Robbie sat on the piano bench, tinkering. "If you don't know happiness, what have you got?"

Margot never says a word these days. George had sunk deeper still within his own reveries. *Except to tell me to shut my trap, and that I'm "uncommunicative," and to complain about my worldly wisdom and distinguished little parties and my hackneyed quotations—I did eat little at lunch, but I'm not hiding in my "safe place." My daughter hasn't had consistent character development.* George had convinced himself of this fact ages past. *Life exists in books, and imagination lives at night. Margot's episodic influence is so disruptive. Ruby refuses to line up to conventional comparisons.*

Robbie planted his leather boots on the slate hearth, set his shoulder to the fire, and began singing a ballad. The cuffs of his pants were frayed, but he wore a gray silk ascot.

Will lifted an embossed volume of *Treasure Island* off the shelf, and in so doing, fragments of the burgundy leather spine fell to the waxed floor. He slid the rolling library ladder back into position, then handed George an original 1653 copy of *The Compleat Angler* by Izaak Walton.

An ice-laden branch tapped against the windowpane. The evening was late. Rye hadn't stirred from the fire-bath he now dozed in. His bronze-flecked coat glistened in the dark, dense interior of the room.

"Did you hear that?" Owen asked. "The owl screech?"

"Aye," Sybil said.

Nobody was going outside.

"If the owl hoots at night, expect fair weather."

"Flower-Face," Robbie said. "The Welsh call her Blodeuwedd. From the flowers of broom, oak, and meadowsweet, two magicians brought forth a beautiful maiden. Harassed and despised because of her wrongs, she spent her days in the dark as the old white woman of the night."

"Of course she's an old white crone," Ava said.

"What was her crime?" Ruby asked.

The house creaked, holding its own against the fierce, howling wind that set upon the winter night.

"Had an affair and tried to kill her husband."

Max affected a yawn. "Just that?"

"No tale of a man turned into a bear for having an affair?" Ruby asked.

"Plenty," Ava answered. "Man wants to penetrate a woman's maternal universe so that he can complete his paradise—Jean Markale."

"I derive all my warmth and life from my wife," Max said.

"Until the 1950s, people nailed owls on barn doors to ward off evil," Owen said. "The owl canvases the wood for a perfectly sized tree cavity. How do we differ? We search for a mate and a dwelling, some of us living rent-free; then, with our fate sealed, we relax, congratulate ourselves on how smart we've been, only to find out that life didn't turn out as we expected."

"Two owls hunt by day," Sybil said. "The barn and the tawny owl survived the persecution."

"I'll meditate, Ava, about whether we ever stopped on a hill and picked wildflowers together on Hopper's Island," Margot said.

"And if we did, could we change ourselves into birds?"

"Did we have two wolf cubs or one?"

"At best, my mother's attitude to her suitors remains ill-defined."

"What conveyed our mothers' innermost dreams?"

"I ask women what they love above all else," Ava said. "When completed, I will have traveled across the twelve months, and who knows how many states. Women want independence. To be respected both day and night."

"Edwina sat at the center of her world, weaving her own entanglements."

"Violet continues to think and organize her life along different lines than most."

"This library is full of ghosts, literary ones," Anna said.

"My taste skews toward a good generational novel," Max said. "And then there's the classic *Fahrenheit 451*, where books were banned and only a few people remember them."

Wren remained on watch, positioned by the window, wary of the fearsome night wind lashing the frame of Struthan Beag.

"By the sound of it, we're shipmates on a schooner stuck in irons, the sails ripping free from the wooden masts and thrashing violently overhead," Owen said.

"The runaway ship." Johnny glanced at a wooden board displaying useful knots tied in cotton rope, grouped by construction and tying method. "*Fashionable Happenstance*. Summer 1986. I worked at Truro and captained a yawl that, though headed to Turks and Caicos, ended up in Antigua."

"I thought that one was called *The Pisces*?" George asked.

"No, you're confusing that summer saga with *Table for Two*. The year I successfully commandeered an heiress into hiding in Nevis."

"Swashbuckling." Anna stirred in her seat. "If you had lain an owl feather beside that sleeping heiress, you would have known why she went into hiding." She took his hand. "My sister wasn't a virgin at eighteen."

"Love makes fools of all of us," Lisbet said.

"Ovid describes the crow as feeling henpecked by the owl," George said. "I would say 'eating crow.'"

And again his eyes rested on Ruby, and then on William. *The lousy bastard*, he thought, *when will he admit I've done well by life? And I'm feeling benevolent now.*

"Fine game and fine whisky," Robbie said. "The missus and I thank you."

The party dissolved with little resistance, weaving through Struthan Beag, the couples' arms linked, entering rooms where they found their beds turned down in greeting, the fires burning.

It was past midnight. Margot brushed honey and whisky cake crumbs from the front of her robe. Abreast of the stone counter, a crescent moon barely illuminated Struthan Beag's shiplap pantry.

"A crescent moon can either wax or wane." A slippered Will stood beside her. "Where is our moon tonight, Margot, giving or taking?"

"Remembering and giving us Ava," she said, her voice as light as gossamer.

"Wax on. Cut me a big slice to match yours."

CHAPTER THIRTY-TWO

The Fruit of the Tree

*E*ach morning, I go down to the sea. While there, sometimes I think about the Zen masters, the masters of wood, the masters of words, the masters of marvels, all the many masters that claimed my attention. I cannot quite remember all of their names but become convinced nonetheless that to master even a day fully lived, let alone a true friendship, keeps the world in balance. I see my impatience and lack of understanding too. Fishing boats in the bay are anchored till they float away. The wind dropped when the sun was on my face, and this family asked me to be the fire at their center.

The walls are round at Otyrburn. All sound echoes back. It is a word and thought basket that this party moves through, debating cultural revolutions and good design, heydays, and gentrification, a *developed reputation. I'm the gray-mare hobo blowing the conch from the edge of the shore.*

Owen drove the winding dirt road home from the lodge beneath the moonlight. There were power cuts, but his reach of the world survived the worst. The roof had been pulled off his farm shed; the last stretch of his drive impassable, he stopped the truck and dragged a dead limb to the side of the road. The old house, his deep bed, heedful of the dust on the surface of his desk—all of it served as a reminder he'd returned to his rightful place. He read her note.

> *Owen—*
> *You call me your "soul keeper." Maybe we shouldn't trust everything we hear. Perhaps two heavies make a tanker ship, not a day sailor, and we'll end up among those people muttering to themselves. Forgive my sloppy writing, but I sleep as I write. I do love you, and always will.*
>
> *—Margot*

In winter's dry heat, the split-oak panel moved freely over the door jamb, and barefoot, he walked over the cold, sharp-edged river stone, his mind racked by the ambiguity of her words. *Central Park, townhouses, eccentric colleagues*, he thought, *and my simple projects for the home. I know—I'll take out my pocketknife and make her a cheese dome with an oiled birch handle.* In a tangle of dormant elderberry bushes sat an owl, low to the ground, blending into the thicket. But the birder missed it.

The paired candles burned on an oval side table in the drawing room at Struthan Beag where Johnny and George had stayed behind after the party retired. It was as though Johnny had never seen him before in his entire life. What had happened to alter the steady course of his life? George had taken pains to be on good terms with nearly everyone. Granted, he said the usual things, and people accepted his compliments.

"George, do you have something more to tell me?"

It was obvious his nerve was shaken.

"If I get any more flak from the press."

"Note duly taken. Fess up."

"Come off it. Of my quest to bring life to the museum, and for that they've had me suspended, without pay. My off-time activity involves museum business, Johnny; it always does."

"If you need anything, ask."

George broke the meditative silence that ensued. His foot rested on the top of an old steamer trunk.

"It's Margot and Owen that's troubling me."

"You're not going to tell her what to think."

"He's refreshingly simple. I'll give him that," George said.

"You think there's nothing to him, but it doesn't matter what you think."

Johnny moved to the window. The moonlight allowed him to make out the rectangular reflecting pool where Ian had mentioned swans swam in season. He fancied the dry garden in a profusion of perennials and bulbs, full of butterflies.

George winced. "People, even our closest friends, use the misfortune of others as collateral."

Johnny lifted a book off the shelf, *The Poetry of Pablo Neruda.* He'd bought a copy for them both years ago. "The lines between right and wrong melt like an ice cube in a glass of whisky."

"Damnation, we should get depressed more often."

"Was I ever with her?" George asked. "I haven't the haziest notion."

"Possibility sustains a vision for decades, but that doesn't mean it's the right one. Get some shut-eye, George."

A lazy day unrolled with books, and splinter groups riding the grounds at Otyrburn. William "lost" the morning newspaper. The reception was so poor at the house, the majority of phones had been switched off in frustration. Max suggested they hire a tarot reader for the afternoon. There were no takers.

George rearranged the porcelain bird figurines on the mantel, one on either side of a pair of small, gilded bud vases, each holding a branch of coral, white, and red, respectively. He stood for a moment, then placed them back in their original positions.

Lisbet, seated sideways in an armless rust velvet chair, fiddled with the decorative tassel hanging off the scrolled back corner. "It's better the way you had it, George."

Ruby broke her concentration before adding the one hundredth border piece to the veteran puzzle solver's one-thousand-piece California Desert.

"There should be a grade school course preparing a kid to be a cultural theorist," Sybil said over afternoon tea.

George had forged one of Mother's checks, Will thought, *his sophomore year in high school. How upset everyone was. How unlike George—said he owed a friend for tickets to a concert.*

"As far as we travel, we always end up at the same place, the sea," Margot said.

"Seems appropriate that if God were to tease us into a romance, he'd do it at the beach." Will stood to take a plate of caramel shortbread from Grace's hands.

"Life is a most beastly madness," George said.

"Life is akin to hopscotch," William countered. "A novelist enters the Met, stares at Magritte's *The Son of Man*, and sees a motif to justify writing three hundred and fourteen pages, transposing the bowler hat into a desire for unabashed freedom in lovemaking."

"It's called *bricolage* when an artist makes things out of scraps that become a whole," Margot said. She heard a door slam.

Ava's taxi had parked in the drive for a brief goodbye. She handed Ruby a pair of deerskin moccasins, and Margot, goat-milk caramel candy. Ruby had a summer invite to join Ava on her cross-country investigation into the lives of women. *First stop in June, a lobster, corn, and clam bake on the beach in Maine*, she thought as Margot saw her out. It was cold and starting to rain; they pulled up their hoods.

"The house seemed so full of people, yet I saw myself reflected," Ava said; the cab's engine was running, her thoughts chasing. *What would I want our sisterly love to do? Make the road less lonely.* "Old friends of yours, even friends of my grandparents, and my father, distant relatives."

Margot shivered in the wind. "What I didn't know about my past became an almost deeply religious part of me."

"And so for me, something that I fortified against attack."

Margot pointed out the mud nest of a house martin on a beam overhead in the portico.

"What was a moonscape now has definition." She smiled.

"Weather has dominated my life wherever I've lived. Ruby is the best in you and me—the incoming tide."

Margot handed Ava a small brass compass.

"It was Archie's. Maybe it will point beyond all that Archie swerved to avoid."

CHAPTER THIRTY-THREE

Blowback

*L*ose your heart and find it again, in a celebration of sexuality and the divine. Arousal is beyond the limits of the conceivable. A petal on the page, pressed between the pages, a picture of your face on the pillow.

I swam on Hopper's Island as a teen with one eye on the lifeguard. Together, we asked a million questions of the universe, and went back for more. Fitz grew old, when not all of us teens were so lucky in 1968. He'd seen 2001: Space Odyssey after dropping acid. And once he changed a flat tire, in his slippers and his bathrobe (the folks were asleep; his brother had asked him for a ride to catch the ferry) and didn't notice that the spare was flat, too, until after he'd lowered the jack. Like a nameless mile, he didn't complain. Sometimes all that remains at the foot of a hill is unearthly music and mysterious light. He *honestly cared. I honestly loved him. If forced to take a vow of silence that lasts ten years—improvise.*

PERTHSHIRE, DECEMBER 31, 2018

Filled with what he thought was a healthy proper resentment, in the silence, George dried his face after showering, splashing Vetiver, and parted his silver hair on the left with a fine-toothed comb. *Our large ivory muslin embroidered sheets were part of the inheritance; my grandmother's white-and-gold Viennese tea set; Archie's stag antlers in the entrance hall at Otyrburn*, he thought. He glanced in the mirror and continued.

"It goes beyond all decency, Margot, but I won't tell you what to think."

"We have party guests to think of."

His left eye twitched in pain. He'd been jumpy all week.

"And we will not let them down."

Swallows moved, their rhythmic calls echoing through the foothills.

"We fail to connect in some of the most profound ways imaginable."

Wrapped in her robe, she folded her arms at the window. She held the edge of her index finger against her lower lip, not turning from the glass pane, highlighted by the rising sun.

"The dagger tucked in the cuff of his sock is more impressive than he."

"Don't start pontificating, George. You could attend an auto-da-fé and eat a sandwich at the same time."

"Rich. I see Owen's put some spring back in the old mattress. What is the logic here? Why aren't you stronger?" During the debacle, he had a thousand questions. "You sound like a shrew.

What about the night your high school chum asked if he could bring a guest to dinner, and it turned out to be the Black Widow?"

"I've loved Owen since I was sixteen."

Her insouciance, he thought. *I must be dreaming.*

"Men and women are collaborators, not adversaries." George noted his nails were atypically unseemly, gnawed, and imperfect. Her behavior over the past months had incensed him to distraction.

"When everybody leaves, we'll finish our discussion privately. What about Ruby?"

"She'll love us both regardless."

The bedroom was a mess—nevertheless, she persisted. "Let's try to hurt each other as little as possible," he said.

Margot bolted to town after their agreement. The cooks were short on coffee. She ran into the bank. The safe deposit box held an onyx high school ring, a copy of the deed to the property, Edwina's and Alistair's birth certificates (both births were "checked" legitimate) and wedding certificate, and a stack of letters. Those that Owen, at seventeen, had addressed to Margot and Edwina hadn't posted. And one from Rhona MacGregor addressed to Archie Reid, dated December 1972. She stuffed the contents into her purse and left. The house needed cleaning on "First Footing" day; neglecting a messy house on New Year's Eve in Scotland brings misfortune to the occupants.

"Yes, that's right," Margot said, confirming the evening's menu with Agatha and Grace, "baked brown trout, and venison. We'll do a ravioli, and roasted baby artichokes with rosemary, and Ruby's made banana and hazelnut tartlets for dessert."

"What about the love apple soup with claret?" Grace asked, brushing flour off her white apron as she placed a wisp of loose graying hair off her welcoming face.

"Keep it. And for an opener, let's begin with the carpaccio platter with beetroot and horseradish relish you suggested. And a platter of your Finnan haddie as well."

"And lunch?"

"Spelt ribbons with oven-dried tomatoes, tarragon, and feta."

Sybil had entered the kitchen through the far end of the exotic pantry, passing tinned sardine filets and bottled anchovies, three types of sea salt, bags of pistachios, and boxes of dates, and having observed that a well-stocked larder is a splendid thing, she'd paused to jot down "Frank Cooper's Vintage Oxford Marmalade," coarse cut, and "Colman's of Norwich, Original English Mustard," double-superfine mustard powder.

A place for everything, and everything in its place—Otyrburn is like a miniature museum, she thought. *George probably has the inventory cross-referenced.*

"George knows," Margot said.

"How long has he known?"

"Since early morning." Margot, distraught, poured her full cup of freshly brewed tea into the dishwasher. She winced. "Celts aren't interested in dogma."

Sybil sat her down and reheated the kettle. *Margot could drag her feet to slow the inevitable conclusion down, but do no more.*

"You lost me."

"The bride in the *Song of Songs* is black," Margot said.

"And?"

"The earth goddess is 'the veiled one.' A black shadow holds what you want to see or keep hidden."

"What did you tell George?"

"Not much. We were rather unmistakably civilized. Owen will deal with the situation. He isn't afraid of the dark."

"He smells of cedarwood."

"He's an on-call firefighter."

"Does Owen know? In a remote, tucked-away corner, stones fly fast."

"George is all decorum and fastidious reason."

"Why did you marry him?"

"Stability. He was kind and mad about me. Archie liked him." Margot fiddled with the ends of her auburn hair. "We fell in love. I thought no one in the world could be so optimistic and considerate. And I, so grown-up."

"In the fashion of the moment."

"He had just won a contested seat on the city council," Margot said.

"That's right. And he not yet thirty." Sybil paced. *Women and men alike told the story of their world in interior monologue.* "The Isabella Stewart Gardner Museum connection was a nice piece of history. Though Newport mansions and a pet lion on a leash on Beacon Street simply isn't you."

"It never was."

"You married the last of the Edwardians."

"I saw quickly how self-contained he was." Margot exhaled. "Then I gave him thoughts and experiences I thought he had."

"George has a way of framing things that I would find difficult to cope with."

"We'll 'ring 2019 in with aplomb.'"

"Now I'm fascinated."

This old house is dear to her, Sybil thought.

"I thought I had Owen out of my system. And made the mistake of making Ruby the one happiness in my life."

The day trailed into late afternoon, with spitting rain, more like hail. What the meteorologist deemed a "wintry mix." The piper arrived at 5:00 p.m. Surprised to find a house of amiable, kitted-out guests, he strolled, warming his pipes, past figures clad in Gordon Dress, Blair Atholl, and Bannockbane Silver.

"The flying angel rode the high-wire over Saint Mark's this morning," William said, arrested by the sight of Lisbet pinning her kilt and her hair for the New Year, upstairs in the Lilac Room.

"I don't miss the crowd in Venice one bit."

She wore her 'il capodanno,' or New Year's underwear, he thought, *the new red panties and bra she swears repel the evil eye. Worn snugly—how lovely—the powerful forces of good luck amplified in the coming year.*

Her Neapolitan purge included throwing out all old underwear, alongside any broken appliances, damaged dishes, or furniture. For the month of December, the whole of Italy becomes a panorama of window dressings displaying red undergarments.

"The best humor in life is telling the truth," he said.

Pleasure and sensuality were in the air, though the earth beyond lay frozen.

The room was cold. Owen threw another log on his fire, and it tumbled into place. The more time he spent with her, the more he saw truths stare him in the face. *I could always identify that mysterious tree in the wood,* he thought. The wind freshened, another storm burst in the distance. They still shared an intimacy that had them whispering without realizing it. He got spruced up while Rye waited at the door.

Owen turned over the engine and blasted the heat. The tires sputtered in the muddy, wet snow as they took the corner at the gate. Swags of tiny white lights swayed from the clipped yew, illuminating Otyrburn with a meteor shower, and in each window, a candle burned. The smoke rose from the fore and aft chimneys. As his boot heels scraped over the shoveled path, the piper's notes within worked over an intricate bar from "Heilan Laddie."

Opening the kitchen door, he found Margot on the other side, as though she had kept vigil, and the two were alone. Between the piper's breaks, animated voices could be heard coming from the Blue Room, where the party was in full swing.

"I'm not replying to your last message," he said, "the one where you had me in the role of Prufrock, the sneaky trickster. T. S. Eliot's coward in the fog talks too much. 'I grow old. I grow old. I shall wear the bottoms of my trousers rolled.' Hamlet is indecisive like Prufrock—I get where I'm going. And you know that."

"Then you don't need to ask for directions."

"Anyway, I visited with Mother, and she's fit to be tied." His voice was lowered over the background noise in the kitchen. "Says she met Adela Reid at a party, both well on in pregnancy in early spring 1973, at some Edinburgh shindig for the Knights of the Green Garter or any one of her devotional regalia."

"So we met in the womb and made love after," Margot said.

"Sing out if you need something."

"And George is aware," she added.

"He's *gaun his dinger* over it, has he now? He's clanking his spurs."

"No, remarkably civil."

"That clears it up for me. A hill is just as long going down as it is going up."

The silver buttons on Ruby's Beatle boots jingled as she crossed the slate floor, headed in their direction, and Margot began fussing with coats in the hall closet.

"I'll keep my steel sheathed," he whispered into her ear. "No one ever tramples on his good luck." Bending near, he picked up a felt hat that rolled off the crowded shelf. "And if George has called forth his inner totem, I'll call forth my inner panda."

Decked out, Ruby rounded the corner; she'd woven a white feather into her hair after piling it into a golden nest upon her head.

"Mother, darling, your guests await." She took an overdone curtsy.

The Blue Room glowed with ivory tapers and pillars, positioned on the window ledge, veneered tabletops, and mantel, while the polished brass grates in the dueling hearths competed for attention, once again.

George chatted with Johnny at the far end of the room, appreciating his daughter's charm and the efforts of a well-organized party, as always, restored by the security of social etiquette. He flung his cigar aloofly into the fire.

"She's not a mean little business," Johnny corrected him. "Margot's been your best friend these past two decades plus."

"You know what she said: 'We have a careful blandness to our living.'"

The flickering fire at the opposite end of the well-laid table made the cut-glass spiral, and the white roses that perfumed the room mingled with the hot beeswax from a sea of candles.

CHAPTER THIRTY-FOUR

Bird's Nest

*I*n 1968, at eighteen, just after the New Year, I left Hopper's Island *for New York City. Dr. Thomas Grey was not happy about my rash decision. I was "all over the map." With a healthy dose of disrespect, I remember saying, "Wow, man," having ingested an earful of his moral ejaculations on what a comfortable life constituted. It was as if I had lost* The Art of Pie Making *and would no longer be his dependable eldest, just a weird abstract, albeit in "a profound time of change"(his own words). I told him that I appreciated his hard-won wisdom, his bittersweet bedtime stories, and his history lessons, but we each sang a song we didn't know in our search for meaning. I also added that the Edwardian beard had to go, and that he and the rest of his old-but-not-dead club could gain something from the power* *of vulnerability—that or a blank journal. Everyone who was anyone was in Greenwich Village.*

I was hanging around the Chelsea Hotel because Bob Dylan was camped out in room 225. JOMO, darling Ruby's "joy of missing out." Well, she wasn't there when he was just a freewheeling kid blowing on his harmonica, gazing out the window, barely older than I.

She has no idea who Topo Gigio was, let alone Ed Sullivan, or why, when I lived in the East Village, the ambiance alone of a lifestyle could make you high. It had felt so fucking good then to say, "all-out for originality, and goodbye to fraternities for future success." How hot the stick burns in a political hotbed of activity.

Today, the counterculture rebels live in vans, hoping to escape "trolls" by adopting the "nomad life." Their forever-childhood tiny house, surfboards, stainless-steel straws, plant-based shrimp, gluten-free pasta, wide-angle lenses, clam digs, and barbecues, may it keep Ava, Ruby, and their fellow travelers warm and safe. See the white doves fly.

"L'Chayim," Sybil saluted. It was early evening on New Year's Eve. A night of firsts, Max had enjoyed his eggplant croquettes. In Scotland, the rounds continue till nobody stands on their feet. When King George IV in 1822 had visited Edinburgh, forty-seven toasts were raised in his honor. Mark me, forty-seven.

PERTHSHIRE, DECEMBER 31, 2018

"Till we don't know if we're walking or riding a horse," Owen said. *To life, love, and loss,* he thought, *fresh water for flowers.*

"Till we couldn't pour water out of a boot with instructions on the heel," Max said, then leaned and put his hand on Owen's shoulder.

"What the hell" is always the right answer, Owen told himself and sipped his whisky, *with a walk around the block, when everything else was shushed and pushed aside, we, she and I, have become experts at emotive expressions—sadness, anger, silliness, shyness, and everything in between.*

The venison, served roasted in red wine with delicate morel mushrooms and red currant jelly, was the same stag Owen had felled on George's fall hunting party. The brown trout, buttered and herbed, ran baked aromatic juices across the platter. Lemon and goat cheese ravioli satisfied the vegetarians.

Our hostess? All her life Margot had been obliged to keep her enthusiasm at a certain pitch. The years after her mother's death, when she'd sat cross-legged in front of a color television. All that she knew faded into memories. Her teen years reading Lorca, those imprisoned and tortured for writing truth—to have risked one's life for a principle. She wore a scarlet dress that accentuated her breasts. In a land where the old crofters sat in stark houses, she recalled Owen's commitment as a teen and how he had said, "I promise."

"It's a tummelberry," he told Ruby, "like a raspberry but bigger."

Margot and I have begun the walk of a lifetime, without generations of fans to cheer us along, he thought. *I'll always be the one who broke a family.*

"We don't need a Gordon Dandy or a Slippered Contessa flaunting themselves in these hills, telling me the dish needs more salt." Robbie forked the flaky flesh of trout to overflowing.

"Sprouts, Margot?" Max mumbled, incredulous. A radish sprout dangled from his lips. "Who would want one—you can't suck it up, and you can't spit it out. You can't throw them across the room and start a good food fight."

Owen raised a toast to Robbie Burns.

"That's a lovely way to put it—'happiness is shy,'" Anna said.

"People drive around looking for a view. Cut a few trees, and there it was in your backyard all along."

"There it is, then," Margot said. "We each long to go where nothing is ordinary."

The color rising in Margot's cheeks brought Owen's mind to a halt. "I prefer the garden of the poet, not the architect," he answered Sybil, seated on his left. "If our soil becomes exhausted, we've got nothing left." He looked away from Margot's large, clear eyes, took a spontaneous deep breath, and heard George pragmatically tell Elisabetta his trending favorite line, "The city life is a marriage of consent."

"Old hamlets, old crofter's house, everything's mildewed here, and so am I," Robbie joked in an ironed shirt.

"The British are coming." George smiled.

The ivory tapers dripped, forming iced waterfalls of wax that spiraled down the silver candlesticks to pool across the banquet linen. Butter knives that belonged on butter plates slipped off. It smelled like a happy house. The purple sprouting broccoli caused a sensation, but not the clootie dumpling. The cast-iron radiators clanked, tirelessly hard at work, in the compact and worn-at-the-edges Regency manor.

Sybil watched as Lily returned from the powder room. "I passed through the kitchen, made a wrong turn. My muddy boots have made a mess of your floor—my apologies, Margot. Where do you keep the recyclables? A paper bag will do."

"The first closet on your left in the pantry."

The freckles of Lily's youth were not bleached by time, Sybil thought. She rubbed her hands together, noting the dryness of winter. *One could only take so much of this.* She worried for Margot. Owen looked trustworthy. If they were traveling on a train, she would ask him to watch her stuff. Margot looked radiant, like she had in her youth. Sybil had a sudden tenderness for her friend, for their familiarity, for their darling Ruby.

"Mom always wanted a sister," Ruby said, "and now she's got a historical period drama."

"Ava's a thought formulated in Margot's childhood and hidden in the depths of her subconscious that, at any moment, could rise to the level of consciousness," Sybil said. *Abandoned and decaying boats could be found in almost every corner of Margot's life, and now Ava's.*

"Tell that to my father," Margot said.

"Ava's a long drive north with no stops," Max said.

"Theoretically, each of your lives acted as an interlude for the other. And after a hiatus, your histories were forged," Lisbet said.

"The burgeoning playwright," Will teased.

"I had hoped to study Breton, and she hopes to visit Brittany," Ruby said. She asked Lisbet for a second helping of creamed potatoes. "Something about 'women and moral superiority,' and it being the only independent Celtic state that carried into the sixteenth century."

"Some things can only be disguised for so long—love, a sister—and neither can be invented," Lisbet said.

Lily stood in the doorway of the dining room, holding the open newspaper, one hand pointing out a photograph for the party.

"Isn't this George in the paper?" she asked at the edge of the spacious, busy room, over the clanking of silver, chuckles of laughter, and tipping of tumblers.

William, who heard her, sprang from his chair and backed her gently into the hall. "Let me have a look at that." He snapped the crease out of the page. "Nope. That's George's cousin's son, George Lowell the third."

"A remarkable likeness."

New Year's Eve, and George had, at that moment, complained to his guests about his sensitivity to noise, then rattled on about a tough week ahead of him.

"I think I'll join you at TEFAF next year, Will," he said, without reservation, as his brother returned to the table.

With that declaration, both Will and Johnny rested their knives, lifted their glances from their overstuffed plates, and locked unknowing, yet responsive eyes. The long narrative of ultimate satisfaction, which George invested in the "wishful and the good." The ambition of years had left a mark on him. "Now I will show you my latest find, such delicacy," so cagey, as though his behavior were unconscious, rather than unconscionable. The unselfishness of his prowess, rolled into a neat rendition of house-proud, and wife-proud, mutually codependent.

It is no good denying facts that stare you in the face, Johnny thought. Yet it was George, friend and also brother. *In his heart of hearts, who is he?*

"I bet my reporting life daily on easily reading the demarcation," Johnny said, eyeing George for signs of regret. "The question is, how long did Archie's abeyance from romance last on the island, and who's knocking next?"

Johnny had started his day, in the early light, with a moth-eaten blanket wrapped around his shoulders, poking through the sifting ash for a living ember. It was capable of being revived. At her grandfather's house, Ruby had floated one of her childhood toy boats in her morning bath and saw the New Year swell in salmon and lavender tones.

*For Max, there was a welcome ease to the place found in the churn-
ing goodness of an old house at work, protecting and providing for
the inhabitants. Anna had awoken on the eve of a new year, having
dreamed she slept in a barn on hay. Everything stashed beside her,
ready to travel. Ready to open an antique shop with a café that plays
1930s tea party music. It was evening, but she heard cicadas humming
on a late afternoon. That morning, the "Innkeeper" had slept with
"Saint Lillian," emptied the slop bucket in the pig yard, and tripped
when cutting through the hedgerow. It was years since he had mentioned "the child." She'd found his emptied flagon of ale in the henco-
op. Lily had never served a cold supper, nor planned too far ahead. She
had been a flower once. As the week closed, they were each intrigued,
and soothed, by Otyrburn and the window it gave them into the mis-
eries and joy that spelled their lives. Beyond the light reflections in the
panes of glass, a full moon rose.*

When the dinner plates were cleared, Will, Sybil, and Johnny rose
in unison and moved to the card table, dessert plates in hand, near
the fire at the entrance to the adjoining library, and sat together.

William stirred his eggnog with a silver spoon. "That
was close."

"I thought you put the paper in the fire?" Sybil asked.

"And have Ruby rail on me about not recycling?"

"The day my father died," Will said, "a voice I knew asked,
'Do you love Jules?'" He gave a laugh of disbelief. "Of all the art-
less phrases."

"Cleanse the doors of perception," Sybil said. "It suffices at the
worst of times and the best."

"Morrison named the Doors for Blake's line." Johnny shuffled
the deck and placed it back on the table.

"Aldous Huxley and Morrison went through the front door and out the back, far too many times," Will said.

He and Sybil had placed their feet side by side on the fender. Johnny's head bent close, not to miss a word. His hair fell over his forehead, covering half his face.

"How many monologues are told to walls?"

Carolers caroling, revelers reveling, celebratory cakes, frosting, and sprinkles. In that moment, Sybil had one perception: "John Barleycorn must die," she announced, then fussed with her hair. "Do either of you have a reefer?"

"Well, this is a pretty kettle of fish." Johnny sighed drearily.

"Huxley Lowell's paperbacks with sex scenes were behind glass," Will continued. "In the end, Dad had sex with his caretaker and told jokes. He hadn't returned to his favorite café or restored the farmhouse in Garfagnana. He had no idea how near his hour was; the last moments irrevocable, a rich funeral."

"The crowd who contented themselves with words and appearances," Sybil said. "That's who we'd never become—our parents."

"Here's to my brother, a man of the bean and the cod. Where the Lowells talk to the Cabots, and the Cabots talk only to God."

"Life has to be undefined in some way, or there's no room left for anything to happen," Johnny said.

"A life full of the springy-fullness of whole-grain bread." Sybil smiled. "Cosmonauts from the International Space Station observed currents lifting particles of sea plankton—atmospheric traces of microorganisms from the ocean—three hundred kilometers or two hundred miles away from Earth." She freshened her lipstick before a black wooden mirror, the top third of the glass painted with a bucolic lake boating scene. "And none of us had breakfast with Einstein."

"Everybody has a relationship with *Doctor Zhivago* but George." Will heaved a sigh. "That frozen room where lovers hide away with their 'what-ifs' banging on the window. Yuri understood everything at first glance."

With each pass around the room, there were fewer people remaining around the dinner table as the stragglers left and joined them.

"I can tell you how to make a pinhole camera out of a mint tin." Johnny's glance followed Margot.

"I am definitely infiltrated or contaminated by parallel dimensions. I kinda like it, actually," Will said.

Johnny finished the last of his tiramisu, in honor of the love-bird Venetians. Will threw a pear log on the fire, then another.

"What would have happened that night," he asked, his voice softened, "if I had said, 'Good evening, Javier, yes, I *do* love Jules.'"

"This is my own lie; this is my own truth," Sybil said.

"I'm already implicated," Will said. "Lunch with Heinke and *whoever* she is."

"The true and what seems to be true don't always coincide," Johnny said.

"When were you aware of George's predicament?" Sybil asked.

"The morning of the twenty-seventh at 5:30 a.m., right before my meditation."

"He'll be extradited to Italy on charges of forgery and fraud. The Italians don't take loss of art lightly." Will shook his head. "But do I give a shit?"

"I don't have any insight into why we behave the way we do," Johnny said.

"He did this thing as a kid," Will continued, "he'd cast, and as the lure would land, he would forget to put his thumb on the spool of the reel to slow it down, and it kept spinning, and the line would tangle. And he couldn't do anything and would lose his fish—cut his line—and start over again. It's called a 'bird's nest.'"

"What we stand to lose is decency and honesty." George's voice floated on the air. He and Max sat together on the green corduroy love seat, drinks in hand.

Max yawned and went to the window, only to return to George's side. He'd been drinking all night. "Those were the real women—our mothers and grandmothers. Nothing like young, tattooed tarts with phone in hand."

"You'll have to live under protection if you say that out loud."

Max studied an oil on board that depicted two fishermen and a mermaid, signed M. R., 1996. He did the math, with difficulty. She was twenty-three.

"Nineteen minutes," Robbie called, "then it's out with the old and in with the new. To Margot, 'I am not led, I lead'—one of the twenty-five greatest clans known to man."

"And to the Donnachaidh chiefs who refused to 'clear' their fellow clansmen for mere profit made from sheep," Owen added. "Where has it left us? A castle is fragile, and tourism is fickle."

"There's nowt so queer as folk."

By moonlight, pressed against the pane, Ruby remarked she could make out the clipped box forms marking the wide entrance steps leading down into An Gàrradh. Who needed teletransport when there was music and darkness? Margot's guests sat down on a Friday and didn't notice time had flown until the following year. The party began slowly, with farewell hugs and kisses, extricating themselves from the deep well of down- and wool-wrapped cushions.

Anna knotted her patterned scarf. "A good holiday brings something unusual."

"The wisdom of the hazel-blessed, as my dear departed mum liked to say, is a trip to the river without leaving home." And with that, Robbie tipped his hat at the door.

Before bed, what Margot read in Owen's letters was expected, the sweet love song of a teenager. What she read in Rhona's letter was another matter. Rhona MacGregor was pregnant.

She had written to Archie in 1972, informing him that the baby was his and the due date in August. It would not be acknowledged thus by her, but she did, in earnest, desire that he should be privy, and respect her wishes, and leave it at that. Their own tryst in midlife loneliness—what had Rhona called it? "An interlude of reckless abandon."

CHAPTER THIRTY-FIVE

County Fair

*T*here are fireflies in the summer, and bears that dance on two legs at any time of the year, especially when the berries are ripe.

John Ruskin ignored his wife, Effie Gray, on her wedding night, then imposed six years of celibacy. In the natural world, a pairing without consummation would never fly. Imagine one's home becoming an isolated location and not having any survival training. The marriage annulled, Effie went on to love and be loved and, together with the artist John Everett Millais, had eight children. Wouldn't she have liked a bird's-eye view? Or to walk with Virginia Woolf's walking stick, highlighting the remarkable workings of creative cross-pollination?

In her marriage—and this is just my opinion alone—Margot has joined the museumgoers, critiquing with George what's on the day-to-day surface. Domestic abuse plays no part in her tale, but abandonment does. George has placed the object of his affection upon a pedestal.

In a collection, works of art exist by a degree of separation, for they are indeed on view, stripped of the fluidity that brought them to life by the uninspired examination of their intent.

Funny how you just can't remember some things, and some things you can. Like the guy who sang in the morning while shaving, "She has freckles on her but she is nice." Then thought he had to explain how, in his rendition, but had two ts, not one. Naughty! He must have heard that one in the air force, one of their oft-repeated lines. Another lover who "bedded violets." Io the cow ate from a field of violets for eternity; violets and Venus, there's a good association.

I do love a man who talks sweetly to his dog, and one whose hand wraps over my back with the warmth of a woolen poncho. Men, too, are gentle, kind, and good.

From what little I've read thus far of Ava's thesis, most women understand clearly why a partner isn't right for them and know when the horizon isn't ideal. They stay out of fear, until they have no choice but to make a change.

Each woman Ava interviews is a churning ocean pushing against that which is precise and specific, looking over her shoulder with curiosity, eagerly impatient to see the story she knows intuitively springs from the sea. A woman walks through the river of peace at rest within her. Only knee-deep, she powers on anyway. See her. See her soul. Women birth life, and with that, the power to conceive other realities.

PERTHSHIRE, JANUARY 1, 2019

Guests packed their bags on New Year's Day, and Margot, bright and early, met George in the stable yard, where they'd gathered at the edge of stone-cold for privacy. *He has devoured bits of my heart,* she thought. *A friend doesn't eat your apple.*

"I know from every standpoint you've done what you believed you had to do," he said.

Margot stamped her feet to warm her toes. The wind was sharp on her face and neck.

"I love you, just not in that way."

The white vapors of their breath floated between them. He shivered. "And you don't find yours is a selfish position?"

She shaded her eyes with a ringed hand.

"Actually, no."

He had always been attracted by her reserve. Then he had control. His world was going up in smoke.

"I'll give you some space, Margot. A hiatus from the ordinary will reveal whether you're a bruised plant and he healed you."

There was a surprising stillness. She fiddled with the hem of her Aran cardigan, noting an abalone button hung by a thin thread, and zipped her coat, the news of a lifetime running through her head: she and Owen were half brother and sister.

"For Ruby's sake," he said, "no snide remarks or boisterous outbursts."

She lowered her gaze to the lawn, to the frosted outline of a stray oak leaf. George's acceptance, understandably, was the making of a jealous man who had not acknowledged himself as such. If he found her different, she was someone else. The entire valley had stretched out and ran, each loch an inkwell.

He took his leave reluctantly, perhaps with relief. Half the party had left Otyrburn early in the morning, and those who remained awaited lentils and pan-seared scallops for lunch.

Johnny and George met in the stable. The barn on a winter's morning smelled of linseed-oiled tack, a summer's worth of June hay days, and that unique horsey smell that works itself into the fiber of your being and won't let go after an hour's ride. Johnny coughed, fighting a cold.

He ran the palm of his hand slowly down the gelding's broad black nose. "When you're in love, you're somewhere beyond third person."

"An unhinged metaphysical exploration of love—so she says."

George got up and moved around the barn, rattling objects, slamming a stall door.

He has lost his head completely. When the marriage collapsed, Johnny asked himself, *what aspect of my friendship with Margot and George has influenced me to rally with one over the other?* George's prosaic ceremonies occurred without rumpus, a place for everything, and everything in its place. *Years on, he will say that none of this happened "that way"; it wasn't his true self.*

"It's a moment of proving, George, one way or another."

"I used utilitarian logic when all else failed."

Not from true altruism but self-preservation, Johnny thought.

They rode until midmorning.

Sybil and Margot worked alone, setting the table. George had removed the orchard harvest vinyl-coated tablecloth, a relic of Edwina's, and replaced it with linen. Will and Lisbet had flown on the early bird, so that made six for lunch.

"You can't bemoan humdrum anymore," Sybil said, not impressed, this late in the game, by George's attempt to understand and accept. He worked events to his advantage. "George is a charismatic and committed conversationalist, though I wouldn't take him at his word. I don't trust him."

They sat down at noon. The Mowbrays, Johnny, and Anna all had a 4:00 p.m. flight.

"Eat lentils on New Year's Day in Italy and welcome posterity. William taught us that maxim," George said.

Sybil watched George, guarding what he knew and what he didn't want to reveal, spreading his monogrammed linen carefully on his lap, one scrolling ebony *R* for *Reid* encircled by sprigs of heather.

"Lentils do resemble little coins," Margot said.

"Give me a double scoop," Max said.

"I smell superstition ad nauseam." Sybil shrugged with visceral disdain. "I don't know what I enjoyed the most, Robbie, the bonfire, or the Highland pony."

"In Catholicism, ghosts are freed on saints' days," Anna said.

Sybil followed the glow in her face as it rose to match her golden dress. Anna was aware of the fundamentals of others and incapable of using the insight against them.

"You don't believe that?" Johnny asked.

"Perhaps."

"Then each day's a stream of feasts," Max said, "and specters ubiquitous."

Margot had neglected to feed Wren and rose to do so.

"A Rodgers and Hammerstein hinterland musical in the spring." Max nodded at George.

"Vlad the Impaler skewered some eighty thousand enemies on poles in Romania." Johnny sliced a scallop. "Then he picnicked beside corpses, dipping his bread in his victim's blood."

"Sustainable farming," Max said.

"What to do with heretics and unchaste women," Anna said.

Johnny's silver hoop earring glimmered.

"He's considered a hero. The Romanian tourism board, despite local opposition, is in full swing on a 'vampire tourism' campaign."

"How to ruin the last medieval landscape in Europe," Max said.

"Prince Charles is a descendant of Vlad Tepes. We'll rent one of his restored farmhouses in Viscri."

"Then George won't have to worry about 'barbarians,'" Sybil said, and then thought, *He'll probably flee to Malta.*

"They drive donkey carts," he said. "Why begrudge them an upgrade to Teslas and television?"

"Gutsy business, poltergeists, and bloodletters," Max said, "gothic demons, shapeshifters, and vampires."

"Heathcliff and Catherine are closet vampires," Margot said.

"In the tenth grade, I tried to burn my copy of *Wuthering Heights*," Max said. He rose and filled the water pitcher at the farmhouse sink.

"Queen Victoria spent eighteen years with John Brown." Anna, glancing at the party, sipped peppermint tea in porcelain, a thistle painted on the bowl of her cup, her pinky extended. "Almost as long as her marriage to Albert. A royal love affair spanned social divides between an aristocrat and the stableman-cum-gardener."

She reached for a second barley scone and began spreading it with thick folds of freshly churned butter.

"Owen's the hero with a thousand faces," George said matter-of-factly, and yet his grimace betrayed his vulnerability.

"I admire anyone who's full of initiative," Max said. "And you, George, must find it convenient having someone around in a pinch."

Sybil suppressed amusement.

"I'm still reading the account of their love affair." Anna flashed her brown eyes, and a piece of Sybil admired her exuberance. "I brought it with me. Johnny and I toured Balmoral while you played poker earlier in the week. I have a complete gallery of postcards. Victoria carried a leather case in her pocket with a collection of John Brown photos, including a colored photograph in profile—and a lock of his hair. And when she died, she asked that his pocket-handkerchief rest on her body." She tightened the back on the post of the aquamarine earring dangling from her left earlobe. "I envy you, Margot, to live in such natural splendor."

"Red squirrels are allowed in Balmoral." Johnny gave a coded nod to Sybil. "Thank the Prince of Wales."

"The queen bumblebee uses old vole and mouse nests, which she covers with moss," Sybil said.

"Sybil's ledger," George called, closing the kitchen door, having let Wren out.

"I'll give it to the Scots for having a perpetual oomph," Max said. "They've got firecrackers, and they know how to use 'em."

"I'll give the place that," Anna agreed. "But leave out the hunting, beef, whisky, and feats of overt manliness."

Sybil, eventually, stopped kicking Margot's ankle under the table, lost in her hunt for a golden raisin in the middle of her scone.

"Johnny snapped a photo of me," Anna said, "in front of the full-size bronze statue Victoria erected at Balmoral after John's death."

"Mrs. Mowbray would like a landscape gardener," Max said, enjoying his wine, his cheeks flushed. "Maybe one day, Owen can be persuaded to make a bed of roses for you, Sybil. What was that Highland maxim that he kept repeating all week?"

George had opened his phone and checked the departure schedules of his guests—still on time. "It goes like this: 'Life is merely froth and bubble, two things stand-alone. Kindness in another's trouble, courage in one's own.'"

"Those Victorians, though, what a twisted bunch," Max said squarely. He barely squeezed in forkfuls. "They photographed the dead. Propped the head of the household at the table, pinned his eyes open, colored his cheeks, then captured a memento for that locket of yours, Anna."

"Max!" Sybil shouted. "When do you ever shut up?"

"Look at the time."

George set down his coffee and, with a coolly detached friendliness, pushed back his chair, cringing as the wooden legs screeched across the slate. He wore his sweater-vest, an Argyll tie, and sports coat—it was New Year's Day. He grabbed his keys, and on his cue, the gang rose, ready to be driven to the airport.

CHAPTER THIRTY-SIX

Hazel

*T*he full moon flooded its brim in Camden, where Ava had finished her potato seed order. Something she would have already accomplished if not for the "meet-and-greet" family event of a lifetime in the Highlands. The new "delicious and diminutive" French Charlotte was sold out in the five-pound, but she could secure a two-pound, or two, for her organic potato patch. Wise gardeners warmed their seed potatoes at room temperature for a week or more prior to planting. The sprouts would emerge from the eyes and make it far easier to expertly trim a well-cut seed piece.

Ruby was the Prairie Blue; Margot, the Dark Red Norland; Owen, the Huckleberry Gold; and George, the King Harry. Ava, the All-Blue, stored well if kept cool and dark.

Ava had texted: I'm an aunt! *Ruby was boxing some of "Nana's" dishes, outbound and labeled:* Ava Kerouac, Moose Corner, Down-Under. *When would that kid run out of amusements?*

The vast epic Reid tableau was structurally based on three essential elements: one goddess, one queen, and one mistress of the orchard. When would Ruby, Ava, and Margot switch roles? Oaths were sworn, divine curses dealt, in the name of prohibition, taboo, magic, and religion, obviously debatable, but that was the purpose.

PERTHSHIRE, JANUARY 2019

Margot sat writing warm wishes to old friends for the New Year when Sybil texted a link from the airport in London: WTF. Then a second text flew in from Ava: I hope all is well. Ruby had gone AWOL.

Later that night, when George and Margot had Otyrburn to themselves, she wanted answers. At once shocking, the Egyptian acquaintance she'd met multiple times, there was something off about him from the first. And the mysterious Doña Maria de Trujillo y Merlo, Margot doubted if the Spanish publishing heiress had ever read a newspaper.

"It will be resolved in good time," he said.

"I need more than that."

"It all started when the Rijksmuseum claimed that I owed 'damages.' As though I knew anything about twentieth-century abstract expressionist art."

"You're not even in painting."

"These landscapes with town views are mostly copies of larger ones painted by Claes Jansz." George polished his eyeglasses on the hem of his pajama shirt. "I came across one once."

"And what did you do with it?"

"The cultural chauvinism of the art world and inequity is quite remarkable."

"George!"

"All our investments are secured by the estate." He opened the top drawer of a brass-buttoned tall chest and began folding his underwear into his suitcase.

"Shut the fuck up."

"What a hothead."

"Thank you for that."

"I don't want you to worry."

The winter wind whistled through the cracked windows, a slight surge, and the crystal drops in the chandelier chimed. The first and only Valentine's card he'd handed her had a fishing lure on the cover, and the inscription said: *You're a catch!*

"You're such a Goody Two-shoes, George, seriously? You're killing me. I get it—my love affair is a diversion."

He reached for her hand. She pushed his away. The gilt frame on the bureau held a photo of toddler Ruby in a red snowsuit, her mittens dangling on a string. She held a Scandinavian wooden doll dressed in sealskin.

"Your reason has heard nature calling, saying that you're free to do what you want to do. The new garden, new home, new love, isn't that it?"

"Women are more courageous than people think."

"I'm usually working and often indisposed," he said, "but you aren't, for an instant, going to think that this is novel. You risk disaster in the name of truth, in the guise of 'I do as I will.'"

"Life is delicious, George. Excuse my cynicism, but as I age, I become less convinced it's possible to change things, to change human nature."

"And my question to you is, are you confusing your desire for independence with desire for Owen? I must admit, I once thought you were too smart to do such a stupid thing."

"Stupid!"

"I'm leaving tomorrow, early."

"Good."

A long black cloud lifted as the moon reached its highest arc in the night sky, casting brilliant white light across the bed linens. *The lonely can see the longing of lovers that the joyful forgot*, she thought. *The lament of crickets. The silence of spiders. The moon in a nest.*

In the empty house, she lifted the AGA's heavy chrome lid, freeing the french top to blast concentrated warmth, and fixed the copper-bottomed kettle to boil. She set the timer, the whistle clogged with lime scale.

At midday, she loaded Wren in the Rover and headed out to the crofter cottage. Her head hummed with images of Victoria transcending class barriers and George behind bars. A sudden movement brought Owen and Rye to the window.

"George left early this morning. He has a few work-related issues to deal with."

"Come in; it's bitter out—Sybil sent me the link."

"She didn't."

"She did. We struck up an accord." He leaned in for a kiss, unshaven and rough around the edges. "I stargazed last night, and suddenly I found myself out there—*out there* in space. The earth seen from the cosmos turns into one big blue eye. What's the message in that? And why didn't I notice it before?"

They sat by the fire.

"That the eye of the beholder is in everything." She rubbed her hands together before the woodstove. It made a hissing sound as the pot of water on the iron lid steamed.

"Have you tasted fruit, and the world's on fire—your power undone?" he said. "I warned you."

"That's what Sybil said."

"Are you afraid to jump? I'm behind you, and the moon is already afloat."

"I know." She smelled onions cooking. He had made a stew. "It's a lot of rapid changes."

"Are you thinking of lapsing back into a marginalized sense of self?"

"No."

"When you repeatedly misfire with someone, life becomes meager fast. If you clear the wood, it grows back twice as strong."

Rye brushed against her leg, weighing his side heavy against her calf, waiting for some love, as Wren stretched out on the hide by the fire. Owen's private world hadn't changed. Margot removed Rhona's letter, in the original envelope, from her bag and set it down on the desk.

"Archie and Rhona had a brief but memorable tryst the autumn of 1972," she said.

"My beyond-reproach mother?"

"Yes, Owen, apparently, there's a reason we 'get' each other."

She picked up a purple tea towel printed with plums, eggplants, pansies, and thistle—one blackened edge had caught a flame—and she wiped a pool of water off the counter.

"Oh, hell."

He started walking between the kitchen and the sitting room, with his hands dug deep in his pockets.

"We aren't having children, cleared that hurdle—thank God. So in the end, what does it matter, considering the alternative is I never see you again?"

He wrapped his arms around her, pulling her close.

"Like poured earth—the Grecian twins, one with red hair," he said. "Go on, read me the letter."

> "When I brought the orchard ladder by, who would have known?
>
> I stopped by to pay my respects to Edwina after her mother's death, and helped myself to the portrait on the mantel of you barefoot beside your bicycle in ripped cut-offs, that summer.
>
> Tiger, tiger, burning bright. I can't possibly forget you now."
>
> —Rhona, 26th December 1972

"Burn after reading," Owen said.

"Seems 2019 ushered in the three-strike law."

"Anything beyond three is unimaginable."

All those many years ago, Rhona had slid a black-and-white portrait into the envelope intended for Archie. The summer of 1969 while he camped out at Woodstock, she had lived in a yurt at Findhorn.

"Our hippie parents," she said.

"Keep the photo. The top of the hill reveals what to do."

"You've repeated that line since you were a kid."

"In the face of obstacles, Margot, efforts are united."

"We couple like there's no tomorrow."

"Everything about us stands in defiance of the elements and renders me helpless."

The draft of fire and the spitting sea-brine had transformed them both.

"The Kabbalah teaches the 'soul of man is a miniature universe.' If it's true, one life has many stories," she said. She spied a gyroscope stashed on the bookshelf. "Live long enough, and you learn lots of secrets."

"Hold that thought. We both have a sister."

They cried. They cracked up.

"What will we do, Owen?"

"We'll shack up like teenagers and work as we've always done. The difference is we'll be together. Somehow, we see the unfamiliar in the familiar."

"Tell me about spring in the Highlands, Owen."

"Can't you wait, my impatient beauty? The cheerful poppies or the March hare?"

"All of it."

"My father found a young hare who'd tangled her foot in the netting from a hay bale out in the stable. As mad as a March hare, she struggled so to free herself that she broke her leg. He would have put her out of her misery, but I wouldn't hear of it and nursed her back to health."

"What was her name? How old were you?"

"Hazel shared my eleventh summer. A shy thing, she made herself at home in the house and, when fit, returned to the moor." He started from the bed; she pulled him back down. "I have a photo of her here somewhere."

"The March Hare and the Mad Hatter had tea."

"Something like that."

"Archie gave me a rabbit's foot for good luck. I never knew quite how I felt about that."

He rose, strolled over to his pondering desk, and rifled through a drawer containing random photos.

"She's sniffing the lip of the glass candelabra on the window ledge as if it were a heavily scented bush. She revisited that spot over and over again. Maybe the beeswax tempted her. Taken just before her release, she's steady on both hind legs, ready to peel out at thirty-five miles an hour on a straight run, and fisticuff a suitor next spring if she isn't ready for his advances."

"And the poppies?" she asked.

"We planted those lovelies in your garden. Poppies turn up wherever the soil is disturbed—the red remembrance of regeneration."

"I hope I am brave enough."

"What foolishness are you talking about now, Margot?"

Owen had lost his footing, but he had all his senses.

"You are fearless. I am not. A part of me, a significant measure, is death-struck."

"You're storm-thrashed, but storms lift—rest a bit—I have to put a log on the fire."

The everyday creak as the iron door lifted, and the log landed with a thud before the lid dropped. The wood ash shifting, the iron poker in the corner; fiddle with it once so that it won't slide. His footsteps stopped to fill two glasses of well water at the old copper farmhouse sink.

"It's deeper than that." She sighed. "I'm aware of a shifting border territory, in the background to be sure, but vividly awash in mortality. It's a place I fear. This landscape doesn't need me, but instinctively, I've come to depend on it."

"I'll do my best to understand your sadness."

She kissed him.

"If you have a story, Margot, paint it. Get into the dark side, with all the soft shafts of light, needle turns, and sad moments."

"Something in a manner reminiscent of a fifteenth-century Flemish panel. Something I can't be parted from, like the *Mona Lisa* was to da Vinci. He honed the composition of his life at the same time he worked the landscape she inhabited."

"Something new and unrecognizable will arise."

"A lot of tension builds in a relationship." She laid her head on his chest. "What if we fail?"

"Then I'll kiss you and remind you that I love you."

"Loss taught me to respect the complicated pieces more than if my life had been happy-go-lucky."

That most profound night, she thought, *the rainfall in my mouth, the rain tasting of lilies and wine. He, just seventeen.*

"It's a skilled exercise—how to be happy in one room with yourself," he said.

"Ours just got a bit more complicated."

CHAPTER THIRTY-SEVEN

Dear Rhona

S ince childhood, I'd describe Ava as self-contained, crisp, and *neat—a steeple on a seaside chapel. How does that happen? Are there origin molecules at play anywhere between us? This brings me to the topic of boyfriends, lovers. The big-ticket items in my life all boiled down to the question of risk level. The enjoyment found in my Taos condo, the gains made in my portfolio, the big boat, and the small— the risk of translating endurance, to be specific, into a stand-in for achievement. Though it does happen . . . Look at that, fifty years! Even practiced sailors have a hard time figuring out why neighboring patches of water, where the river meets the sea, move in counterintu- itive directions.*

"I saw you when I looked through the keyhole," Ava said.

(This was going to be bad.) Her eighteenth year, and she had hand-sewn twenty-seven scrap leather patches onto a pair of threadbare saddle-brown corduroys.

"You took off your dress, Mom."

His cool kisses. "I'm sorry we woke you." (There were too many ropes on the bed—I mean the ship—and anyway, he was too tied up for the reign of my free spirit.) "When did you get in from your party, sweetheart?"

"I can't ever leave you." Her hands went on her hips. "Who will take care of you?"

I was happy. My daughter was capable of genuine expression.

"I had another of my psychic tension headaches." I tightened the emerald-green tassel tie on my caftan. "Miguel gives great neck massages."

"Too many unknowns. Too many men." She rolled it like thunder. "You're too much of a hippie."

"Holy crap!" (That got me riled.) "At least I didn't furnish your world with IKEA hacks."

"You're a fucking fruitcake."

"Were you ever wild and young?" I was looking at someone I didn't know. "Do you know what it was like coming of age during the sixties? The world exploded, Ava, from the center of the color arc of the rainbow."

"Not this again: Ideals, Hope, Change, Love, Peace, Make Love Not War—see the white doves fly."

I thought I smelled Old Spice aftershave on her sweater.

"Where are we, really? I'll hazard a guess," I said. "Awake in a universe yet explored; awake in a brilliance we sleep through as though it were exchangeable."

"Why the psychic tension headaches, then?" she asked.

"I forget to take my electrolytes."

"*No. You get them because you have 'unemployed mirrors.'*" She tightened the wristband on her smartwatch. "*I read that in one of your poetry books. I think it was the guy from Jerusalem.*"

"*Yehuda Amichai.*"

"*You make the same mistakes over and over again.*"

"*Wear your hair long, wear it short, trade flowers for tattoos, eat tofu, trade plowshares—all I'm asking for is truth. Not the good son, or dutiful daughter, neither who they were meant to be. Accept no lies or infractions on your soul, Ava.*"

"*You're not getting any younger.*"

"*And maybe you're being a little revisionistic.*"

"*Only if you're lucky, Mom.*"

Perthshire, January 25, 2019

Margot answered a call from George in New York City. Barely twenty-four hours since his departure. The fire burned in the Blue Room, where she sat reading, with Wren staring at her.

"George, my actions are my own."

The phone on speaker amplified the situation. The decades of their life together echoed in the stillness of Otyrburn. *How sad, and how beautiful.* He'd cared for her when ill, and she in turn, him. Unsuspecting George holding newborn Ruby, the love they shared. She missed their house.

"It's hard to fathom the fact that the fall of our marriage is wrought by something as mundane as encountering an overgrown garden," he said.

"And your career?"

"Do you have any idea how many 'orphans' are in private collections and dealer warehouses simply because they couldn't produce a paper trail of providence back to 1970?"

"The UNESCO convention on illicit trafficking made your job easier, not more difficult."

"Is there any less beauty apparent in a questionable piece?"

"Has the distinction between legitimate and corrupt antique dealers been obscured? Or is it that you had a symbiotic relationship with your ceramic archaeologist?"

"Heinke Hessel is not a heister."

"I figured he was a slippery Dutch dealer."

"The old conflict."

"Your excellence in epistemology?" she asked.

"Knowledge and psychology are behind every interaction in life."

"Including sacked, pillaged, and plundered objects."

"Have faith."

"In the art of deception?" she asked.

"Trading in sacred objects can be a shady business."

"How many times? No, don't tell me."

Despite the poor reception, she heard him add ice to crystal, pouring a drink. The incessant pharmaceutical ads of the evening news droned in the background. He had called from the living room—*their* living room. His method of pouring drinks nagged her, three thousand miles distant.

Margot needed sunshine. "I couldn't grasp how far we had drifted, but now I do."

He had dropped his phone. "What'll I tell Ruby?"

"I'll talk to her."

"And what about the house?" he asked.

"If necessary, I'll sell a couple of acres to make ends meet. Wren needs to go out."

"I give you six months of grim gray, and then you'll be ready to entertain civilization again. And order take-out from Nobu."

Owen busily stacked logs by his back door. Checkered silver birch, its bark curled on edge, lay atop a smooth-faced quarter log. He pushed the sharp crown of his brown felt trilby to the top of his brow with a shove of his gloved hand, allowing the narrow brim to frame his face and granting his pupils a few moments to adjust.

"*Shh*," he whispered.

"What?"

"The *chack-chack-chack*, more like a cackling witch than avian. By the pear tree, the big thrush with gray head and rump and brown back—the fieldfares are helping themselves to the drops. There's a surprising ingenuity to a bird. The bird with the biggest brain doesn't live in a large flock of casual relationships but devotes his brainwork to forging enduring bonds."

"Something's stripped the crimson berries off the hawthorn at home." Margot slipped her hands into his front jeans pockets and pulled him close. "Where are you taking me?"

"To meet my mother; a visit is long overdue. She thinks I parted from this world. I told her that you found her letter to Archie."

"And?"

"She asks that you read his letters to her."

He leaned forward on the butt of his axe and kissed her slowly, and again felt the world slip away.

"She and Archie cooked on pear and applewood. How on earth did they find the liberty to do that?" he asked.

"Your mother understands emphatically that we won't be having children. That we aren't beyond redemption."

"Aye, of course, and the 'prisoners of soul' analogy, which actually placated her mood."

"She gave you a copy of Gibran as a child."

"They had a hidden cut-flower garden. God knows where."

"Is she able to talk about it?" she asked.

"Not now, maybe never."

"Has she unraveled any of her dismay?"

"My mother? Over an issue dealing with the moral molecule, not till spring will she relent—then she'll turn her grief into the soil like hot compost, fork it over, and watch the amethyst crocus bloom. There must be an acre and a half of heart-rent bulbs waiting to surface. Rhys calls it her 'tulip fever.' He won't be home when we come calling."

"Have you mentioned Ava?"

"Increments, not tidal waves."

She leaned down to the snow and picked up a pebble threaded with quartz. "Edwina left me a note with the letters in the safe deposit box."

"And I'm hearing about it now?"

"I have to continue alone on my way through some of this. Her words are like seagulls circling."

Dearest Margot,

Queen of the orchard I tried to shield you. Life had already delivered enough blows. Archie's diplomacy left little on the table. I can't speak for him, nor the catalyst that drove him, or his ring of invisibility. Man is born again through woman, he'd say. One of the blessings of being old is becoming less picayune; the details matter less. And as your lovely mother liked to say, "Life is a river of spectacular mistakes, and far greater still, barely witnessed everyday achievements, with a soupçon of existential angst."

With the letters locked away, my will and determination wouldn't drift.

Someday, someone would find the key and your story be remembered.

May your bid for freedom succeed, the birds sing sweetly, and you find your basket filled with ripened fruit at the orchard gate.

—Nana Reid, June 2000

"Who would have thought?" he said.

"We'll each write letters to everyone we love and stash them away in a safe deposit box."

"Or try to do better."

Margot entered the house to freshen, noting on his desk *Why Are We in Vietnam?* and *Black's Veterinary Dictionary.*

By midafternoon, Rhona's small, high farm became visible in the distance. The arable, stark land, set with frost, lapped into the green seawall.

"My uncles, the Johnny-come-latelies, arrived here in 1320, Welsh before that, but we won't mention the dreadful mistake on Mother's side."

"Inverness is said to be the happiest place in Scotland."

"The northern reaches are home to long-forgotten feuds that resurrect themselves overnight. Getting through one year in these parts is hard enough, but wrangling with centuries-old wrath, that's quite a different matter."

"That must be why Archie said, 'The virulence of venom can split a man's spleen.'"

"My brothers, Percy and Kyle, both got in trouble with the law. Petty infractions, which my father couldn't squash, had led inevitably to larger forays. My mother feared they'd drift down to Glasgow, and then it'd be all over." He turned the radio on, hoping for the weather report, and had no luck. "Down-to-earth people, the Glaswegians, but some crazy bastards as well, opioids, heroin, and bloodletting gangs. Percy doing just that, adding a scar to his face, bragging about being brave enough to piss in a guy's beer can."

"You never fit in."

"What did my mother get out of it? Her boys were cheering on the international soccer team as one crowd, then killing each other on Saturday afternoon. Make a choice. Make a promise. The love of her life had children by three different women."

"She got you."

The coppery fieldstones led to the weathered blue door. Rhona, her petite shoulders bent over like the crown of a tree at the sea, answered, apron in hand.

"*Tha I breagha an duigh,*" Rhona greeted Margot in her sing-song Scots voice before casting a dismissive eye.

Owen yielded to his mother's steely pleasantries.

"She said, 'It's a lovely day.' Any Highland day that doesn't produce all four weather patterns across twenty-four hours is a miracle."

"A pleasure," Margot said as they shook hesitant hands. *Adela, and Violet, but he may've loved Rhona best*, she thought.

The house smelled of cardamom and cinnamon. Was love indeed incompatible with marriage and not governed by laws?

Her sensation-seeking father, concerned consciously, or otherwise, with pushing his rebellions underground. Each love, begun in secret, refused to remain submerged and ended in the birth of a child. Archie carried "to love one's neighbor" a tad too far.

"Is he teaching you a simple way to propagate your roses?"

Rhona led the pair over the creaking floorboards beneath the low, splintered ceiling beams to the formal sitting room.

"And other useful lessons."

Margot trailed behind Rhona in the narrow hallway, smiling over her shoulder at Owen.

"A garden is all experience and mystery. It's meant to disrupt the scale of things," he said. "You appreciate that, Mother."

"If I pull the long trailing stems of rambler roses," Margot said, "scratch the stem, plunge it in the soil, secure it with a brick, wait a year, and cut the leader, I'll have a ready-made garden."

They sat together in a cozy sitting parlor papered in a blue-and-white pattern of cloud-pruned hornbeams.

"Henry Ward Beecher comes to mind." Owen sat down in one chair, then moved to another. "Flowers are the sweetest thing God ever made and forgot to put a soul into."

"As a boy, Owen kept meticulous journals, sketching dragonflies' wings because they were 'the best at flight.' Rhys and I used to joke that the volumes were his 'Codex Atlanticus'—if Leonardo had gardened, not invented. I would have sewn Owen a purple satin cape with an Arabian hood to wear on his travels, but Rhys wouldn't have it. No son of his strutting around in a pink cap and rose stockings."

"Mother, I poured a sprinkling of fantasia over my reality like sea salt over your battered cod, I grant you that."

"My mother taught me to read when I was young." Margot motioned to a wandering Wren, using the "down" command.

"Shortly after my fourth year. Each word had a special power behind it, and its own story."

"You look like your mother. We worked together on the conservation committee for the river Greeley."

"So I've heard. Though there's more of my father in me."

"At the crossroads where spring met winter today," Rhona said, "I told spring's loveliness, 'Keep on the steady.' It worked. It's thirteen-point-three Celsius, but it shouldn't be."

"Fifty-six Fahrenheit," Owen interrupted.

The two are much alike, Margot thought, *fenced in by memory, the sky clear and dark.*

"If you bump into a climate denier, have him parade past my door in his Speedo, and I'll give him something to chew on. It's above freezing in the Arctic."

"Where poppies sleep, spring is in the air."

"I was once at home in this world," Rhona said.

"We each swim childhood's river, Mum, sigh our fast-fading youth, and write poetry on the banks," Owen said.

"Archie and I met once, ten years on." Rhona placed the quilted tea cozy over her teapot. "At the house, while he orchestrated Edwina's expansion of the wood, with the planting of one thousand trees and shrubs—his gift to her. She had chosen some trees for their spring flowers, and some for their summer scent, and many for autumn color. 'I'm happy,' he said, 'my titian-haired child sings mornings, and afternoons, she plays beneath storm clouds.'"

"That's a wonderful insight, Rhona."

Rhona made a picture seated on her damask sofa, surrounded by a profusion of climbing yellow roses.

"Owen was a decent archer by the age of seven, and the weight of his bow grew with him. He'd spend two hours at longbow practice on Sunday."

"Grip is key. The correct draw is a little like holding a baby bird. Too tense, and the bow shakes. I preferred the two-fingered hold, less friction on the string, then a draw to the corner of the mouth as my anchor. I'll show you one day."

"Kept a copy of *Ivanhoe* under his pillow."

She sliced into the crumbly topping of her apple shortbread pie.

"Go carefully with a full cup."

Her eyes fixed on Margot as she handed her tea with plenty of sugar from a round, tilt-top table by the ivory-linen-draped window.

"Owen was a queer one. He used to place a spare bowstring coiled under his cap in case he met the 'white boar.' A dry string snapped, and to be 'highly strung' meant a bow in danger of snapping."

"And you'd say, 'Go ahead—keep it under your hat,' and remind me not to be pompous, like a two-bit squire patrolling an acre of wet sod, lest I end up the 'butt of the joke,' stomping off to slay my target sack. You see, Margot, a medieval archer called his targets a 'butt.'" He picked up a family photo off the old television. "That white boar was a mythic creature invented by a woodland tramp, scouting underbrush for hours on end for fairies and magic portals."

His glance rested on Margot in a way that made her blush.

"The key is fixing both eyes on the target, then letting instinct take over."

"Aye," Rhona said, putting her oar in, "sleepin' between the roots of trees. He tried to make ink out of an acorn."

"While you were busy milking a sheep. I think you got a certain amount of pleasure out of my antics."

"The fatted sheep that is entangled in the brambles leaves her wool in the bush."

Owen pushed back.

"No man ever broke his bow, but another man found a use for the string."

"And it's no wonder that the cat smells of the herring that it holds."

Margot stirred lemon honey in her second cup of tea while waiting for the skirmish to finish. A moratorium invited a welcome sustained lapse.

"Some of us chase windmills," Rhona continued. "Edwina did one better. A woman who could tan a hide in the spring, pull out a row of pink-flushed new turnips, and take up the baton of drafting a life around Alistair's whims. She aimed to show things exactly as they are, and Alistair, as if seen for the first time—and the current merry, but not too fast." She pulled a wilted blossom from a cluster of hyacinth bulbs on the windowsill. "It's a long while since I've enjoyed such a half hour with a Scots woman."

"All my life they were a blessing."

Edwina gave me my backbone, she thought, *and I made an absolute mess of my life. I valued what I feared and not my intuition.*

Rhona remained by the window, smoothing away the wrinkles with the flat of her hand from a length of her refined embroidery on linen. The juxtaposition of an embroidered pea in high relief inside a square box pleased her, and beyond, the hillocks and mountain chains, hedged in clouds.

"I wouldn't trade you for the world, Mum."

With that, by late afternoon, the firestorm had sputtered out.

"We'll be skedaddling *aff*, Mother. Call if you need anything."

Rhona placed a block of her cheese in his parting hands, with a kiss. The dulcet, creamy whey settled any acrid odors remaining in the parlor. Owen still had plans for the day.

"At her worst, she can be a mean-ass woman," he said, striding the path. "But in the end, it's a wee transgression."

"I expected worse on two fronts." She pulled up a sleeve to look at her watch and gave a parting glance at the salty wall of sea.

"There never was a high wind without some rain."

CHAPTER THIRTY-EIGHT

The Letters

*I*n total, I've attached my hand to six messages that sailed in green
and amber glass bottles. The first was launched in 1963 at Swan
Pond on Hopper's Island when I was thirteen.

> Hi, just hoping your wishes come true, each day is
> special, your friendships are warm, real, and that
> the sun sets beautifully.
> —Miss you a lot, love, Violet Grey

*I don't know whatever happened to that one. Maybe the Russians
picked it up. The night of my high school graduation beach party, I
sent the second, again from Hopper's Island. That was in 1968. We
were taking acid hits. I wrote it before I peaked—something about*

voluptuous nightingales and being stuck in life's shallow, habitual groove. I had nothing to prove, no problems. I was, at that time, made relatively of home-loving stuff. I would make my own nest from the sweetest spells.

In 1974, a message sailed off the coast of San Francisco. Then in Berkeley, hungry and yet not starved, a charming song was the sweetest thing under a roof. "Norwegian Wood" under the stars, your face, your wild eyes, perched above right and wrong. I wrote the opening to a song about unwearied lovers: "The night there was no albatross. What love, so near, so far?" You had to be there, somewhere between here and there.

The fourth time inspiration hit, I was aboard in Barbados with the barbarian. That was a verified message in a bottle, a plea for help. SOS.

The fifth floated along the rocky coast out to the sea in far northern Quebec, with my mother, Anne-Marie, on a pilgrimage to Kamouraska, where her drop of Montagnais blood originated. And a visit to family in London inspired the sixth, and the last, so far, the London Bridge drop, dedicated to Tennyson.

I need you to understand that the charm of my mission lay in its ephemeral nature. The goal wasn't to attract disciples. God no. I wrote more along the lines of one who authored a detective story with an open ending. I liked the idea of common friends engaged in a volley for no gain other than the pure joy of it. Not to buy or sell anything.

Though a little obscure, the messages weren't in the least prosaic, or temporal, nor composed of witticisms, or bon mots, but rather, I hope, euphonious when read aloud as intended. Those little Homeric heroes that put an oar in, after I put a cork in, bobbed with levity and goodwill, which is why one of them survived and reached land. Like a sum you had done nothing to earn.

You see, in the good old days, you licked a stamp, S&H Green
Stamps, and issues of LIFE or Time or Astrophysics for Amateurs
were mailed with a paper label glued on the lower-right corner of the
cover, which easily peeled off. I reused them on the backs of my holi-
day cards and seafaring messages. Hoping against all odds I'd make
contact, like ET, or the Central Intelligence Agency. (Don't blink, not
just yet; NASA said UFOs are legit—and I got a reply.) The footwork
of stardust in propulsion, we do seek magic. Complexity in nature, not
stand-alone elements. It's an open-and-shut case; living is allegorical,
transcendental, and simmered in surprise. Like a message in a bottle,
it's meant to be read and deserving of a response.

Hi Violet Grey,

Sorry it's taken me forever to reply. Forty years is a long
time. My apologies. I found your bottle in the sand while
walking my dog, at my beach cottage in Orust. That's
not far from Göteborg. In Sweden, the "wild west." It's a
good thing your bottle didn't make it through the narrow
straight into the Baltic Sea, for then the Russians might
have picked it up. I doubt you'd have received a reply.

I hosted a graduation party on the beach for my
eighteen-year-old daughter that same night. This would
have been in 1978. Yes, ten years after you dropped it in
the Atlantic. Where had it been?

By strange coincidence, my favorite wine is Chateau
Pradeaux. The cork was faded, but still recognizable.

"My heart, my nerves, the shadow and sunlight of girls and boys in love."

Your friend,
Ingalill Sjöberb
September 7, 2008

PERTHSHIRE, JANUARY 25, 2019

In the early evening hush, Margot listened as the engine sputtered. The cobbles on Victoria Street in Edinburgh would be crowded with the mad rush of last-minute shoppers before they headed to the town hall for the bard's birthday.

"Rhona gave me a fleeting smile," she said. The broken yellow lines whipped by.

"High-spirited, Mother laid her cards on the table. Now I understand her pious tirades."

"Plenty of resourcefulness, and devotion."

"One of her uncles owned the No Mend Hosiery Company in Edinburgh, 'tested, and approved by Better Fabrics Testing Bureau for highest quality.' There are no loose threads on Mother's side of the family." He moved his hand over the steering wheel. "The elder MacGregor brother owned Cleercoal—'less than a barrel of ashes to the ton.' Unlike you, I was raised in a tight ship."

"What are you concocting now, Owen?"

"I'm taking you to town to buy a dress, and a new dress needs new shoes. It's Rabbie Burns Night. Mother always said it was her favorite night of the year because she got her *one* new dress, and oh, there was nothing nicer than new shoes."

It had begun to rain, and the rain came down sideways. They had one working wiper.

"Archie rambled on about the cakes, stories, and music, and how the celebration lasted all night."

The slightest smile made her light up. *Summer sowed*, he thought, *and winter gathered.*

"As a boy, I waited on the evening because of the epic poetry reading."

Dickensian shops with wooden counters and bare floors lined the street where the "Wizard of the West Bow" had once lived, who was accused of witchcraft in 1670. A right on Candlemakers' Row was Greyfriars Kirkyard, home to the grave of Greyfriars Bobby. Owen left him a stick when he made it to town.

"Ah, tidy."

Owen sighed in appreciation, admiring Margot outfitted in green.

"Definitely the malachite, not the Antwerp blue—that's what you called it, aye? It makes your hair play brilliantly. In that dress, you give the town a reason to *blether*—and gossip they will."

"Oh, stop."

"I've held a place for you." Owen reached in his vest pocket for his pipe, then put it back. "Somewhere across the long, wintery night, I'll be Pan, and you'll be the Fairy of the Waters."

"And I'll weave our wishes into the blanket that covers us." She leaned into his face, and they rubbed noses behind the dressing curtain.

They arrived home after a long day to find the fire had left a scattering of ash from which it reignited. The dogs were where they were last. Rye had confiscated the wing chair and turned his head over his shoulder to glance at them, as one interrupted from a good novel.

"Did you get lonely, pup?"

Owen smiled, with a nod at Margot.

"We never should have gotten him those new reading glasses."

He moved to the kitchen and stood tasting his recipe with a wooden spoon, adding a pinch of nutmeg, thyme, and salt to the pot he'd left slowly roasting, keeping his eye on her, then pouring two glasses of champagne.

"I loved you from the day I met you."

"What is the order of festivities tonight?" Margot asked, then sat in the vacant linen wing chair to the left of the woodstove, one of her cheekbones rosier than the other. The beeswax tapers in the wall sconces flickered and dripped as Owen joined Rye opposite in the partner chair.

No sooner seated, he rose dramatically, rested one elbow of his moleskin shirt on the mantel, and slowly crossed his left foot over his right, to land on the toe of his brown leather shoe.

"The banquet commences at five thirty with the Address of Welcome, delivered by the chief. Shall I be Archie for you? Give me a year, and it's Rabbie Burns Night, Margot, in New York City."

"Nineteen thirty-three."

"Scotsmen today have not forgotten the immortal William Wallace or Robert the Bruce."

He looked for approval, received it, and continued in the theatrical vein.

"They will always uphold the tradition of the Tartan, with the fire and fury, which has distinguished the Scots in battle from age to age. Some people claim that a man cannot love two countries. Those who say so do not speak for Scotsmen. We love the land we left. We also love the land of our adoption. They both stand for Freedom and Liberty."

And when he had finished, Owen placed three flat fingers, his thumb and pinky tucked in, sweeping first upon his forehead, then his lips, to rest on his heart. He ended in a bow, ascending to the ground.

"My mind, my lips, and my heart."

"Lovely. That sounds like him. And then what?" she asked.

"Rousing applause, *for our father*, before 'The Road to the Isles'—'A far croonin' is pullin' me away' performed by voice and a harp, and a handful of equally sentimental songs, including 'Bonnie Dundee' and 'I Love Loch Lomond,' all before the Scottish Dance. The Malcolm sisters were the best, Alice and Wilhelmina."

"Who?"

"I had a good time with that pair at Hagget's Pond on at least one clan gathering. How they could step."

The house smelled utterly delicious.

"Aye. There'd be a few duets, without a doubt, 'Hunting Tower,' and then it was on to the poetry reciting—Rabbie Burns, 'the Ploughman Poet,' listening to 'A Man's a Man for A' That,' 'Ae Fond Kiss,' and the evening closes with an ear-haunting rendition of 'Auld Lang Syne.'" He fiddled on the sparse mantel with a fish fossil from the Devonian period, when Scotland was volcanically active, with hot springs around Aberdeen. "And by then, everybody's balling, smelling the scent of pine, and longing for the wildwood and a *wee thackit* cottage."

Rye yawned and vacated the chair.

"A place just like this." Margot rose to sit curled in Owen's lap.

"Aye, *hame o' mine*."

She snuggled into his neck, his arm wrapped around her. "Tell me another." She'd entered the woods where dappled light falls.

"One more story, then dinner. Have I told you about the Fiery Cross?"

"No."

"The Fiery Cross—or *Creau Tarigh*—the Cross of Shame, was the chieftain's summons to his clan when danger threatened. And disobedience to the symbol conferred infamy. Making a cross from any light wood, the chieftain slew a goat, searing the tips of wood in fire and extinguishing them with the blood of the animal."

"Is there a different version?"

"Brave up. The messenger delivered the cross—every village had one—and he ran with it to the next hamlet, and so on throughout all the lands of the neighboring chieftains. Encountering the Fiery Cross, every man capable of bearing arms was obliged to come running to the place of rendezvous. He who failed to appear suffered the blunt edge of the sword and the ire of fire."

"You'd think one of the Reids would have told me. I feel robbed."

"Robbed—I'm not a fifth-generation agrarian! Be glad of what you did have. It only takes a few enthusiastic Scots with an ardent love of their native land to carry the torch. You have to understand one thing—the clans existed, and so today, to serve the people. There are two sides to a tree, the 'material side' that faces north grows moss and represents protection and succor, and the 'ideal side,' facing south, exists to give birth to new ideas. When one man went down, a sum would be gathered and paid out to the widow and her bairns and any of his legal beneficiaries—this was the north side of the tree at work." He stood and adjusted the damper to slow the burn down. "And on the south side, the *leal* and true upholders of the Highland institutions cultivated our history and traditions, our literature and ideals, our minstrelsy and song. The customs we abide by today. Let's eat."

"Can you believe how ludicrous this is?" he asked.

"More and more so, yes."

Owen sopped up his broth with a crust of bread.

"We're always the person we were at birth—we just keep finding a new way to express it. In our case, embrace it."

"Not remotely funny," she said.

"Mother says you have Archie's mottled gray-green eyes. And she gave me two letters."

They read them together by candlelight.

Dear Rhona,

There is no explaining it. I apologize for my indiscretion, and for pulling you away from your husband. What would thwart our desire? We couldn't stop even before our fingertips met, just as in our youth.

I wish you peace with Rhys, and only happiness within your beautiful family.

—Always, Archie
November 9th, 1972

Dear Rhona,

Late in life now, I have the leisure to scrutinize the recesses of my solitude. The random compelling pieces of my life. I never married again.

There were blue holidays. My life a large dusty room like a loft, or the garret at Otyrburn. When I think of the times that Margot made a bored gesture when I tried to tell her details about a woman, I want to cut and rearrange the world.

Margot married and found herself in ancient Rome, talking to Cicero. I have a beautiful granddaughter, Ruby, who is my solace.

What discoveries are made by accident? A frozen river cracks and spring is born. I will forever remember when we huddled together on the cold steel frame of a mattress in that garret at Otyrburn. And the fog began to blow from the sea and closeted us in our zeal. But now I am grown so old, and though a little tired and cynical, my Happy Nightingale, I think about how things might have been if I hadn't left for New York. If we had married instead.

—Always, Archie
November 30th, 2001

"The daydreams of two solitary souls," she said, rubbing her forehead with the flat of her fingers.

"The secrets."

"Did he love my mother?"

"Did he love mine?"

"Did he love Violet?" she asked.

"Doesn't anyone wear panties?"

"Your mother was in love with my father, as I'm in love with her son."

"Yep." Owen broke a bar of dark chocolate in half. "We can arrange it either way. It's a palindrome of sorts."

"Aye." She licked chocolate off the end of her finger. "I have to make a flowchart to absorb all this."

"Better to start with the family tree."

"And jump out of my skin."

"Fiona and Edwina's friendship began in childhood." He had stretched out on the floor, fireside with the dogs. "Mother gave her letter to Fiona, who delivered it to Edwina, under the guise of forwarding to Archie the annual reports on the River Greeley

Conservation Program. Something Rhona and Archie had joined in high school."

"A faded summer love."

"Mother assumes the missing photo of Archie made Edwina suspicious."

"What a lot of baggage."

"And needless second-guessing of what something signified."

"I sabotaged my life," Margot said. "Rhona hers, and Edwina kicked the can through the town."

"A good observer is a bad listener and gets taken advantage of."

"Does this make Violet my stepmother?"

"And my mother, 'Happy Nightingale,' the songster. And my father?" he asked.

"Archie played recordings of birdsong in the weeks that led up to his passing. He said that his birthday in the fall was a time of power, of coming back, each year, to who he was." She held a photo of Rhona and Rhys in a narrow boat, summers past, and thought of the challenges they'd faced and neither of them expected. "Then he said, 'Just look at you, Margot, to cull such lovely images, tongue-in-cheek clever.' I can't forget that day, trees all in white, the snowflakes tumbling down. He had left me."

"My mind works exceedingly slow."

"It's a mind fuck." She smiled with heightened passion. She would no longer live a double life. "My New Year's resolution, 'thou shalt not swear.'"

"It's a bitch, but you break that one daily."

"And the shepherd?"

"To remember that we're little more than a flash in the hot-oiled pan of life."

CHAPTER THIRTY-NINE

Flight Patterns

*L*ife on an island influenced Ava's belief that the world churned out imaginary friends specifically for her benefit. When I told her stories, she waited for things she expected. Objects were almost magic, strung between magnetic poles.

I sent her to Argentina on a language study-abroad program her seventeenth year, to give her some perspective, as hitchhiking had given me. She always showed a frighteningly competent understanding of complicated matters. Ava went on to study with world-class luminaries at Cornell, found a work-study job in the library, and taught sailing in the summer. Dated the grandson of a rabbi, broke up, moseyed back down to South America, and fell in love with a guy she mistook for Octavio Paz.

Why do we let someone fuck with our circles? Sometimes only a thin membrane separates us from memory and ambition. In the elasticity of time, a portal of the past is already imprinted.

In the time of psychedelics, and now, in the time of Instagram junkies, when in a lonely place, and frightened, too, this will pass. Keep enough ground to repel bullshit.

Ava's dream is to have to work only one job to have a nice life, have a roof over her head, and be able to afford nice things once in a while, like an avocado. If the storm within that propels leaves for another coast, and Ava can't even produce rain, she doesn't have to explain it because she can't. Festina lente: *hurry slowly. I love you.*

PERTHSHIRE, FEBRUARY 2019

Margot read George's text: **Deep-rooted differences can be weathered by time.** He had booked a flight to Edinburgh.

He arrived in the evening. Wren barked. She sat up and wiped the corners of her eyes, greeted by his cold, hard expression. A moment in time had changed the balance of everything between them. *People are altered by time, and should be,* she thought. *A successful marriage is built upon that.*

"We need to talk," he said.

"No, we don't."

"I finally read Frazer's *The Golden Bough* crossing the Atlantic. A bit outdated, but still worth the read. Frazer's dying gods' sacrifices for the good of the kingdom became the default role of a woman."

"Prompted by your idol's painting of the same, I presume?" She had moved to the bathroom and splashed her face with warm water. "That's so contrived."

"Turner, who lived like a miser, left one hundred thousand sterling pounds to found a retreat to care for artists in their old age."

George smelled of a whole day of sunshine and line-dried linen, as if he were a man visiting his sister, and that sister were a nun.

"And you think that will impress me?"

"Our life has not been merely discontent."

"That is quite true."

He thought, simplistically, that lovemaking would make a difference. She refused him. They made eggs and toast by the AGA instead.

"I love you like a brother. Life's lies have a way of stubbornly hanging on."

She cracked an egg over Wren's bowl and parted the lace curtains from Provence at the kitchen window. *White sails that sparkle,* she thought, *Owen, so placid and self-contained.*

"I take the red-eye tonight." George scrolled through his phone. "You won't even know I'm around."

In the raw morning air, Margot and Owen crossed the frosty coastline, arms twined, over the triangular promontory along Loch Lomond. An outing he had awaited for ages, it seemed. The silhouette of the ruin they sought broke the hill rise on their destination. At the remains of Urquhart Castle, there was no boundary between spheres, just endless grizzled blue. And the mountain beyond a soft gray sky was magnificent. Thick forests bled into the jagged summit like a passport to another world.

"Before they crowned Robert the Bruce the king of Scots, he and his young wife, Isabella of Mar, lived here. Regrettably, she died soon after giving birth. They were much in love. Probably half brother and sister, cousins for sure."

"I slept with Will." She'd run through as many alternating perspectives as she could; they were the hardest four words she'd ever said.

"Lovely. That's exactly what he expected—what did you say?" He lifted his brown beaver felt hat and scratched his head.

"It was twenty-four years ago. The family wedding of a Lowell cousin, when we both had too much fun, and that night, I danced on top of the piano."

"You slept with Will? Who knows?"

"No one. And so it should remain."

"Let's see, which grieves my heart worse? The love triangle, that your husband filched and thieved, or that you slept with two brothers?"

He planted the seed. She moved the clouds. The sky traveled in sweeping gestures around them. The unforgiving tides, the survivors, shocking long-held secrets, crumbling castles, and butterflies against the windowpane.

"We've built a map in our mind—bare minimum; remember to read that the next time you get bored."

"I couldn't let the baby go."

"Will's Ruby's father?"

"I was only twenty, and still pretty mixed up."

He became suddenly agitated around her, the air thin. "That's a little fucked up."

She disengaged from his arm and moved away.

"You're trying my patience, Margot."

"I own my action. I did what I did to protect her."

"Dissimulation is a family practice."

"Who was Archie? He didn't seem to fit in anywhere. Part of him was just completely untamed."

"You protected yourself."

"How do we ever know anyone?" she asked.

"Some birds see at the ultraviolet end of the spectrum where we cannot. Mark my words, Margot."

He leaned forward, resting on his knees, squatting on a boulder, peering attentively at her face.

"A sparrow blindfolded and taken three thousand miles off route will inevitably return to his winter home. He'll hide thirty-three thousand seeds across hundreds of square miles and recall where he placed them. Tell me we comprehend love and creation—genius, for that matter."

She cast her glance along the steep escarpment, where a fox ran as low to the ground as a snake.

"Say what you want to say." Owen squinted in the haze.

"In that moment with Will, the power of love immediately dispelled all the other considerations of my life."

"That's handy."

"It was both something he said and the way I heard it; maybe the wine contributed, but not only that."

The wind blew her hair every which way. He skipped a rock over the terrain.

"Right before we wake," he asked, "between dream and reality, do we have the power to choose? Unknowingly, we stood in defiance, in joint opposition to the authority of a father figure, Archie."

"He was all I had left."

"And why, perhaps, unwittingly, you and I, together, challenged him."

"Because I had to challenge death?"

"No, Margot, to challenge *life*, as after your accident."

"By that reasoning, I take you as my lover to replace my lost brother, Angus."

"Something like that."

"Then who is Ava?" she asked.

"She's the girl of the sea."

"Our father went fishing."

"We are never fully satisfied by anything, sex included." Margot followed the flight, listening to the incredibly speedy song of a skylark.

Where the ground pitched steeply, his boots slid on wet sea tangle. He steadied himself on the slippery seaweed, and calling out to Rye to slow down his canine capers, he let a pucker whistle fly, his aloofness dissipated.

"I brought this on Ruby," she said.

"You should worry." His eyes moved over the landscape, depleted by man of the oaks, beech, and pine. "Trust is not easily won."

They scouted the collapsed masonry, dislodging rubble, running their fingers over embedded fossils and shells.

"George probably told you females have larger brains when they have 'extra pairs,' like a bird, and he flew in to reclaim his territory—pilferers keep a low profile."

She let him roll with it.

"I pity him." He ranted. "His life rock shattered, he hides under a childish delusion."

"I can't defend him."

"Then you've made a hash of explaining his petty tyrannies."

And as quickly as Owen became agitated, like a bee around stands of bilberry, he quieted. He held her close, wrapping his waxed jacket around her.

"This takes squeamish kids not wanting to hear about their parents making love to a whole new level."

He planted a cheerful kiss and continued softly. "In the Judea of the Old Testament, there were uncles married to nieces right and left."

"Oh, shut up, Owen, just shut up."

"Were you a colicky baby?"

"No!"

CHAPTER FORTY

Gone to Ground

*S*o perhaps Ava has a point. Hoping for some quality time with myself, willing to break bread with her but practically nobody else, maybe I was a little bit too sassy. Maybe I rolled my eyes out loud a few too many times. Maybe "he's a bastard" and "she's a bitch" aren't always the right answers. Maybe I didn't see my way into a new understanding of unalterable truths. But I have had a few uncommon friendships.

I've always been a cloud spotter. That's one area I can hang with the cultured elite. At Bread Loaf, the bulletin board was painted in puffs of cumulus and cirrus clouds, and the notes we left were written on assorted bird silhouettes. So your message, whether you were selling a car, bartering for tutorial help, or hitching a ride after the retreat, stood out—it had wings.

That is, if you could grab a patch of sky to soar over. The passen-ger pigeons, and sundry goldfinch alike, predominantly sang a song of love, a coo, a pinch, a how-do-you-do?

> White Male, 31, 5'11" 160 lb, insatiable 8", hungry
> As a man just waking to flee the monotony of
> expectation
> Desires dead flies to feed the bird feeder, promises
> he Will watch closely what happens, and take
> pictures, Expects same

Élan on the Lawn. *The naked couple splayed on the grass with cro-quet mallets and balls—that was my summer affair, or grass stains you didn't know were there.*

Beauty is something wholly inexplicable. If I don't get up once in a while in the middle of the night and write—or answer the compelling hello of a tender soul on the message board, what's life for? Especially if awoken by the soft fall of rain. Not all that much writing happened at Bread Loaf. Part and parcel of being a writer, writers like to talk too much, at home with books.

On a steep hillside in Vermont, secluded doesn't quite capture an overgrown summer. Beside Shelley and Byron and Keats, oh, how we adults, like they, drank, wiled away hours, played cards, caressed, and sexed instead of texted, we, who smiled far and wide. And over and over again told each other how much we loved the other, and healed our flesh, in and out of the sulphur springs that ringed the town.

My immortality, my unquenchable sexual appetite—the summer in the Vermont woods I passed writing. Archie, despite his appearance at Woodstock and his peregrinations from point A to point B with Swami Satchidananda, was provincial. He was a rebel for kicks, not an original. From time to time, I, too, end up a long way from where I want to be.

PERTHSHIRE, APRIL 2019

Margot had barely opened the door at Otyrburn when George telephoned from Manhattan. He had killed Archie. Not single-handedly, but the stress of the argument had brought on the heart attack. She could not be convinced otherwise.

George had a habit of making impossible demands in the friendliest way, with a slightly quizzical smile. Her petulant pout of boredom; there was little time to be bored when Ruby came along; her silence, she supposed, was in itself a tacit agreement. Even if she dragged her feet, she couldn't slow the circle down, even a minimal alteration of routine. *Why are you so grumpy this evening? I'm not grumpy.* He had won and come to a full stop. It was his journey too. Her childhood had ended the fall that her mother and brother died. Spring now would bring the close of her marriage.

"In a susceptible frame of mind, you're submitting to whims, and the elements you no longer want, you've mentally erased," he said, pacing the kitchen. The timer on the stove rang, and he switched his gait, still wearing his wing tips, the leather heels clicking over the ceramic tiles.

"My husband, the gravedigger." He would not have revealed any of what he knew for the world.

"For the love of God, get off your high horse."

"My fault rests in being a coward. But who's the fool now?"

Margot opened the freezer and removed Wren's dinner to thaw.

"And our griffin plaque that hangs in the foyer?" she asked.

"Smuggled out of Estonia."

"Oh, for fuck's sake."

"By the way, Archie left you a present years ago," George volunteered.

"What's that?"

"He said to tell you, if anything were to happen to him before he had the chance, that you'd have to work for it. He hid a package in Alistair's comedic labyrinth."

"And?"

"'*The Age of Innocence*,' that's as far as he let on in the clue department. Edith Wharton."

"Everything in its place," she said. "Out of the clouds falls rain."

The early-spring weeks passed. George led a demanding exhibit on classical Greek vases, coins, and gems, in between court hearings. Sunday afternoons, he held a Met discussion on the Column of Marcus Aurelius, little altered in his professional conduct, and then there was the trip to plan. She answered his texts. Owen and Margot lapped up the increasing daylight found in the Highlands. They read *The Age of Innocence* out loud together; Archer, May, and Ellen, the right partner who came along at the wrong time.

New York City, April 2019

The dark side of the art market, Johnny thought, *and how it influences his enlightened eclecticism.* He was seated in a corner booth at Eduardo's, their local haunt in New York City. George was late. *Bad times*, he said to himself again, then looked down the stretch of street. Absurd times. Maybe that's exactly what George expected him to do—rush off to save him, and maybe, and this was getting convoluted, George expected him to read a simple code, and consider that his crimes were in fact insoluble. Bolster his status by reminding him that only those who fought within the rules would succeed. To accept that criminals who followed the money had adopted George without his knowledge, merely by his asking to see the "pick of the week."

"You have zero misgivings?"

This threw him slightly; he had paused. "In which sphere?" George asked.

"Margot."

Another pause. "Why should I? She gave me her best years. There's never a shortage of intrigue and problems in life."

"True," Johnny said. One thing was obvious; he was never going to get the truth.

"I'll survive. Maybe Greece for the summer."

"Maybe Rhode Island is a better choice."

Johnny was eating the peanuts again, and George apparently couldn't have cared less.

"They've confiscated Doña Maria de Trujillo y Merlo's passport, and that of Heinke Hessel; how is it that you held on to yours?"

"I went to see her."

"Why?"

"She wanted me to make an offer on her late husband's collection."

"You've become intimate."

"The bitch," he muttered. "I bet she did him in."

"When?"

"Over a year ago. It was nothing."

"I think I'm in the way here." Johnny made as if to stand, but didn't, and gave him a hard look, and he returned it calmly. George tapped the table in a friendly way.

"You're in the middle of a half-written chapter," he said. "Don't try to write the end."

"Two policemen showed up at my apartment."

"And I'm still here before you."

"They asked about container-loads of loot."

"In your imagination." A flash of lightning lit up the street. "Shit. I'm not a man of action. You know that."

The place was packed. Well-dressed people sipped cocktails on the sidewalk setup, eyes on the sky, and within, a micro-meadery taproom and restaurant. Dependably, a few big groups celebrated something on the rooftop garden patio, then danced after 10:00 p.m. on a Saturday.

"A tab of incidentals," George continued, "such as taxis and meals, is nothing compared to Hessel, who posed as a bond dealer in antiquities and made off with millions, stealing tiny Tintorettos for his lovers. And Doña Maria is certainly not the first high-profile con woman with an aristocratic alter ego."

Johnny could reliably count on him to say, at least once across the evening, "Wow, what a city!"

"What happened to Lady Courtenay?"

George ordered charcuterie. "Let's make a pact not to talk about it on the trip."

"It's all settled, then."

"It's possible for stories to be real, for events to have happened, and for the stories to be mixed up."

CARPATHIAN MOUNTAINS, APRIL 2019

The connecting flight from Cluj-Napoca taxied the runway in a WWII Soviet Union retrofit. Johnny distracted George after takeoff during the two-hour-and-fifty-minute sojourn by quizzing him from a Hungarian phrase book, but his efforts didn't deter his travel companion from noticing mist rising through the rusted rivets bolting the underbelly. The train was late—and slow. While horse-drawn carts

*rumbled along dirt roads past layer upon layer of mountains, un-
der rolling clouds, dodging mud-filled potholes the size of Joe's Pond,
George drove the rental car, cursing about the flimsy tin body and fum-
ing over the absence of airbags. He shifted gears; the cramped, tiny
vehicle left their shoulders touching as their heads skimmed the roof.*

Johnny studied the map with his knees in his face.

"After we exit the super-high highway in Transfagarasan—
voted most scenic ride by *Top Gear*—and gas up the Soda Can,
we can take the paved road from Bunesti—not bad—or take
Dacia, about seven kilometers of dust, not paved, axle-breaking
but passable."

"No conundrum there—seven—as in seven kilometers."
George asked Siri what time it was, and remarkably, Siri still answered. "Jeez Louise. Time for lunch. I'll pull off at the first cob-
blestoned town."

"If the locals rattle on, don't show any signs of impatience,
George. Romanians play it fast and loose with schedules."

They slipped into the only building with a sign scrolled in
English that read RESTAURANT for their one-hour lunch.

"Is it just me, or does this wine taste like fizzy juice?"
George asked.

"You're not in jail. Here we are surrounded by Alpine snow-
capped mountains, as far away from the North Pole as we are
from the equator—if the wine gurgles when sipped, so what?"

"Cold sweats, nausea, and stomach bugs, that's what."

"You're so risk averse about some things, it's ridiculous, and
the wine delicious. How is Ruby even alive?"

She's extraordinary, he told himself, *feisty and unintimidating,
utterly charming.* The picture matched the caption.

Had felonious secrecy, not unlike attraction to the wrong partner, manifested as a novel thought with velvety good manners that grew more attractive the more he considered it? Johnny thought, watching George distractedly doodle iconic castles on a paper napkin.

"Eighteen Saxon villages in five days by bike." Johnny flipped through his guidebook. "My balls are killing me."

"Someone who takes on mythic status does so because of their idiosyncrasies." George cuffed his shirtsleeves. "I need a cup of coffee."

"Me too."

For some time they sat in a kind of dumbfounded silence. *The weakest thoughts are welcomed by the mind,* Johnny thought, *alongside those with merit,* before the waiter broke his concentration.

They ate polenta and pork and hard-boiled eggs, and for dessert, a morsel-like donut sprinkled with confectioners' sugar, stuffed with sweet cream, surrounded by fresh berries—papanasi, a sweet to rival the nipple of George's Venus, crowning a dollop of clotted cream.

"So preposterous," George said, leaving the tip, "what is guided by reason, and what by passion."

"Maybe not," Johnny offered thoughtfully. "Honesty might be a more fixed proposition."

"It's the way the world wags." George considered for a moment. "If you're interested, there are plenty of books about art scandals."

"I suppose that means your advice to me is to forget what I've found out?"

George shrugged his shoulders. "That's one way of putting it."

In the museum, George could hardly have found a better place to hide. *Claro,* Johnny's thought track had switched fluidly to

Spanish. *No lo recuerdo nada. I don't remember anything. It worked every time.*

"If a man breaks the law, it's everyone's duty to report to justice, is it not, George?"

"We're all careless at times."

Before they left the restaurant, a step behind George, Johnny made a point to examine George's doodle-art napkin and take a closer look. He had drawn a banner flying off one turret. In tiny print, it read: *Nobody told me.*

The food and the jabber went down and stayed there. The car ride resumed, as bumpy as before. Arrived at their destination, Johnny stood on a dirt road. Viscri was far from the main road. The village clock tower peeled. George had checked it off his UNESCO World Heritage Site list. They stood shoulder to shoulder with a dwindling population of Székely people, descended from Attila's Huns. The curving cobble path to the entrance of the stucco-facade farmhouse brought them to a chiseled plaque beside the door with the date "1758."

The guesthouse plank door of HRH the Prince of Wales's periwinkle-blue bed-and-breakfast opened beneath a low-hung, red-tiled roof into a grapevine-draped courtyard, enclosed by the auxiliary buildings. Below the roof was an old horse-drawn wagon parked beside oxen hitches; a warped ladder, which led to the hayloft; and all around, a profusion of clinging green ivy.

In the corner of the kitchen, decorated with hand-embroidered linen wall hangings with cutwork-scalloped edges, was an open firepit. Old Turkish and Carpathian rugs hung on the wall provided insulation against the Siberian winters. In the uncertainty of their friendship, the two of them poked around, ducking beneath the stone lintels that framed the doorways; even the shelves had handmade lace.

"We'll encourage the rural revival and spend money. Mass globalization spells lost identity, and that's a dangerous moment. Three hundred pounds equals an annual Romanian salary. And to make matters worse, George, the Germans and Austrians can't stop culling forests, over forests."

He turned the shortwave radio on—no English station. He trailed George into the room with a pair of twin beds, their matching oak headboards heavily carved with grape clusters and oak leaves trailing along the top rail.

"Two boys at boarding school," Johnny announced.

"Prince Charles has no master bedroom?"

"There's a spare with a pitchfork."

He turned over random objects on a shelf and shook the dust of ages off a length of ivory skirted fleece overflowing from a wicker basket.

"Charles left us a matched pair of carding combs."

"Fiddle with the *Kachelofen* until it burns bright enough to highlight the whites of a vampire's eyes. I'm off to unpack in the better of the two wardrobes—on *my* side of the room."

Songbirds sang. Butterflies visited the soft, feathery leaves of common yarrow, lured by the pungent scent to pasture and wayside, and throughout, the abundant pale-yellow flowers of daffodils proclaimed springtime. Johnny reminded George not to pet the dogs or flash his valuables out in the open. They walked along forest roads, passing large beech and elms, with Johnny steering George away from tables selling holy relics. He made many private phone calls and religiously checked his messages, whenever and wherever the service proved passable. It was an authentic Saxon village with the Germans at one end, the Romanians at the other, and on the outskirts of town—the Roma.

The sole member of the cultural aristocracy wasn't interested in bird-ing. Little bitterns at the water's edge held no charm.

Later that evening, leaning back with half-closed eyes, George repeated out loud, "I can live without her."

"We are all manifestations of Buddha consciousness."

"Of all the asinine things." George watched the shadow of the kerosene flame in the copper lantern flicker. "I'm filling the tub. If you want to live to see another day—do not disturb."

He got out of bed. A candle fell from the wall sconce and landed at his feet, splattering the baseboard with beeswax. In the bewilderment, George stood motionless in the room filled with folkloric knickknacks, reflecting on his impending miraculous good fortune.

"Here's a bee for your bonnet." Johnny chuckled, folding down the corner on a Romanism tourism magazine he was reading in bed called *What's for Dinner?* while George stepped gingerly over the bearskin rug, slipping out in his boxers with a towel draped over his shoulder. "HRH's great-great-great-grandmother was a Hungarian countess—Claudine Susannah Rhédey—and you can bet your bottom dollar, she poured bubbles in the tub before you. Your horsehair mattress awaits."

Thirty minutes passed, and George plodded back, leaving a water trail across the oak flooring, his hair matted in disarray from scrubbing too hard with a bar of handmade goat milk soap, his flesh tinted rose.

"Did you shut the gate?" he asked.

Having rearranged his hair before the pitted mirror, and checked to see if his bed was made with attention to crisply folded hospital corners, he tucked in with a heavy sigh.

"I don't have the foggiest. Why?"

George shifted restlessly, fluffing goose-down pillows. "And grab that bottle of local firewater made from the plum mash, while you're at it."

Johnny acquiesced and walked out the bedroom door.

"Don't howl so loud. People will think we're having fun."

He returned and handed off George's glass. The odd couple lay in bed, staring up at precisely dovetailed massive timbers, sipping ninety-proof moonshine.

"What did they call this gut-warming kick?"

"Tuică." Johnny got up and opened the window. "I'm spending the day in the woods. These days the woods are a pretty quiet place."

"Marriage is often an exercise in watching the landscape inevitably change or decline over the years. Whoever slept under this roof survived the horrors of two world wars, misery, and destruction."

"Get some shut-eye, George. Dream about cobble lanes, bucolic landscapes, and barefoot handmaidens with large busts; tomorrow's another day."

"Drinking this, I'm a traitor to my country," he said, after a fit of laughing and coughing. "What's for breakfast?"

"Polenta with Romanian cheese, topped with a fried egg and smothered in sour cream. You know, George, I don't cultivate friendships basking in the good old days with anyone but you."

"What was breakfast like in Argentina?"

"A punctuation mark." He added a wool blanket to his coverlet. "Everyplace I look here, I see my mother's home cures, gourd planters, and wild strawberries, not hedonistic New York."

"You love the city of your birth."

"Not like you. I get racially profiled all the time." He looked at the moon catching a cloud. "It gave me a perception of difference as normal. I remember to feed the sourdough starter in my fridge. Some things just are."

"Johnny? You still awake?"

"Yes, George?"

"There must be a secret staircase."

Some laws you let slide. Art existed in that realm. Where nobody got hurt, and everybody got what they wanted. He lay there, staring at the ceiling, thinking. *Archie had brought it on, nothing short of blackmail: he would go to the police with his findings. It had been a "hot mess," and yes, in return, I'd pushed him too far; but to blame me for his heart attack—preposterous.*

CHAPTER FORTY-ONE

Brothers and Sisters

When the traffic light changes, a lie still blinks. I have one sister, Jewel, who doesn't glance in the rearview mirror as often as she should. She's my baby sister, a hopeless romantic of a human who lives in London. Jewel's fifteenth summer, our father the philosopher—not to be confused with a philistine—tried to cure her by shipping her off to the White Mountains of New Hampshire to work as a forest trooper. "Carve out the American frontier, my dear!" An endeavor in the untamed wilderness would teach her that from the heartaches of love, there would be no escape.

It was fancifully funny, enough so that in the end, Thomas drove off to "rescue" her from the evil gang of crows and the threatening black bear cubs. They were invading her personal realm again. What a collection of letters and vintage postcards we received that summer.

"*You won't believe where I got poison ivy*"; "*It's extremely steep and rocky here. I'm going to die, or need to be airlifted out.*"

In a log cabin, her interest in Cornish swallows and European royalty grew exponentially. Go figure. We each have our special places. And like a vintage rose, Jewel grew further entrenched in her handpenned sentiments, despite the tree huggers and amateur botanists she cohabitated with. Trees communicated, but why on earth would anyone care what they said?

July broke after June, and Jewel stubbornly and repeatedly refused to "take a walk in the woods." Hell-bent on proving that the world of a longtime mistress, sequestered in a villa (Monte Carlo might do), was a worthy cause, she set off to London, an orphan of optimism, on a moor.

The only problem I saw with Jewel's plan was that she wasn't an American heiress with a vast fortune. After graduation, and one thousand threats of "I'm leaving," she enrolled in one of Great Britain's top professional nanny schools. Where is she now? She wears heart-shaped diamond necklaces and married the first son of a house who crafts Elizabethan "love potions" awarded the Royal Warrant of the Queen Mum. Awash in the symbolism of scented blooms, Jewel's life is a colorful illustration. She lives on Grosvenor Square and has a passel of well-mannered children, Ava's cousins.

The decline and fall of a distant species cried out in that White Mountain wood, where mute birds in a valley flew, and trees sang, and Jewel screamed her truths, too, and landed in a manicured garden, singing.

CARPATHIAN MOUNTAINS, APRIL 2019

Daybreak heralded early spring. *Brotherly love*, Johnny thought, returning from his photo shoot. *Why am I trying so hard to rescue him from his moral vacuum? Or unravel the ruse?* The whistling kettle had begun to roll, and George peered out the bubble-glass sash window.

"Good lord, look at you. You're filthy," he said, holding the door ajar, choking on his orange juice.

"We're part of nature, not separate. *Trans*, 'across,' *Sylvania*, 'the forest'—bears live in that forest and, when not feeling threatened, sunbathe on the meadow. I'm here to post an article in the syndicated press on illegal logging: the Carpathian forest must be preserved."

"Greek *arktos* and Latin *ursus*." George drew the hot tap, his hands cloaked in lemon and aloe suds; he soaked and squeezed the corner of a dishrag. "In Ireland, 'the good calf.' In Wales, 'honey-pig.' In Russia, 'honey eater,' and in Lithuania, 'the licker.'"

He dabbed at the stain decorating the front of his shirt.

"Steel yourself, George, and have a bear claw almond pastry."

"How did it go?"

"Not too bad, an early-morning hike on location, and I caught some bear hugs between shy introverts."

The Americans freshened. George plucked green elderberry, still wet after a sudden shower, from a cluster hanging over his head, spat it out, and drew a ladle from the old-time dipping well.

"You never saw any consequence to your actions?" Johnny insisted, then grabbed his coat and hat. "You owe me, George."

"I'm going to retire and devote full time to establishing the George Wilder Lowell Foundation: the most important and most trusted art house in the world."

"Since donating phony works to museums isn't against the law, I can see you pulling that off."

What other bad habits did well-heeled George have? Johnny mused. *A tap on the wrist wasn't getting his attention. Art scamming, people scamming, his best friend included.*

"Smell it?"

The dew highlighted a spider's web. The somnolent spider, full of wings, played with the strings of his harp.

"I do."

"The distinctive smell of the earth after rain."

"A priest or a future in philanthropy—don't you love yourself enough to tell the truth?"

George swatted the bugs away before his face for the twentieth time in ten minutes.

"Oily plant resins fall to the earth, harden, and dry, only to be released by the first rain after prolonged dryness. Petrichor—Greek petro from the Latin *petra*, 'stone,' *ichor*, from Greek 'essence.'"

Etymology, Johnny thought, *his mantra.*

"*Essence*, that's exactly what I'm asking you to do, George: cut out the bullshit and be straight with me."

"As Margot was straight with me."

Johnny watched closely as the expression drained from George's face.

"I maintain my innocence. I do, as always, have immense gratitude for our friendship and your concern. But you shouldn't worry so, Johnny. It doesn't suit you."

They started walking, listening to donkeys braying, passing a man carrying a scythe with the blade up over his shoulder.

"It took sixteen haystacks to feed one cow through winter." Johnny reached to pull a shaft of wheat, nibbling on the end. "And the horse-drawn cart took five hours to reach the market. The EU allocated two billion for rural farm rebuilding, and not a penny went to Romania."

"And in the not-too-distant past, the peasants took refuge from Ottoman Turks at the twelfth-century church."

A bumblebee alighted on purple clover.

"Are you sure you read that correctly?" George insisted.

"Page two hundred and fifty-seven, 'to obtain the church key, one must knock on a house door.'"

Johnny creased the center of the pocket guidebook flat for George, who read over his shoulder.

"Which blue house?"

"It's not specific, which leads me to believe—any house. They all have keys."

A pair of homemakers in animated gossip sat on a rustic bench, their arms folded across full chests, heads wrapped in colorful floral scarves, feet clad in homemade woolen shoes resembling mukluks. The visitors picked a house and knocked. The door with red potted geraniums opened.

"*Helló, jó reggelt,*" Johnny greeted, and before he could say "*szeretnénk meglátogatni az egyházat,*" the man reached for something hanging on the wall.

"*A kulcs.*"

He returned the smile and handed Johnny the weighted six-inch rusty iron key.

"*Köszönöm,*" George added, not to be outdone.

He could always say polite things in languages that he knew little.

"Tourists think we crawled out of shallow graves." The local spoke perfect English. "We are poor, but our souls are clean."

And with that, they set off to tour still more iconic relics. The wooden bells in hidden valleys rang. George had stopped to ask, "How much do you want for that?" at least seven times.

"If we hadn't successfully jump-started the Soda Can without jump leads, we'd still be in the petrified wood. That's a sobering thought."

"And that storm broke right while we stood in the mud of the ditch."

"I'm so glad I caved and purchased the boots." George stood in a traditional black leather three-quarter pair, filled with a quiet happiness.

"Count Lowell, was there ever any doubt? I just wish you'd wear the matching cummerbund and not save it for special."

Again, George broke away to take yet another call.

"Really, George, no news to relay?"

"Damn little."

"You think you're a karmic charm, is that it?" Johnny asked.

"The universe has no beginning and no end, and here you are, truly strung out on rumors and gossip."

"I think there's something rather moving about honesty, beauty, and wonder."

George leaned on a split-rail fence. "You'd have me driving an Uber for the remainder of my days."

"You ought to have had more foresight. I doubt whether you're capable of comprehending just how disastrous the situation is you've wrought, not just for you, but your family."

"As my grandaunt Isabella Stewart Gardner said, 'Don't spoil a good story by telling the truth.'" He tucked his shirt collar down and adjusted his belt. "Are you satisfied with your shoot?"

"Relatively." Johnny walked through a day that glistened. "Maybe in ten years' time, they'll let you out for a tour of the monasteries of Moldavia or the Danube delta. Did you ever send that postcard to Margot?"

"And one to Ruby."

George, sporting the new black fedora, lagged paces behind Johnny, fascinated by a swarm of bees buzzing with abandon over the wildflower grasslands.

"I think they prefer purple," he said softly to himself.

"Hurry up, or we'll be late for the train," Johnny yelled as he dashed. "An expedition in Alaska."

"A moss fishing pool in Iceland." George cracked a faint smile. "Or the Hermitage in Saint Petersburg."

"You're not slipping on my watch, or implicating me within your situational ethics."

The wheels rolled, and the steam engine chugged, passing fortified family compounds and watermills, and leaving the little village brought wide-open countryside for miles, until the next collection of low-roofed houses nestled within white blooming shrubs, and seventeenth-century church spires that rose 250 feet skyward, highlighting the graveyard. Left behind were hand-tied hay bales and workhorses adorned with red wool tassels and bells tied to their ears.

Somewhere, deep in the Carpathian Mountains, they ran into trouble and collided with a dump truck, and the train became mired in a massive load of overturned pig shit, and so it remained for two solid unthinkable days. George consoled a crying woman who happened to be a colleague he had met that fall at the London symposium on Aphrodite of Knidos. In the dining car, he had thought she looked familiar.

"What a coincidence." Johnny was incredulous. "On the peak of a snow-capped mountain dotted with the ready castle ruin, you bump into an acquaintance. It's truly quite remarkable when you stop to think it over."

"And what about Anna?"

"Delightful, but still off the mark."

"She's an Austrian archaeologist who goes by the name of Gigi, but her real name is Georgiana Peabody." He complained about the train getting a bit stuffy. "When she isn't digging and dust-ing off femur bones, she's casting in chalk streams in Yorkshire, where she has a second home—caught her first fish at the age of five."

George paused to watch teams of horse-drawn carts haul wreckage slowly away, and like a stream that came alive during mayfly season, he continued, walleyed, "She prefers nymphing to fishing the floating fly. There's an ephemeral intensity about her that I do find rather attractive."

"In the midst of a quagmire, your middle-aged thoughts bend to the faint hope of resurrection."

"There is profundity even while contemplating the shit on the bottom of my heel."

George dawdled on the platform. He had been silent for a few moments, and not interested in asking him to hurry, Johnny wait-ed for George to compose his thought.

He recited, in flawless German, a proverb: "And 'if you don't want to be deceived, you must have as many eyes as hairs on the head.'"

Johnny was startled. In the moment, his old friend gave him chills. George was, in a word, someone who colors another but has little color himself. Each point of contact, once entertained, involved a semantic bleaching, on his part, of the individual, event, or landscape, by the reduction of its intensity. At any given time, almost everything he ut-tered was half-favorable and half-derisive.

George was arrested briefly in Switzerland on the homeward end. His missteps misfired; the shit on his shoe had left a trail. Momentarily spooked, upon entering Swiss customs, he paid a twenty-five-thousand-dollar fine for his unscrupulous dealings. George had tried to fob some trinkets off, stashing them in Johnny's checked bag. Where had the rendezvous transpired? How had Johnny missed it? He didn't have a clue.

Landing stateside, the threat of three months in prison nearly destroyed George, but ancient Greece saved him in the end. Seafaring merchants had the option to purchase maritime insurance, or "bottomry." Charging 30 percent, the insurer reaped a profit if the voyage was successful. While ships sat idle in port, the Greeks had invented insurance fraud. A fraudster uses ingenuity. With an edifice of artifice, George had flipped the coin and played both sides. He'd collected money from both the insurance company with his authentication and Lady Courtenay on the sale of misappropriated, as well as bogus, pieces that she exploited. George, being George, got off relatively Scots'-free.

CHAPTER FORTY-TWO

Aunt Ava and Niece Ruby

"Violet Grey speaking." That's how I answered the phone as a child, and so today. I mentioned toward the beginning of this book that in the interest of economy, short stories were my specialty. I began writing this novel without ambition, simply because stories are nothing without a voice, and a voice gives a sense of belonging. Besides, I regained something of my youth when I became a "mother" to a full house at seventy. I am a woman who keeps myself to myself, though in this instance, I can only repay the kindness.

In the twenty-first century, without a defined war, per se, Ruby and Ava, among the more pronounced conscientious objectors in my story, and dear Sybil, still question the proliferation of arms and "progress for profit." We did that too. Vision versus "Victory in Vietnam," Karl Marx versus "Kidnapped by the Blue Light Special."

They protest corporate contracts written in vanishing ink, which place an invisible burden on each of us who weren't even in the room. The woes of the homeless, who have names we don't remember, and the cries of the abandoned, as lowly as a farmed fish who swims in endless circles, have stories we walk away from. Someone has to take love home. A political movement, of any sort, is people working for peace while society is asleep.

At Bread Loaf, where I teach creative writing during the summer months, I ask my students to tell me what a room would contain, a room in which no one else is allowed and to which they alone possess the key.

Then I ask that they build a house around that room, using only words on paper as building blocks. Aspiring or published, in my class, all are writers. Some summers produce a monopoly of phallic skyscrapers and stark Norwegian lake house inspirations; others, soft-bellied yurts; one of George's Amsterdam houseboats materializes routinely, and then again, the more esoteric lines of Bucky's geodesic dome manifest, or the wilderness hermit hut of a Chinese poet.

This house of yours! What constitutes your wild idleness? What was gentle and undemanding? What exists if you don't feed it anymore? How can that which we love ever make sense on one plane?

When they've finished composing, arranging and rearranging what advances and what retires, then the character of beauty, and all that they've waited for, remains in that clear stream.

If you're inspired, send your design, along with a self-addressed stamped envelope, to:

Violet Grey
General Delivery
Hopper's Island, Maine 04997

If I could build Ava a house, it would have walls that sing and floors that dance.

NEW MEXICO, ROUTE 66, JUNE 2019

"Anytime I visit with Violet, I pray she isn't having one of her psychic tension headaches," Ava said, changing lanes in New Mexico on the way to spend the night. "Those scare the bejesus out of me."

"My mother called me 'bijou,' and I liked it because it sounded like the name of a secret, rare Pokémon card." Ruby clocked the distance on their anticipated one-hour trip. "I can't even. She threw away my *first edition* cards."

Ava beamed, almost with a maternal pride; Ruby was such a wonderful creature, and those freckles.

"When Violet smoked pot on Hopper's Island, she said things like, 'Ava, you are a natural child of God,' 'Creative work cannot be dehumanized,' and 'The present cannot foresee the future.' But my favorite of all time, stoned or straight, was, 'The imagination is fearless.'"

"Does that mean that Archie fathered two children by two different women *and* smoked pot?" Ruby asked.

"Spilling the tea."

"Pics or it didn't happen."

"It's true, Ruby. There's nothing past tense about us. You and I are royal renegades."

Ava felt for Ruby. Her entire world had flipped upside down. Welcome to the school of suspicion. All contracts could be revised.

"Violet never told Archie she was pregnant. Why not?" she asked.

"Because she knew who she was by herself. Because, as she said, 'When you're in love, wonders happen, and when you get married, you start wondering what happened.'"

"Twenty nineteen, and a woman of little means can't get elected because of the high cost of campaigning." Ruby broke into a granola bar.

"Or raise her children on one salary."

"It's your 'overlapping systems of disadvantage.'"

"All these years," Ava said, "and I thought my father was a spy who infiltrated Violet's vulva."

"Men want women to be not too nice, but not too bitchy. Bye, Felicia."

"That's what Violet typically thought; 'You're leaving, and I don't care.'" Ava scanned the radio dial for the *Weekend Edition* and instead found only country music. "And, Ruby, having pubic hair is not a sign of not taking care of yourself. FYI."

"Do you know why girls go to the bathroom together, Ava?"

The V-dub bounced over a bump, tipping side to side and spilling a bag of peaches.

"No."

"Because when Hermione went to the bathroom alone, she was attacked by a troll."

"And I bet he was *waayyy* too hot for this world." Ava grinned and shoved her sweater beneath her butt, the springs shot.

"And he tried out the toilet in an apartment before signing a contract to be sure he could sit down and his cock wouldn't touch the water."

"Like a girl's body count matters."

About one hundred miles of sagebrush and a few dead tumbleweeds had passed along the roadside. The sun was high and the road clear. Off in the distance, they thought they saw the faint outline of dust storms, the apocalyptic *haboobs* on the horizon.

"Ruby, did you jot down the woman in Albuquerque's answer to question number nine? I seem to have misplaced it."

"Yep. She's the one who said about her husband, 'There's something at the bottom of his well, and it ain't pretty.'"

"That's right." Ava nodded. "She said she was living his fears and lies because he did not love himself enough to tell the truth."

She shifted into fourth, and the tiny engine in the back vibrated like a washing machine.

"What did you mean by the 'modus operandi of sex'?" Ruby asked.

She shielded her face with her hand and squinted in the sun's persistent glare.

"I almost know how to explain it. Sex is a means, not an end. Like math or science. You cannot join two beings together when their minds are far apart."

"I know that." Ruby wiped the windshield with a hand wipe. "It's better to be alone than to wish you were."

"How many women have I interviewed who said, 'I didn't know who I was apart from him, or her'?"

"Because this, because that, because the house needs to be maintained and the children cared for, when love, as you said, is something inherently without limit—that's what you called it, right, Ava?"

"It's sad how many of their marriages were sexless."

"And the last couple of years have been hot-girl summers."

"And what does that mean exactly, Ruby?"

"Show your swag; live your best life. Don't let the Karens of the world rule."

"We've met some Karens," Ava said. "Seemingly entitled, and permanently-angry-at-the-world-and-everyone-in-it types." She tipped her sun visor. "People are genuinely getting dumber."

"The literal downfall of human civilization, that's what it means to be a Karen."

"Ruby, every straight man in existence is not a piece of shit. And every white woman isn't using her privilege to demand her own way."

"The volume inside of this bus is astronomical."

"Just remember, Ruby, that you have the right to claim considerable damages whenever life becomes fabricated and intolerable because your voice isn't heard."

The wind hissed as it blew from side to side.

"YAAAAAS! Originality rules!"

"Originality that isn't *just tolerated*, Ruby."

"Are there lobster claws in Maine as big as my head?"

"Yep. You'll be foraging fresh seafood and raking clams before long."

"*Hit it!*" Ruby yelled and waved her arm out the open window.

Ava laid her palm down hard on the pummel of the air horn, and it blew, *Ah-oo-gah*.

"*Free the prairie dogs!*" they both sang.

"Are you going to write about Archie and the pain that he caused in that doctorate of yours?"

"I don't even know what the most painful part of it was," Ava said. "And here I'm studying what psychological factors are peculiar to women."

"Mom was the one in a blind alley."

"Edwina aided and abetted the lies of her son, as if Margot's and Owen's faces were the faces of an audience, and she the director."

"The son's rebellion against his father is expected," Ruby said, "and the daughter's not even discussed."

They passed yet another shrine in the desert to a traffic accident victim—a wooden cross and a bicycle.

"If I want to move forward, I have to leave all that was backward behind." Ava asked Ruby to open her water bottle lid.

"Did you know, Ava, that women's eyes are like a grotto?"

"Dark and mysterious, like our vaginas."

"I hated it when Dad told me I'd made my eyes look 'big' in the presence of a boy—and to cut it out," Ruby said. "I was a monster to shine, and be sensual, and so on. But he could spread his legs, seated in a chair, and talk on about how a key that opens many locks is more valuable than a lock that has been opened many times."

"Live by your reason and instinct, Ruby."

"When do we get to Taos?"

"Almost there," Ava said.

"This life as a vagabond is GOAT."

"Violet always said, 'Angels exist all over the world, and they're called strangers.'"

"I love talking to strangers, Ava."

They pulled off the road to study the map, and Ava's phone dinged.

"V cute. A text from Johnny."

CHAPTER FORTY-THREE

Wolf Whistle

I do see a little of Ava in Ruby, something about the nose. In the *fall, Ruby is pursuing her master's in philosophy, cosmology, and consciousness-integral ecology. A bird of the night, never celestially bored. She tackles historic global challenges.*

George pleaded an insanity defense, and he found one of the messages I had stuffed in a bottle while casting with Gigi on a shady bank: JUST OVER THE HUMP.

I crank out a new poem once a month, in between stabs at writing a memoir. Margot and Owen remain of the earth and happily active in a culture of their own making. Do not suppress your personality. Give up all that. I wish you more than I can say. See the white doves fly.

PERTHSHIRE, JUNE 2019

Along the garden path, wrens hopped about, skirting in and out of the undergrowth in the lee of a cedar hedge, where a songbird perched on a low branch. It was summer. Owen's cottage saw improvements daily, a lime wash, and the fruit trees planted. Wren had learned to bark at the new lambs and, eventually, the old ewes. The robin had made his nest in an old lantern left by the compost. The Highlands had no use for slackers. *Digging around unearths details,* he thought, *and the garden that is complete no longer thrives.*

"A bonny time to be here," Owen said, with high-noon pleasantries.

"I think they call it 'commonplace lunacy,'" Margot said.

"What do you say we have a wee gander?"

"I couldn't conjure a summer such as this. A bird made a nest in the boxwood again."

He reached with his hand to free a profusion of wind-tangled coppery-lavender heads. Some of them were four feet tall.

"You have a gift with things," she said. "Ruby decoded Alistair's message."

"And what did the old buzzard have to say?" he asked.

"HAVE A HAPPY DAY."

"That'll do."

"I did some digging around in the land of far and beyond, as per Archie's instructions."

"Which letter hid the surprise?" He wiped his brow with a bandanna. "And why didn't you ask me to help?"

"The 'V'—a small tin box under an apple tree held a note that said *Veni, Vidi, Vici.* Archie left me these." And she dug in her pocket and opened her palm. It held a diamond, a ruby, and an emerald. And one small bag containing three apple seeds.

"Set for life."

"The dissenter on the bench loved the orchard after all."

It rained down out of the sunny blue; they shook it off, and the songbirds kept on singing.

"Have you heard from the traveling duo?" Owen asked.

"The V-dub broke down between Albuquerque and Needles. Somewhere on a three-hundred-mile run of Route 66, but neither Ruby nor Ava was fazed."

"Then I reckon Ruby's still singing 'It's an Ava Kind of Afternoon?'"

"Yep."

"Do they still have that stray they picked up in Nebraska?" he asked.

"They couldn't shake her."

"Then Heel Along is doing just fine."

The sun rose higher. They sat together on the stone step at the front door of the cottage.

"They said she was pure pride after they gave her a bath," Margot said.

"Loving that grass-fed beef jerky."

"We'd be lousy explorers." She picked a daisy.

"They pitch camp in pleasant places."

"Ava isn't lazy. She fixed the broken axle single-handedly. Stripped a Maine hardware store, before leaving, of anything fit to take on rigorous conditions."

"If the springs ride any lower, they'll be pushing coming home."

"I worry about them traveling alone." She entwined her fingers in his.

"Ruby crammed in enough canned goods to save a village from starvation."

"She should have left the bistro table and chairs behind."

"Have they kept on making turkey and turmeric bone broth with fennel from scratch for Heel Along in that pint-size camper's kitchen?" he asked.

"Did you have to ask?"

"Ruby will adopt a buffalo calf before they hit San Francisco."

"Ava is no better." He paused to listen to a willow warbler. "The Corn Goddess stops at each farm stand and used bookstore, where she's working on filling her second forty-five-pound crate."

"They both liked the RV meet and swap at Amarillo best. Ruby said they're becoming 'pioneers of American craft and comfort.' They traded a stainless-steel grease-splatter cover for a wool throw with a map of Lake Minnetonka."

"Any more unidentified spinning tops along the horizon?" Owen asked. He didn't have to hope any longer that one day, she'd join him.

"A few. And a whitish oval object."

"And we have to make do with the Northern Lights."

"Ava keeps asking where the sea is. She isn't at home without lumber trucks."

"Ruby will give her a good time." Owen nodded.

"And on the homeward end, Ava will show her how to eat lobster."

"And Johnny?"

"He and Ava are spending August in Camden."

"And Violet?"

"She'll be here for New Year's."

He let a hand whistle fly, calling the dogs from the loch. They would be covered in mud to their snouts if they left them roaming.

"How many whistles do you have? I only have one."

"It's on account of the gap between my teeth," he teased. "It makes my mouth ambidextrous. Hand whistling is the act of resonance in the cave formed by cupping my hands."

He let a second whistle fly. By inserting his second and third fingers into his mouth to shape the opening, he resembled the Bocca Della Verità. The sound was forceful and loud.

"That there's a wolf whistle. *Far* more mysterious."

He pinched his bottom lip, sucking air inside his mouth, releasing a piercing relay.

"The bottom-lip whistle, that one requires regular practice to master."

He let the fourth fly. The bewildered canines stood clueless.

"Teeth whistling is the jim-dandy of the whistling world. I've been called uppity for favoring it too much. The difficulty is drawing through my central incisors. Don't ask me how I do that one. Then there's the little girl who whistled in her throat—Molly McGillicuddy. She was quite quirky. She could imitate songbirds with her mouth closed. I shadowed her on the playground all through fourth and fifth grade. Tried to figure it out but never did. She'd run through the skylark, the blackbird, and the marsh warbler, then finish off the repertoire with a rendition of her favorite, 'Lullaby of the Leaves.' Boy, could she whistle."

Margot's a willow warbler with a necklace of gold who made her nest of fern, he thought. Holding hands, they strolled behind the cottage, where fiddleheads unfurled in early June and Owen had attached a target to a round hay bale.

"Watch how my arrow sails through the air," he said.

He let one sink with a thwack, then sidled up behind her as she held the bow, getting into position, heeding his directions. "Is your bracer on correctly? No need for string-slap."

"Don't clench my teeth or fidget; stay straight. Nock—draw —loose."

"Hold it for five seconds." He repeated their lesson. "Don't breathe in too deeply; sometimes it can take your breath away." His arms rested lightly on her shoulders. In the full draw, she wore a cape of encouragement. "Now—*loose.*"

He watched, with pride, the fletch soar and land.

"Aye, you took your porridge this morning," he said with praise. "But next time, open your eyes."

"It's a surprisingly effective weapon." She spoke matter-of-factly, with softness in her expression.

"Something secret and mysterious?"

"Like stringing a bow—stay straight, mind relaxed."

"Then come into your draw."

"I V-dub you."

"I V-dub you too."

"I V-dub you more."

"More love than we were built for will rebuild us. Then we'll parade through our gardens in our pajamas." Owen smiled.

"I don't know about you, but I'm not wearing pajamas."

"Ruby."

"Yes, Mom."

"You were born with a dimple in your chin, and your eyes flecked with emerald."

"Oh, Mom, I love you too."

"We come from a long line of raconteurs, daydreamers, and pretenders to whom the imagination matters."

"Mom, don't cry. What's wrong?"

Margot had crushed the violet beneath her heel, and with three words, privileged truth: "Will's your father." In so doing, she'd released the gift of forgiveness, infused with love. The color violet at the outer arc of the rainbow spanned the distance between mother and daughter.

Like a River

HOPPER'S ISLAND, SEPTEMBER 2024

I have no hesitation when asked if I'll join the gang at Otyrburn again for New Year's, knowing full well we'll smile and say the now customary greeting, "Fancy meeting you here!" We'll shut off our phones, and drink, and eat way too much; the reception at Otyrburn remains lackluster. Five years ago, I accepted my first invitation to the spectacle of excess. Plenty of time to learn that *ecology* in Greek means "household." (Thank you, George.) And a multitude of experiences to learn that trust forms the constellation called "family."

Heel Along gave birth to a spanking litter of pups shortly after they parked the V-dub in Camden. Of course, I adopted the runt, Topo Gigio.

Ava has conceived, and Johnny's on board. He is indeed the father! Older sister Olympus turns four just weeks shy of the baby's expected due date on April 29. A bumper crop was planted on rich loamy soil in Orwell, Vermont, where Ava and Johnny bought an old farm and turned it into a goat dairy. They are excellent parents. You can see that they're well and happy, this new family. The grapes in Johnny's vineyard are beginning to fill out. Desire isn't the same as passion. Johnny and Ava have found passion, and it suits the privacy of their spirit.

Lily passed away, and Robbie joined a monastery. They say he paints, but I can't comment, as I haven't seen any of his work. I think he "went to church" so that he could eat the world-class black raspberry and rhubarb jam crafted by the monks at the abbey.

Sybil and Max have opened a bookshop devoted to mystical literature.

Will closed the gallery, and he and Lisbet, like a pioneer species, moved to Puglia, at the heel of Italy. They have two homeschooled boys, Rainier and Wolf. They're still trying for a pair of girls. Will has his heart set on teaching "Etna" and "Tula" how to throw clay. Lisbet's play, *Undisturbed by Delight*, was picked up on Broadway. Having joined forces with the transcendentalists, the ethos of the divine at work in the human soul, and the individual's precedence over society, informs Lisbet that New York City is no place for her or her loved ones. Self-reliant and independent, they've survived the lack of water historically plaguing the south, and the malarial aspect, so why on earth would Lisbet and Will abandon the commune and the royal menagerie they've established? Their eldest, Rainier, bakes and sells his own strawberry frangipane—elderflower galettes, with fresh-squeezed lemonade, at the end of the donkey path leading into their property. Little brother Wolf is never beyond an arm's reach of Vigilante, their Abruzzese, the large milk-white sheepdog of the region.

I've begun writing a novel: *In Search of What Remains of the World's Extinct Characters*. Somewhat of a surprise package, somewhat of a pop-up card, and one part matryoshka doll, it deals with falling deeply in love with now-vanished forms.

I went to the drive-through at the bank today and closed two accounts. That's what an epilogue is: you're handed a cashier's check for the amount left over. Your statements and recent activity are brought into stasis, like an otter at rest on his back, seaward looking skyward, reading clouds.

HOPPER'S ISLAND, SEPTEMBER 2030

It is another year, another September, and six years on; I'll call the new manuscript a slow stalk through the weeds without scientific instruments.

This old white farmhouse of mine has a wraparound porch. They've gathered inside the sprawling rooms and outside on the clipped green lawn. Ava and Johnny, Margot and Owen—the whole gang. Someone is talking to someone in the bathroom, delivering advice on hemorrhoids after the long flight. I want to help, but I don't. Why I let Ava make such a fuss over my eightieth birthday, I'm not sure. She knows I don't like that sort of thing.

The smell of the sea is what brings them. Though this year, with all the heat, everything's ripening sooner; unerringly at the tail end of August, when the last of the blueberries willingly plunk in tin pails, the children chase the fireflies well into the night. Will and Lisbet's daughter, Etna, asked for ponies at Great-Aunt Violet's party, so ponies there shall be.

Two drive a cart down the path to the sea into the magic of a late-summer day. I walk over to peer at the edge, at the happy party below, step down the embankment, and slip in my leather sandals, grabbing a small tree trunk to brace myself from falling, where the land drops to touch the ocean.

Rainier didn't want a pony ride. Will and Lisbet's eldest found me, lent me a hand, and we scrambled back home together, lying beneath the low-hanging branches of one of my sweetly fragrant flowering quince trees. He couldn't stop talking about the Spanish moss—like delicate bloom of cobweb beauty on the tip of ever so many branches. We'll ask Sybil about that and if it's an invasive species. Rainier said, for reasons only known to him, that we should name the tree "Mr. Fletcher." Then he asked me to tell him Owen's story about the door into the mountain, and the rings of Saturn, far away, far out on the horizon where seals bark. His father, William, had this to say on being a dad: "My voice makes the little one sleep and the other two whine."

Olympus, my firstborn granddaughter, communed with a baby hawk here this summer that had fallen from its nest. Giant brown eyes, she wanted to know how his iris worked and pupil dilated. And again, we sat in the branches of a tree beside him. Olympus spends August with me on the island. Ava kept her house in Camden, but there's no place quite like Hopper's Island. When her sister, Oakley, is old enough, she'll have her ten days too. She's a little whippersnapper. I showed her the book you now hold in your hands and turned to this page to show her the letters that spelled her name. Oakley said: "I came alive in a book."

Ruby packed her telescope, as always, and this summer, her new, older lover too. They met in Puglia at "the commune." A good friend of William's, Umberto has a degree in semiotics but prefers working out of his food truck. He can make honey from a weed. His *Carciofi Fritti con Parmigiano Grattugiatto* have made him famous in Park Slope, where they live.

Everyone has suddenly burst out singing. Ruby baked me a magnificent cake and decorated it with cosmos. The gift of an articulated origami bluebird Etna made, attached with a kilt-pin to the hem of my blouse. It carries her handwritten note in its beak: "Nonna ~~People~~ Purple Violet, I love you too."

In the midst of the commotion, a lanky young man appeared at the screen door, asking for directions to the O'Toole house. He said he was looking for Archie Reid; the resemblance was undeniable. I'll draw him a map after I finish my hazelnut cake.

Jewel joins us on the odd years. She makes a point of telling me that I avoided family, only to collect it. I tell her the subconscious rules in the end. And that our truths are hidden behind the heart-shaped leaves of the violet.

THE END

CPSIA information can be obtained
at www.ICGtesting.com
Printed in the USA
BVHW090616041022
648588BV00004B/13

9 798986 120508